HITLER'S GIFT

The Story of Theresienstadt

George E. Berkley

BRANDEN BOOKS
Boston

Library of Congress Cataloguing-in-Publication Data

Berkley, George E.
  Hitler's gift : the story of Theresienstadt / by George E.
Berkley.
    p.   cm.
  Includes bibliographical references.
  ISBN 0-8283-1954-4
  ISBN 0-8283-2068-0 (2002)
  1. Terezin (Czechoslovakia : Concentration camp)
  2. Holocaust, Jewish (1939-1945)--Czechoslovakia.
  3. Czechoslovakia--Ethnic relations.
  I. Title.
  940.53'174371--dc20   92-42127
                                           CIP

Branden Books
BRANDEN PUBLISHING COMPANY Inc.
PO Box 812094 Wellesley MA 02482
Boston

For
HARTMUT LANG
and the many thousands of his fellow-Germans
who are helping to create
a new German-Jewish relationship

Ich kenn' ein kleines Staedtchen,
Ein Staedtchen ganz tip-top.
Ich nenn' es nicht beim Namen,
Ich nenn' die Stadt als-ob.

(I know a tiny city,
As nice as one could see.
I call it not by name,
I call it just would-be.)
   Leo Strauss
   (Resident of Theresienstadt, 1942-44)

TABLE OF CONTENTS

ACKNOWLEDGMENTS

The idea for this book was born in the Newton, Massachusetts living room of Louis and Ditta Lowy some years ago. I was interviewing Mrs. Lowy for a book I was writing on the Jews of Vienna under Nazi rule. Since she was deported from Vienna to Theresienstadt in the fall of 1942, our discussion eventually touched on this unique Holocaust institution. I listened with fascination to what she had to say about Theresienstadt, and when, in describing some of its many ironies, she referred to it as a "theatre of the absurd," I became convinced that another Holocaust book remained to be written.

Once my book, *Vienna and Its Jews: The Tragedy of Success*, was finished and published, I returned to the Lowy living room, this time not only to interview Mrs. Lowy at greater length on Theresienstadt but also to interview her husband who had been a teacher there. This marked the beginning of a research mission which took me to Connecticut, New York, Israel, Vienna, Prague and, of course, Theresienstadt itself. Geographically, it ended almost where it began--in the Newton, Massachusetts living room of another Theresienstadt survivor, Mrs. Netty Schwarz Vanderpol.

In carrying out this research, I chalked up a large number of debts to a large number of people and institutions. Among the latter are Yad Vashem in Jerusalem, Beit Terezin at Kibbutz Givat Chaim, the Wiener Library at the University of Tel Aviv, the Simon Wiesenthal Documentation Center in Vienna, the Jewish State Museum in Prague (the Terezin Memorial Museum in Theresienstadt itself was not then even on the planning boards), the Leo Baeck Institute in New York City, The Massachusetts College of Art, and the libraries of Brandeis University, Hebrew College and the Goethe Institute of Boston.

The staffs of these institutions were almost uniformly helpful. I am especially grateful to Ms. Alisha Shek and Ms. Alisa Schiller at Beit Terezin for the information, both written and oral, which they gave me, and I only hope that my book may help create more awareness and appreciation for their untiring, and largely unsung, efforts at documenting Theresienstadt's history and maintaining its memory.

Among the many others to whom I am indebted are: Lisa Gidron for giving me the names of the Lowys as well as for describing her own experiences in Theresienstadt; Professor Karel Margry of the University of Utrecht for giving me in writing much useful information, especially concerning the Gerron film about which he is writing a book of his own; Dr. Gabriella Anderl of the Documentation Center of the Austrian

Resistance, who airmailed to me a copy of her paper on the SS at Theresienstadt; Professor and author Arnost Lustig for patiently submitting to several lengthy and, for me, most helpful telephone interviews; Professor Leonard and Dr. Phyllis Ehrlich, who supplied much data on Rabbi Murmelstein, whom they had interviewed at length for a forthcoming book of their own on ghetto leaders; Professor Joza Karas for putting me in touch with Ella Weissburger; and Attorney Ralph Vanderpol for allowing me to examine a manuscript he has written based on interviews with his grandfather, Adolph Schwarz; and Siegmund Levarie and E. K. Rothblum for various efforts to help.

I should also like to thank Cyrille White, who, on her own initiative, sent me a copy of Gerda Haas's book, and also Gerda Haas herself who, at my request, supplied some supplementary information. Sam Berger was similarly helpful in regard to his own work.

A special note of thanks should go to Ernest Seinfeld, who virtually worked with me not only in providing information from his own experiences in Theresienstadt, but in alerting me to, and sometimes providing me with, various written materials. His assistance was invaluable.

None of those mentioned has seen the final version of the manuscript and all therefore should be absolved of culpability for any errors or misstatements it may contain. Eyewitness accounts and even statistical records about Theresienstadt vary and one can only try to weigh them all carefully and come up with the most accurate depiction possible of this most unusual community.

Finally, I would like to express my appreciation for the support and encouragement of others who have no direct connection with Theresienstadt. They include my special friend, Dorothy, my two sons, Sean and Serge, my crackerjack typist and semi-editor, Adelle Robinson, and my new publisher, Adolfo Caso.

My thanks to you all.

PRELUDE:
THE GIFT

The first reports appeared in the German press in early summer of 1942. Suddenly, and magnanimously, the Fuehrer was presenting an entire city to the Jews. The news accounts identified the city as Theresienstadt and gave its location as northern Czechoslovakia some 39 miles from Prague. Theresienstadt's regular residents were being evacuated but would leave behind their furniture for the city's new, and seemingly fortunate, inhabitants.

It soon became evident that only certain Jews would benefit from the Fuehrer's generous gift. Foremost among them were the German and Austrian elderly. They had merely to sign contracts turning over all their remaining assets to the SS; in return the SS pledged itself to take care of them for the rest of their lives. Since such arrangements had been common in pre-Hitler Germany, and since living conditions for Jews in the Reich were becoming increasingly intolerable as well as hazardous--deportations of middle-aged and younger Jews to the "East" had been going on since the previous fall--most of these elderly Jews readily signed up.(1)

Some of these elderly Jews were eager to go, for northern Czechoslovakia was known for its resort spas, such as Carlsbad and Marienbad, and as the SS described it to them, Theresienstadt seemed to fall into that category. Indeed, SS officials asked them to specify in advance where they wanted their rooms, such as on the lake, by the square, etc. They were also urged to take along their nicest clothes. So they packed their parasols and summer dresses, their top hats and frock coats, and prepared to depart for "Theresienbad," a name the SS sometimes used in referring to their new home.

Word of Theresienstadt's role as Hitler's haven for older Jews soon spread throughout German-occupied Europe. In Paris, officials at the General Union of French Israelites, responding to anxious inquiries about impending deportation of the elderly, said the old people were probably being sent to Theresienstadt, the "model ghetto" whose creation had been reported in the Nazi-controlled press.

But elderly Jews were not the only ones eligible for the new ghetto. Another category included those Jewish war veterans who had earned high decorations for bravery or who had suffered severe injuries in World War I. The specific standards imposed on them for deportation to Theresienstadt instead of to the "East" were certainly high; they needed to have won a medal higher than an Iron Cross, 2nd Class, or to have suffered at least 50 percent disability from their wounds. But so fiercely and loyally had German and Austrian Jews fought for their countries in the Great War, that nearly 3,000 of the less than 200,000 Jews remaining in the Reich in mid-1942 met these requirements.(2)

Another group destined for dispatch to the privileged ghetto were those Jewish partners in mixed marriages which had been dissolved through the death of the Aryan spouse. Even those whose marriages had ended in divorce were eligible if the marriage had produced half-Aryan children. Then there were those Jews whose mixed marriages had remained intact but who had run afoul of the Nazis' many restrictions on Jews. Though they lost their exemption from deportation through such misbehavior, their marriage to an Aryan often qualified them for Theresienstadt.

The case of biochemist Ernst Eichengruen, an employee of the Bayer works, who had discovered a marketable form of aspirin, illustrates how easily such violations of anti-Jewish regulations could occur. Married to an Aryan, Eichengruen had been allowed to continue working for Bayer until he submitted, on Bayer's behalf, a patent application for a new drug. In signing the papers he had forgotten to include Israel as his middle name. Since this middle name was now required of all Jewish men--Jewish women had to have the middle name of Sarah--the biochemist, who had done so much to bring fame and fortune to the German chemical industry, was packed off to Theresienstadt.

Then there were the German, Austrian, and Czech half-Jews. Although not normally subject to deportation at all, special situations continually arose for which Theresienstadt provided a solution.

The case of 12-year-old Liselotte Neuhaus offers an illustration of such a situation. She was the illegitimate offspring of a Jewish woman and an Aryan man now serving in the German army. Her mother had subsequently married a Jewish man with whom she had had more children. The SS deported the mother along with her husband and the other children to the East, but sent Liselotte to Theresienstadt.

Some of the special cases vividly illustrate the bizarre turns which Hitler's racial laws could take. Oswald Pawder, a respected poet from Hamburg, was only one-quarter Jewish. As such, he normally would have escaped not only deportation but most other forms of discrimination as well. But he had married a Jewess in his second marriage and was preparing to follow her and their daughter to America when Pearl Harbor dashed his plans. So he too was earmarked for deportation even though his son by his first marriage to an Aryan was serving in the German army. (His son showed up in uniform at the train station to try to get his father released from deportation altogether but could not do so.)

Still another group which met the criteria for Theresienstadt were employees of those Jewish organizations in the Reich and in the Czech section of Czechoslovakia who had worked under the Nazis. They included not only functionaries and office workers but also doctors and nurses from Jewish hospitals. Most of these hospitals were now being shut down and their patients were being sent to Theresienstadt as well.

Then there were those whose prominence or previous positions warranted, in Nazi eyes, favored treatment. These were Jews who had once held such positions as Prime Minister of the German state of Saxony; Vice Governor of Indonesia; French cabinet minister and Mayor of Le Havre, France; President of the Dutch Red Cross; Surgeon-General of the Dutch Army; Vice Field Marshal of the Austrian Imperial (i.e., pre-1918) Army; General of that same army-- there were at least two of these--and Minister of Justice in the Czecho- slovakian government. There was a Jewish Baron from Bavaria (Rudolph von Hirsch, nephew of the Jewish philanthropist Baron Moritz Hirsch), a Jewish Baroness from Berlin (Ellie von Bleichroeder, granddaughter of Bismarck's chief financier), and a Countess from Vienna who later gained her release from Theresienstadt by convincing her captors that she was half-Aryan.

Many prominent performers, artists, and academicians also ended up in Theresienstadt. Perhaps the best known was Kurt Gerron, who, prior to the Nazi era, was widely considered Germany's leading character actor. He had acted in films with such stars as Marlene Dietrich--in *The Blue Angel* he played the male sublead--while his recording of a song from the stage version of *The Three-Penny Opera*, in which he played the police captain, had become a best-selling record in the German-speaking world.

Most performers sent to Theresienstadt were not actors, however, but musicians. They included the former conductor of the Royal Danish Symphony, the former concertmaster of Holland's Concertgebouw Orchestra, the former Deputy Concertmaster of the Czechoslovakian National Symphony, and a bevy of well-known violinists, pianists, singers, etc. from around German-occupied Europe. One singer was Julie Salinger, whose two sons had married the daughters of a Hohen- zollern prince. She herself had given recitals before the last German Kaiser and had received a medal for entertaining the German wounded in World War I.

There were also numerous *Prominenten* from other fields, such as economist Leo Taussig from the University of Prague; Elsa Richter, a University of Vienna professor who had helped develop the science of phonetics; Emil Klein, the physician who had launched Germany's natural foods movement; and Artur Weinberg, who had co-founded the huge chemical concern, I. G. Farben. (The company's current board chairman had strenuously sought to free Weinberg from deportation by pointing out the 82-year-old man's services to Germany, which included several decorations for valor as an army major in World War I. His efforts, however, proved no more successful than those of Pawder's soldier son.)

Many Theresienstadt deportees were relatives of world-famous figures. Among them were Franz Liszt's granddaughter, Elsie Bernstein; Franz Kafka's youngest and favorite sister, Ottilie; composer Oskar Strauss's son, Leo; and Mimi Mann, divorced wife of writer Heinrich Mann and thus an ex-sister-in-law of his more famous brother, Thomas.

Many of these latter deportees had claims to fame of their own. Leo Strauss was a well-regarded opera librettist; Mimi Mann had become Germany's foremost translator of Scandinavian literature; and Elsie Bernstein, now in her 70s and blind, had published several well-received works of poetry under the pen name of Ernst Rosner.

Theresienstadt thus became something of a center for the cream of continental Jewry, or at least for those members of it who had failed to escape the Nazi threat. When Leo Baeck read the names of the Dutch deportees arriving in Theresienstadt, he felt he was seeing a list of Holland's Jewish aristocracy. Many distinguished deportees got to meet equally distinguished colleagues whose acquaintance they had always wanted to make.

Baeck was the most prominent of the more than 20 rabbis who would eventually come to Theresienstadt, for he was the most respected figure in Reform Judaism. His disappearance from Berlin had occasioned great concern throughout the Jewish world, and when word of his new residence reached his American colleague, Rabbi Stephen Wise, during a dinner in New York, Wise hurried from table to table joyfully announcing, "Leo Baeck is alive. He is in Theresienstadt."

From Vienna came two famous Zionist figures. One was Robert Stricker, a leader of Zionism's militant wing and a co-founder of the World Jewish Congress. The other was Trude Neumann, the 51-year-old daughter of Zionism's founder, Theodor Herzl. She had been in a mental hospital since 1918, the year her son was born. (Her son, meanwhile, was serving as an officer in the British army.)

Some of those sent to Theresienstadt had had direct or indirect alliances with the Nazis themselves. These included some informers and collaborators for whom deportation to Theresienstadt was a reward. They also included several special cases.

One very special case was Ida Steinhuber. She was the fully Jewish widow of the one-time head of Bavaria's storm troopers. (Her husband had become head of the Bavarian police after Hitler's takeover.) Another special case was Luian Dawber, a Jewish attorney who had defended certain Nazi leaders when, prior to the Nazi takeover, they had gotten into trouble with the authorities. Still another was Jewish editor and publisher Paul Cossmann who, as an ardent German nationalist, had used his influential magazine *Die Suddeutsche Monatshefte* (the South German Monthly Journal) to propagandize the myth that Germany had lost the war because it had been stabbed in the back. (Hitler had subsequently used the myth to attack the Jews, claiming they had wielded the dagger.) There were also a few German army officers from the current war and even a former SS man, all of whom had later been found to be Jews.

Although most of these deportees would have preferred to stay in their own homes, many felt privileged to be going to Theresienstadt instead of some place else. Had not the press described it as a model ghetto? Had not letters and cards come back from new arrivals attesting to its pleasantness? As one card from a Dutch deportee reported, "It is a friendly town with broad streets, lovely gardens and single-story houses," while another had mentioned how "those who wished could take a nap in the afternoon."

No wonder that a Dutch Jewish mother, who had hidden her infant son with a Dutch Christian couple who were willing to keep him, decided instead to take him with her. No wonder that a Viennese couple, fearfully awaiting deportation to the East themselves, wrote to their son, "Uncle has had a lot of luck. He and his whole family have been sent to Theresienstadt." No wonder that when it came to handing out destination tags at the Berlin deportation center, "those who received a 'T' (for Theresienstadt) dared to breathe again, while the others, with an 'O' (for *Ost* or East), turned pale." Although not many details were known about Theresienstadt, continues this observer, "one thing was clear: it was infinitely better than the East. The type of people who were selected for Theresienstadt gave some indication of this fact."

The Nazis themselves seemed to concur in this conclusion. Those wishing to assist any Jewish friend or other Jewish connection destined for deportation sought to have them sent to Theresienstadt. Thus, we find Hermann Goering, the second most powerful man in Nazi Germany, directing the SS to deport a Jewish couple of his acquaintance to the Czech community, adding, "They should be allowed to stay there as long as the town is available for this purpose."

As Theresienstadt's first commandant told the town's first Jewish administrator, "You people have no idea how good you will have it. We are going to make Theresienstadt into a paradise ghetto."

---

1. Actually, the Nazis did not bother with the contract scheme in Austria even though Austria was now an integral part of the Reich. Presumably, this was because the crackdown on Jews had proceeded faster and more furiously i Austria, leaving its elderly Jews with nearly nothing to turn over. The Nazis also probably felt less need to keep up pretenses before Austrian Gentiles who, being much more anti-semitic than Germans, would experience and express fewer qualms over seeing their elderly Jews sent off.

2. It is one of the many ironies of Jewish history that more Jews died fighting for Germany and Austria in World War I than have died fighting for Israel in all six of its wars.

PART I

MARCH 1939 to JULY 1943

CHAPTER 1
AN END AND A BEGINNING

March 15, the Ides of March, proved as fateful to Czechoslovakia in 1939 as it had to Julius Caesar 2,000 years earlier. At 4:00 A.M. Czechoslovakia's aging, ailing President Emil Hacha, after an all-night meeting with Hitler in Berlin, had finally yielded to the Fuehrer's threats and verbal bludgeoning and signed a statement requesting the German leader to "rescue" his country from rupture and ruin. By 6:00 A.M. the already mobilized and fully motorized German troops had crossed the border and were streaming toward Prague. By noon they had disembarked and were parading through the city streets. Central Europe's one remaining democracy had ceased to exist.

This rapid-fire turn of events had caught most Czechs by surprise. True, Hitler had annexed a substantial slice of their country the previous September in the infamous Munich agreement. But that section was the Sudetenland whose mostly German population had yearned to be part of the German Reich. At the time, Hitler had said, with a convincing note of disdain, that he wanted only Germans in his Reich, no Czechs.

Since then, the Czechs, aware that the Allies had abandoned them, had gone out of their way to placate and even pander to the German leader. The Czech government had renounced its pact with the USSR and had granted the Slovaks substantial autonomy, a step which Hitler had long insisted on. It had even offered to let Hitler nominate a Czech German to its cabinet, for although most of Czechoslovakia's large German population had lived in the Sudetenland, ethnic Germans were scattered throughout the country including a substantial number in Prague itself.

Unfortunately, and unbeknown to the Czechs, Hitler had always regarded the Czech provinces of Bohemia and Moravia as German territory lost by the Hapsburgs, the Austrian ruling family which he despised. He had long wanted these provinces for the Reich; he had now made his move.

Among those caught off balance by Hitler's bold step were the leaders of Prague's Zionist movement. But their executive secretary, Franz Kahn, a still youthful former army officer who had lost an arm fighting alongside the Germans in World War I--Czechoslovakia was then part of the Austrian empire--hastily called a meeting. The Zionist leaders gathered at noon in Kahn's apartment and, with the sounds of

German troops marching and motorcycling through the streets below, they deliberated on what to do.

Two alternative courses of action arose. They could either try to get themselves, their families, and as many of their fellow Zionists as possible out of the country, or they could stay and help their fellow Jews cope with the Nazi menace. The rationale for the first and seemingly selfish strategy was that, as the country's most visible and militant Jewish leaders, they would bear the brunt of the Nazi persecutions. Up to now they had been busily working to help the Jewish refugees who had fled to Prague from Germany, Austria, and, most recently and most numerously, the Sudetenland. Now they owed it to their families to think of themselves. Furthermore, once outside Czechoslovakia, they could continue working for a Jewish homeland. Most of them had, or had access to, the few highly valuable Jewish immigration permits for Palestine.

But a forceful, persuasive advocate for the second strategy emerged. "For years," he said, "we claimed to be the real and responsible leaders of the Jewish masses. Now, when the crucial moment has come, we cannot desert the Jews of Czechoslovakia. Our place today is at the forefront of the Jewish community."

The member making this case for the stay-and-struggle approach was the 35-year-old, pudgy-faced head of the Palestine Agency's Prague office, Jakob Edelstein. A native of Polish Galicia whose family had fled to Prague during World War I--Galicia was also then part of Austria--Edelstein had grown up in a Yiddish-speaking, religiously observant home. He had, however, attended German schools in both Galicia and Czechoslovakia. After graduating from a commercial high school, he had become a traveling salesman until his natural talents for public speaking and organizing, plus his passion for Israel, drew him into full-time Zionist activity.

Edelstein differed from most other members at the meeting in more ways than simply his Galician background. With only a diploma from a commercial high school, he was the least educated of them all. He still, in fact, spoke a less than perfect Czech, while his German, though fluent, was marked by a pronounced Yiddish accent. He was also a socialist and though the Zionist movement contained a socialist component, most Jewish socialists had disavowed such nationalist ideals. Finally, he was an observant Jew whose wife, a former teacher of English named Miriam Olliner, kept a kosher home, and whose 8-year-old son had a Hebrew name, Arieh. Edelstein in fact was at his morning prayers, wrapped in his *tallis* (prayer shawl) and *tefillin* (phylacteries) when he received the call for the meeting at Kahn's apartment.

But despite the differences separating him from most of his fellow Zionists, Edelstein's argument carried the day. The Czech Zionists would stand by their fellow Jews and seek to help them survive the Nazi evil.

Following his troops' triumphant march into Prague, Hitler moved swiftly. Within two days he had lopped off Slovakia, transforming it into a puppet state under his control. Then, after allowing both Hungary and Poland to seize slices of Czech territory for themselves, he transformed what was left, namely, the provinces of Bohemia and Moravia, into a "Protectorate." his "Protectorate" would have some of the trappings of an independent state but which would be under the firm control of a "Protector" whom he would appoint.

The Protectorate at this time harbored just over 118,000 Jews, one-quarter of them refugees from the Reich. Most of the Protectorate's Jews, however, no matter where they were from, now wanted desperately to flee, but their prospects for doing so were hardly promising. For one thing, the pipelines to freedom were already jammed with German and Austrian Jews seeking to escape Hitler's iron heel. For another, few Czech Jews had relatives abroad and the American quota for Czechoslovakia was only 2,700. Moreover, the Nazis themselves were not initially inclined to facilitate their departure, for they wanted to get rid of the German and Austrian Jews first, thereby making the Reich *judenrein* (cleansed of Jews), and did not want Czech Jews taking their places. Finally, one-half of all the Protectorate's Jews lived outside of Prague, which made contact with foreign consulates difficult.

The Nazis realized, however, that the scarce British immigration permits for Palestine were being spread around Europe, with some earmarked for Czechoslovakia. Furthermore, their experience in Vienna had shown that illegal immigration to Palestine was also possible. So, to take advantage of these opportunities to get rid of some Czech Jews while not interfering with the exodus of Jews from the Reich, they ordered the Palestine Agency's Prague office to resume its activities.

Edelstein and his fellow Zionists responded enthusiastically, believing that one way or another they could get at least several thousand young people to Palestine. In May, with Gestapo permission, Edelstein journeyed to Palestine, Trieste, and Geneva to spur on such efforts. (His wife and son stayed in Prague as hostages to ensure his return.)

Thanks to these and other, more individual initiatives, by mid-summer some 10,000 Jews had managed to escape the Nazi yoke.

The outbreak of war in September worsened the plight of the Jews in many ways. England and France, along with their colonies, were now virtually closed to them. So was the Polish border, while to the south the new Nazi puppet state of Slovakia had begun arresting fleeing Jews. Daily life in Czechoslovakia itself was becoming steadily harsher. Jews had already been banned from working in the professions and from frequenting public events and parks. Now they were being fired from even menial jobs and were prohibited from walking on the main streets during the weekend, from owning radios, and from shopping at other than designated hours.

But the worst, or what looked like the worst, was still to come. After speedily conquering Poland, the Nazis decided to establish a Jewish reservation in a swampy section of south Poland along the new Russian border. (Their original intention was to dump gypsies as well in this area, thus making it, in the words of SS chief Heinrich Himmler, "a garbage pail.") In early October the Nazis ordered the Jewish communities of Czechoslovakia and Austria to assemble transports of 1300 and 1600 men, respectively, for departure to a site called Nisko, where they were to build a new Jewish entity. They chose Edelstein to lead the Czech detachment and another native Galician, a Viennese rabbi turned administrator named Benjamin Murmelstein, to head the group from Vienna.

From the outset the project was a nightmare. On the train the SS men physically abused the men and refused to allow any stops for water. Nisko itself turned out to be a muddy field along the tracks, with no buildings, water lines, or other facilities. Though ordered to construct their own accommodations, they had no building materials and only such tools as they had brought with them. The first night a group of neighboring Poles raided their camp, killing 21 Jews and injuring many others. When the men asked for weapons or some means of defending themselves, the SS guards laughed in their faces.

Fortunately, many of the men had brought along leather shaving kits which, to the Poles, looked like pistol holsters. They gathered up these kits and gave them to their younger and tougher members to wear on their belts. They also fashioned clubs from tree branches. Then those who were doctors began visiting nearby villages to offer their services. Gradually, the attacks subsided. The men also found some boards and under the supervision of the engineers among them started to build.

The Nazis, however, had already decided to abandon the project, for Hitler was now planning to invade Russia and did not want to launch his attack from a Jewish settlement area. Consequently, instead of encouraging the Jews to create the reservation, the Nazis sought to get rid of them, either by allowing them to die from cold, hunger, exhaustion, or Polish assaults, or by forcing them to swim across the San River into Russia. Many drowned while trying to do so and many of those who did make it across perished later in Siberia. In April those still alive in Nisko were brought back: 457 to Czechoslovakia and a mere 198 to Vienna.

Among the Czech survivors was Edelstein, who returned with two firm convictions. The first was that Murmelstein, his rabbinical counterpart from Vienna whom he would encounter again in Theresienstadt, was never to be trusted. Just what led him to this conclusion remains unknown, but, as we shall see, it tallies with what many Viennese Jews had come to believe. The second was that he and his fellow Zionists must exert every effort to prevent further deportations to Poland. The Czech Jews could only hope to survive under Nazi rules by staying in Czechoslovakia. These two convictions, especially the second, would shape his strategy and condition his behavior for the remaining four years of his life.

One factor which steeled Edelstein in his determination to keep the Czech Jews in Czechoslovakia was the behavior of the Czechs themselves. Although anti-Semitism had been rampant in the country at the turn of the century, even producing a trumped-up ritual murder trial (the Hilsner case), it had since subsided considerably. A variety of developments had produced this change, the most recent and significant being the tensions between the Czechs and their own ethnic Germans who made up 22 percent of the country's pre-Munich population. My enemy's enemy is my friend, runs an old saying, and the Jews, having become the enemy of the largely pro-Nazi Czech Germans, had become, to some degree, friends or at least allies of the ethnic Czechs.

Understandably, the Nazi occupation strongly sharpened anti-German feeling. Although the Nazi's were willing to grant more status and services to the Czechs than to other Slavs coming under their control, the Czechs produced fewer collaborators. In the amorphous darkness of motion picture theaters, Czech audiences laughed at German newsreels and in Prague coffeehouses waiters often served Nazi newspapers upside down. As one Gestapo report put it, "The ordinary

Czech no longer views the Jewish question as a problem. His only emotion is . . . hatred for the Germans."

Edelstein's experience in Nisko had persuaded him that the Nazis would willingly kill off the Jews, and the Poles would willingly help them do so. But the Czechs, he felt, might actually help the Jews survive. So he persuaded his fellow Zionists to agree not to take part in any more deportations, even if it meant being deported themselves. He even offered them an example. The Nazis once ordered him to draw up a plan within 48 hours for transporting all the Jews out of the country. Failure to present the plan would, he was told, result in his own speedy dispatch to Dachau. After consulting with Kahn, Edelstein told his superiors that they might as well ship him off right away. The Nazis backed down.

On other matters Edelstein was prepared to work with the Nazis, believing that only through such cooperation could he secure more viable conditions for the community. He spoke scornfully of those "delicate souls" who recognized the necessity for such dealings but declined to dirty their hands by engaging in them themselves. Still, he scarcely enjoyed his role as a rising Jewish leader. "For him," writes Ruth Bondy, "the constant contact with the SS was an incessant battle with fear. Edelstein was no dauntless, heroic figure. It was enough to look at him: a bespectacled Jewish clerk who shrank from violence and had never raised his hand against anyone. Sometimes, when he was unexpectedly called to the Gestapo, he would feel a sense of weakness, turn pale, and have to go to the toilet. And yet he went, his stomach in turmoil but never betraying his fears."

Although Edelstein accepted the need, and indeed the necessity, of working with the Nazis, the question of how far one could and should go continually haunted him and his fellow Zionists. When the Nazis demanded a list of Polish Jews currently in Czechoslovakia, a dispute arose within Jewish ranks as to whether they should comply. Kahn wanted to refuse, but Edelstein argued that doing so would only lead to worse consequences, for the Nazis already had lists that were merely incomplete. The Zionists finally decided to submit the list but to do everything possible to warn those who were on it before complying.(3)

As these incidents indicate, Jewish organizations were now playing a greater part in Jewish life. "The more the external world receded," writes Bondy, "the more functions the Jewish community institutions assumed." The staff of the Jewish Gemeinde, the official organization of the Jewish community, increased twelvefold and its activities twenty-fivefold. It even added a department to assist those Jews who did not consider themselves Jews but who now found themselves classified as such.

Within this expanding Jewish organizational network, Zionist institutions were playing an increasingly greater role. For the Nazis' rigorous enforcement of the Nuremberg racial laws seemed to be making a mockery of those who had maintained that Judaism represented only a religion, not a nationality, and therefore Jews needed no nation. More important, the Zionists controlled some of the exits to freedom through their possession of a few official immigration permits to Palestine and through their involvement in illegal immigration activities being carried out primarily by their fellow Zionists in Vienna. Consequently, parents who initially sneered at suggestions to sign up their youngsters for *Aliyah* (emigration to Palestine) were now almost coming to blows in trying to get their offspring at or near the top of the list.

The increasing role of the Zionists meant an expanding role for Edelstein. In March 1940 the Nazis appointed him Deputy Director of the Prague Gemeinde. (Neither the Gemeinde's director nor its secretary were Zionists.) Shortly before, they had allowed him to visit Geneva again, this time to address a conference of high Zionist officials. He impressed his audience with the severity of the conditions confronting the Czech Jews. He also impressed them with his simple sincerity and his firm commitment to his community's welfare. One audience member, Moshe Sharrett, who as Moshe Shertok would later become a foreign minister of Israel, described himself as "awed by this unknown hero" who described the abuse, including beatings, which the Nazis had inflicted on the Jewish leaders, but who did not say that he had suffered such abuse himself. "Only later did I learn that Edelstein had experienced those beatings in person," wrote Sharrett.

The spring of 1940 brought the German conquest of Denmark and Norway, followed by their lightning sweep through the Lowland countries and France. It also brought Italy's entry into the war. These developments drew the noose still tighter around the Czechoslovakian Jews, drastically narrowing the few remaining avenues of escape. The Nazis now closed the Palestine agency office, though they permitted a last illegal immigration to Palestine in early September. The following month the U.S. council in Prague suspended operations. There were few visas available and still fewer ways to use them. The nearly 100,000 Jews still remaining in Czechoslovakia were, with very few exceptions, trapped.

To facilitate their handling of the Jews and to prepare for their later deportation, the Nazis shut down all Jewish agencies outside of Prague. The Prague Community Center now became the only link between the Jews and their Nazi rulers. More and more Zionists had moved into managerial roles within the agency and had become its dominant presence.

Adolph Eichmann, who now headed Jewish affairs for the SS, appointed a 29-year-old captain, Hans Guenther, as overseer of the Protectorate Jews. Tall, slim, and truly Aryan-looking, he was one of the few people in Eichmann's operation who was a native German and not, like Eichmann himself, an Austrian. Guenther's second in command, however, was a former Austrian school teacher named Anton Burger, while his personal aide was a machinist from suburban Vienna, Karl Rahm.

One factor helping the Zionists was that many of their Nazi superiors were far from bright. Burger, for instance, once ordered Edelstein to prepare a report. Edelstein did so, but when the time came to hand it in, he told an associate, "If I don't return, it means they understand that the report says nothing." But he did return--to announce that the report had pleased them. On another occasion Burger ordered Edelstein to prepare a speech for him on the German Orders of Knighthood. Burger liked the speech, but when Edelstein read it to his colleagues afterward, they burst into laughter.

In the spring of 1941 the SS sent Edelstein and one of his associates, Richard Friedmann, to Holland to help the Jews there set up an organization along the lines of the Prague Gemeinde. The Dutch Jews were at first suspicious of the pair, regarding them as Nazi puppets. But Edelstein soon won them over with his sincerity and diplomatic skills.

Both he and Friedmann sought to impress on their co-religionists the gravity of the situation. Edelstein, for example, told a meeting of Zionists in a private Amsterdam home that the Nazis intended to destroy the Jews, and the only solution was to try to hold them at bay until the war ended. Edelstein also warned a local Jewish leader, Professor David Cohen, that he, Cohen, would have to announce horrible things which would earn him the enmity of his own people.

Edelstein and Friedmann returned to Prague just as Hitler's Balkan invasion got underway. This development dashed whatever hopes remained for further emigration. So the Zionist leaders decided to turn their Palestine permits over to Jews in Budapest who could still use them. Understandably, many were reluctant to take this step, but

Edelstein sought to console them. "I, too, am here, we're all here," he said. "We'll stay together and leave for Palestine together later."

The Jewish community had long been operating training courses aimed at equipping its members with manual skills which might help them as immigrants if they got out, and make them more likely to survive if they did not. By the summer of 1941, some 100 such courses were being given, including one for repairing fountain pens. Edelstein visited the Lodz ghetto at this time, and the sight of its workshops and small factories busily turning out goods strengthened his conviction that becoming economically useful to the Germans would give the Czech Jews their best hope of surviving the war.

While the Nazis had not yet fully ghettoized the Czech Jews, they were increasingly concentrating them into distinct and demarcated districts. Then, toward the end of the summer, the Gemeinde, presumably at the Nazis' behest, established a new department called simply "G". Its purpose: to prepare plans for a ghetto in the Protectorate.

Chosen to head the new department was Otto Zucker, former president of the Bruenn Gemeinde. The 50-year-old Zucker had won several medals as an officer in the Austrian army in World War I. After the war he had won acclaim as one of Europe's more brilliant engineers who, prior to Hitler's advent, had executed several outstanding projects in Berlin. These included the construction of a pedestrian tunnel in a single night to avoid disrupting traffic. He was also an accomplished amateur violinist and a lover of the arts in general. Edelstein had chosen him as his own second in command when the Bruenn Gemeinde closed down, in part to provide geographic balance but also because Zucker furnished an intellectual and personality balance as well. Zucker, for his part, regarded Edelstein as somewhat exhibitionistic and disorganized, but the two generally managed to work well together.

Two developments in September spurred on the new department's efforts. One was a further crackdown on the Jews, including the requirement that they wear a yellow star. The second was the appointment of Reinhard Heydrich, the feared head of the Gestapo, as the Protectorate's Protector. At his first press conference Heydrich vowed to purge the Protectorate of Jews in eight weeks.

Virtually all Jewish leaders were now willing, indeed eager, to aid and abet ghettoization, hoping thereby to head off deportation to Poland. Fortunately, the Nazi administrator for Lodz had balked at accepting any more Jews, while work on the Polish concentrations camps had only just begun. Edelstein also sought to suggest subtly to the local SS that keeping the Jews in Czechoslovakia would enable their SS overseers to stay in Czechoslovakia as well, thereby avoiding possible service on the Russian front.

The Jewish leaders hoped at first to create a ghetto within Prague itself, but the SS quickly rejected the idea. Although Zucker claimed no other city in the country could accommodate the Protectorate's nearly 90,000 remaining Jews, Guenther told him to look for sites with less than 6,000 inhabitants for the projected ghetto. The choice eventually narrowed to one town: Theresienstadt.

It was not the choice of the Jews. Though it was a somewhat scenic community with broad streets, a large square, and two large and two small parks, Theresienstadt was also a fortress town named after the Austrian empress Maria Theresa. The town was encircled by a double layer of embankments, each several yards thick and containing dark, dank chambers (casemates). It also had a high level of underground water, for the Eger, a tributary of the Elbe, flowed just outside it. This would make construction difficult. But most relevant was its role as a garrison town with no industry to speak of. This feature, plus its small size, would make it difficult to develop the economically useful activities which Edelstein regarded as the key to Jewish preservation.

The Nazis, however, thought differently. A town built in 1780 to keep Austria's enemies out would now serve well to keep Germany's enemies in. Moreover, Theresienstadt was smack on the border of the Reich itself, for the Eger separated Bohemia from the Sudetenland. Should the need ever arise, the SS could summon help from Leitmeritz, a German city less than two miles away. They could also count on assistance from the SS garrison at a former Czech prison known as the Little Fortress which lay just outside Theresienstadt. The Gestapo had taken over the prison and was using it to house Czech political prisoners.

Moving out Theresienstadt's 6,000-odd inhabitants would pose no particular problem since the demobilization of the Czech army had deprived the community of its main economic base. The question of housing 88,000 Jews in 219 houses plus 14 military barracks and administrative buildings also posed no critical problem for the Nazis, for when it came to the long-term future of the Czech Jews, they had other ideas in mind.

Life for the Czech Jews was becoming increasingly hellish. This was especially true outside of Prague where even Jewish teenagers were occasionally hung for such offenses as failing to wear a star. But the real blow fell on October 14 when Prague's chief of police issued orders to send 5,000 Jews to the East.

In accordance with Nazi practice, the job of selecting the deportees was given to the Jews. But when the two men charged with this task appeared to be dragging their feet, and when only 300 showed up for the first transport instead of the scheduled 1600, Karl Rahm, who was sitting in for Guenther, became furious and dispatched the pair to Mauthausen, the harshest concentration camp within the Reich. In about two weeks, word came back that both had been fatally shot "while trying to escape."

As the deportations went forward during late October and early November, the Jewish leaders realized that Theresienstadt provided their only hope. They therefore worked feverishly to prepare for its establishment and operation. On November 6 they presented their plan to the SS. It envisioned an elaborate administrative apparatus, including a post office, a telegraph service, and even a "travel bureau," the latter presumably to assist those Jews who might still be able to emigrate.

The Nazis made little comment on the plans but asked both the Zionists and non-Zionists to submit lists for a Council of Elders who would supposedly run the community. Edelstein, who headed the Zionist list, was chosen by the Nazis to head the Council, with Zucker as his deputy. They would work under a Nazi commandant, a 29-year-old SS captain from Vienna named Siegfried Seidl. (Seidl was one of the few SS officers with a Ph.D., but as we shall see, his degree may have been obtained with Jewish assistance.)

On November 10 the Nazis ordered the Gemeinde to have a construction crew ready to leave for Theresienstadt in 15 days to prepare its transformation into a Jewish ghetto. Since the Nazis promised not only to exempt the men and their families from deportation to the East, but also to allow them to write freely to their families and friends and even to return for Sunday visits, the Gemeinde experienced no trouble finding volunteers. The first group of 342 left for Theresienstadt on November 24, followed by a second group of 1,000 on December 4 and a third group some three days later. The last work detail arrived in buoyant spirits, for at the train station they had seen headlines reporting the Japanese attack on Pearl Harbor. Already infected with the desperate optimism that would grip so many of Theresienstadt's future residents, they believed America's involvement signaled a speedy end to the war.

Edelstein, Zucker, and about 30 of their associates had come to Theresienstadt on December 4. They too had arrived in a good mood, having joked and told stories on the train. The nearest train station to the new ghetto was in Bauschowitz, a Czech town nearly two miles away. After getting off the train, they got lost but eventually found their way to Theresienstadt. Carrying small suitcases and unaccompanied by any police escort, they passed through the gates of their new community.

---

3. During this period Kahn often sought to dissuade Edelstein from cooperating closely with the Nazis, but he nonetheless admired his courage. Once, after seeing Edelstein voluntarily take responsibility for the failure of another Zionist to fulfill an SS assignment, Kahn said, "I could not have done that."

CHAPTER 2
GENESIS OF A GHETTO

The SS did not wait for the Jewish construction crews to complete their work before sending other Jews to join them. On December 4, the day the second work group as well as Edelstein and his fellow functionaries left for Theresienstadt, two more transports of 1,000 each from Prague and Bruenn departed for the "paradise ghetto." Included were women and children along with many elderly and ill Jews. By the end of the month, 7,350 Czech Jews were living in the town.

The deportations accelerated during the first half of 1942, as over 50,000 more arrived by train at Bauschowitz from where they walked or, if elderly or infirm, rode in a truck to Theresienstadt. By early summer the vast majority of the Protectorate's Jews had arrived, and so in July the Nazis sent most of the Gemeinde's functionaries to Theresienstadt as well, keeping only a skeleton staff in Prague. They also retained a small group of Hebraic specialists to work in the Jewish museum, for Nazi scholars wanted to maintain the artifacts and archives of what they intended to be an "extinct race" and had selected Prague as the center for this enterprise.

In late June the Nazis cleared out the 3,400 Czech Gentiles still living in Theresienstadt and on July 2 formally turned the town over to the Council of Elders. The evacuation of the Gentiles opened the way to a new wave of deportations, this one from the Reich itself. Beginning in June, but mounting rapidly during the summer and continuing into the fall, trains from Berlin, Hamburg, Vienna, and other German cities poured 33,000 German Jews and 14,000 Austrian Jews into Theresienstadt, along with some 213 from Luxembourg and 3 from France, namely, former Le Havre mayor and French cabinet minister Leon Mayer and his wife and daughter.(4)

The first half of 1943 brought further deportees from Czechoslovakia, the Reich, and Luxembourg, and in April the first group of 297 arrived from Holland. These newcomers, however, were all former German Jews who had fled to Holland before the war. The 4,597 privileged Dutch Jews who would end up in Theresienstadt would come later, as would smaller delegations from Denmark, Slovakia, and Hungary.

The new arrivals not only swelled Theresienstadt's population but changed its composition in many ways. By March 1942 women made up a slight majority of its inhabitants, and by mid-1943 they outnumbered men by nearly 3 to 2. Only in the 16-and-under age group did males have a slight edge.

The city's age level also rose dramatically with the influx of the mostly elderly German and Austrian Jews, and by mid-1943 nearly 40 percent of the residents were over 60 years of age. Although it was in this group that the numerical discrepancy between men and women reached its highest level, still, even in the 16-to-55 age group there were 25 percent more women than men.

Among the later arrivals from the Reich were employees of various Jewish institutions, for with the widespread deportation of Austrian and German Jews now underway, most being sent to the new concentration camps in Poland, these Jewish institutions were required to scale back or phase out most of their operations. Many employees of the Vienna Gemeinde, including doctors and nurses from the city's only Jewish hospital, began arriving in the fall of 1942, while most of those from Germany reached Theresienstadt early in 1943.

On June 10, 1943 Jewish life in Germany officially ended as the Gestapo came to the offices of the Berlin Gemeinde, the last Gemeinde still operating in the Reich, to announce its dissolution. Two hundred of its employees, along with 300 patients from the Jewish hospital, were ordered to the collection center from which on June 16 they left for Theresienstadt.(5)

The Council of Elders selected to run the community consisted of six Zionists, including Edelstein, three non-Zionists, and three "specialists." Since one of the latter, an engineer named Jiri Vogel, was a communist, all main sectors of Czech Jewry were represented. Zucker was also on the Council and continued to serve as Edelstein's second in command.

The plans previously drawn up in Prague, minus a few niceties such as the travel bureau, had been approved by the SS. They envisaged five major departments: Executive Office or Internal Affairs Administration, Economics, Technical, Finance, and Health and Welfare. Later, three more departments--Labor, Youth Welfare, and Recreation--were added. All administrative offices were lodged in one building, the former Magdeburg barracks, and Edelstein and his personal staff lived there.

The most elaborate of these departments was the Internal Affairs Administration. It included a legal section with both criminal and probate courts, a security division which operated a ghetto police force and fire department, and a central registry for births, deaths, marriages, etc. There were also offices to assign housing, maintain buildings, and operate an internal mail service.

A Jewish police force, the Ghetto Watch, came into existence early in the ghetto's creation. From an initial membership of 35, it gradually swelled until by early 1943 it counted 420 members plus a reserve. For a community which was only a little over 700 yards long and 500 yards wide, and which was already policed by about two dozen SS men assisted by over 100 Czech gendarmes, this was an extraordinary figure. Its members were mostly younger men who had completed their military service in the Czech army, many as reserve officers. It remained virtually all Czech despite the arrival of German, Austrian, and, later, Dutch and other Jews, for these groups included few physically fit men in suitable age brackets. All members of the Ghetto Watch, however, were required to speak German.

The Jewish policemen were not, of course, given any real weapons or, for that matter, uniforms, although they did wear a special helmet and arm band and carried small clubs. Each took an oath saying, "I swear by Almighty God to serve the Elder of the Jews to the best of my ability and conscience, fearlessly, faithfully, in body and soul, for the benefit of the Theresienstadt ghetto."

Separate from the Ghetto Watch was a detective bureau headed by the former executive director of the League of German Jewish Front Fighters. The Nazis allowed the bureau to investigate and prosecute all crimes among inmates, reserving to themselves crimes between ghetto residents and the outside world, such as smuggling of contraband material into and out of the ghetto. During its first year, the bureau investigated over 5,000 crimes, most of them minor infractions such as spitting on the street or insulting a member of the Death Watch. (The latter offense constituted 10 percent of all the Ghetto's reported "crimes" during the first year.) Most of the more serious crimes consisted of stealing. Ghetto records indicate that almost no violent crimes occurred that year or any other year, and given Theresienstadt's small area and dense population, it would have been difficult for any such crimes to occur without coming to the bureau's attention.

At first, the SS administered the punishments, which most often took the form of *Stockschlaege* or caning. The number of blows would vary from 10 to 25, but the higher number had to be approved by Prague. Later the SS required members of the Ghetto Watch to inflict the blows themselves, and any member who did not strike hard enough would be caned himself. But as the ghetto's own Justice division took shape, the SS turned over to it the punishment function for all crimes within the Jewish administration's jurisdiction and also entrusted it with the operation of two jails, one for men and one for women, set up in the basements of two separate barracks. The SS established a jail in the basement of its own headquarters for those whose crimes it continued to prosecute.

The ghetto judges, all of whom had been judges prior to the Nazi era, handed out mostly lenient sentences, though occasionally they could be somewhat severe. Thus, while most convicted offenders received short jail sentences of a few days or a week or two, a physician found guilty of taking the earrings of a deceased woman received a three-month jail term and lost the right to practice his profession in Theresienstadt.

All sentences needed approval from Seidl, who usually went along with them and frequently, in response to Edelstein's request, released prisoners early. But even the mildest of sentences stigmatized the offender and, as we shall see, usually created dire consequences for the culprit's future.

Milder, less consequential sentences were handed out by a labor court which adjudicated cases of chronic lateness, absenteeism, etc. This court imposed fines, overtime work, reassignment to less desirable positions, and similar punishments.

An engineer, who had once taken a training program in firefighting and had then served for a time as a volunteer fireman, organized a fire department of some 50 men. They took over the town's existing fire apparatus, which consisted of three vehicles, only one of them motorized. The other two had been horse-drawn but were now pulled by the firemen themselves. During their first year they put out 200 fires, allowing none to become serious blazes. The men also served as medical orderlies and sometimes took on other duties. Like the Ghetto Watch, the fire department remained virtually all Czech. Also like the Ghetto Watch, its members developed a high degree of solidarity and a marked *esprit de corps*.

The Jewish administration was even more successful in setting up and operating facilities for children and the ill and in running cultural and athletic programs, all of which will be described in more detail in later chapters. But a main focus of its attention now and in the future was to ensure that the ghetto turned out goods which the Germans could use.

All newcomers on arrival filled out detailed forms covering their education, skills, work experience, etc., and after being examined by a doctor, were placed in one of four categories: heavy work, ordinary work, light work, and work exempt. All those in the first two categories were initially grouped into 100-member labor brigades to do whatever needed doing until they were assigned permanent positions. Women were also expected to work, although their labor brigades usually handled cleaning duties while the men worked at construction and maintenance.

By the end of January 1942, hardly more than two months after the first construction detail had arrived, facilities for locksmithing, sewing machine repair, carpentry, glass making, house painting, shoemaking, leather craft, and packaging were busily in operation. The carpenter shop alone employed 39 workers plus two foremen, and the tailor shop employed 33. Initially, most economic activity focused on producing goods for the community itself, but soon Theresienstadt's workshops began turning out leather boots, uniforms, inkwells and fountain pens, lampshades, salt shakers, and even toys for the Germans. In September 1942 alone the community produced, among other things, 1,000 dresses and 400 pairs of boots.

Some worked just outside the town, tilling fields and tending animals at an extensive farm which the SS maintained for its own use. Others volunteered for special work details elsewhere in the Protectorate, and in late winter of 1943 some 400 men left for the coal mines, while in April 1,000 young women departed to do forestry work. All were returned to the town in June.

In the summer of 1942 the Nazis set up a plant for splitting feldspar. Since this task required a highly delicate touch, it employed only women. Three of the 150 to 300 women involved were blind, their sensitive fingers more than compensating for their lack of sight. This project greatly heartened Edelstein and his associates, since the work seemed vital to the Nazis' war effort and hence more likely to help the ghetto remain in existence.

The following May the Nazis inaugurated another, much larger war-related activity. They stretched an awning over the town square and put 1,000 men and women to work packaging special kits designed to help tank engines start in frosty weather. The circus-like aspect of the large tent gave rise to a popular joke. "Theresienstadt has the only circus in the world where the people work and the animals [the SS] watch."

Another project which the Nazis deemed quite important, though it bore no relation to the military, was the Hebrew library. Housed in its own small building, it employed 30 to 40 rabbis and rabbinical scholars in cataloging various Hebrew works for the Prague museum and archive project mentioned earlier. Those engaged in this effort received extra food rations since many were elderly and could not be replaced. During his frequent visits to Theresienstadt, Eichmann liked to drop in on the library to check on its work and to show off his few words of Hebrew.

But there was other work for rabbis besides cataloging. Although the SS permitted no official rabbinate, Edelstein created one *de facto* by setting up a section within the Internal Affairs Department to handle burials. He appointed Sigmund Unger, former Chief Rabbi of Bruenn, to head it along with two other rabbis to assist him. The trio also held a rabbinical court (*Beth Din*) which performed marriages (there were 124 marriages in 1942 and 233 in 1943), granted divorces, and supervised Jewish religious activities in the community generally.

There was a fair amount of such religious activity, as most of Theresienstadt's other rabbis held services and performed Jewish rites, such as bar mitzvahs, in whatever space they could find. A good many Torahs, prayer shawls, prayer books, and other religious objects had found their way to the ghetto, many brought by new arrivals, while the Red Cross supplied matzoh for Passover seders. The most conspicuous component missing from the community's religious rituals was wine.

Judaism was not the only religion practiced in Theresienstadt. Nearly one-eighth of its residents considered themselves non-Jews, and while some of these declared themselves *konfessionslos*, i.e., without religion, the rest considered themselves Christians. They included over 1,130 Catholics and about 830 Protestants.

In the fall of 1942 two Jewish Catholics from Vienna, one a former professor of engineering, founded a Catholic congregation, and a rather bemused Edelstein allotted them space in an attic for Sunday services. (There was a large Catholic church in town, but the Nazis had locked it up, neither using it themselves nor allowing the Catholic Jews to use it.) The organizers found a religious leader in Brother Kuhnert, a monk who was also from Vienna. Only 15 worshippers turned out at first and, frequently shivering from the drafty cold, they would stand around the Jewish monk in a semicircle, making their responses as he said the Mass. As one of them later recalled, "We felt very close to God in this hour and were conscious of an affinity with the early Christians in Rome and what they must have felt in their catacombs."

The number of regular worshippers at Catholic services soon grew to nearly 100, with 200 or 300 showing up on Christmas and Easter. Later they organized a branch of the Leo Society and held a lecture series on "Christian Personalities."

The Protestant congregation came into being soon after the Catholic one. It was organized by a former Hamburg judge named Artur Goldschmidt. Although raised as a Protestant and married to an Aryan- -he had lost his exemption from deportation when his wife died-- Goldschmidt had never been particularly active in church affairs. But now in Theresienstadt at the age of 70 he assembled a few former friends and fellow believers and together they began reading the Gospels on Sunday. Others joined them and soon they were holding services in work sheds and other such space as they could find until Edelstein allowed them to share the attic used by the Catholics, holding their devotions at a different time. Goldschmidt would conduct the service and preach the sermon, while a former music teacher directed the choir. A non-Christian woman violinist supplied instrumental accompaniment.

Soon Theresienstadt's Protestant congregation was also flourishing, with Goldschmidt visiting the sick, giving communion, and officiating at funerals. The two groups of Christian Jews got along remarkably well, especially when one considers the tensions which then colored Catholic-Protestant relations in the outside world. One of the Protestants created an altar which could be used by both groups, and Goldschmidt, making his hospital rounds, would often say an Ave Maria for a dying Catholic. As one Jewish observer noted, "The Theresienstadt ghetto is the only ghetto in the world where Catholic and Protestant services are held. In an attic room Protestants and Catholics pray. Here the Ecclesia have reconciled." In a sense, therefore, the ecumenical movement which would sweep through the Christian world after the war may have first shown itself in this Jewish ghetto.

Despite all these activities, religion did not play a major role in the life of the community. The marriages and divorces--there would be 20 of the latter during the community's entire existence--had no real legal validity. (As we will see, however, they did figure importantly in one very crucial aspect of Theresienstadt life.) Most registered Jews attended services only on the High Holy Days, if at all, and many regarded holidays such as Chanukkah and Passover more as nationalistic celebrations than religious events.

A more significant though far less sizeable group were the communists. Although they numbered only about 100 active members, they made their influence felt, not so much from having a member on the Council of Elders, for Vogel owed his position more to his technical than his political qualifications, but through their zealousness and close-knit organization. Edelstein maintained continual contact with them.

But the real driving force in Theresienstadt were the Zionists, especially the Czechs. Though split into various groups--there were three distinct Zionist youth organizations plus a small Mizrachi or religious Zionist youth faction--their loyalty to Edelstein and their goal of creating the first all-Jewish community in the diaspora united them.

They occupied many, though by no means all, of the key posts in the administration, operated the children's houses, and maintained a disguised registry which listed their 6,000 members under a card file entry innocuously entitled "Interested in Jewish Lectures." They held meetings and secretly elected candidates to a 28-member council. They even paid dues in the form of margarine and sugar from their scanty rations.

The younger Zionists cooperated with the communists to set up a secret 200-man self-defense force. All of its members had served in the Czech army and its leaders had been officers, though usually in the reserves. They began establishing a central storage depot with a radio, but closed it down when the SS became suspicious. Subsequently, they installed a radio in the attic of a bakery, and one member who knew English monitored BBC broadcasts regularly. In this way, they heard reports of the gas chambers in Poland, though most, including Edelstein, refused to believe them.

They made no plans for an uprising, realizing its futility. Instead, they assigned their members work in the electrical plant, water division, fire, police, and other sectors, where they could take some defensive action should the Nazis decide to destroy the ghetto. They also surveyed and identified those sites which seemed most defendable and familiarized themselves with the sewers leading out of town. They had no access to weapons, but some members experimented with homemade bombs.

The Nazis, however, were showing little interest at this point in annihilating their model ghetto. In September 1942 they allowed residents to send a card of 30 words each month to anyone in the Reich or the Protectorate. Later the residents were allowed to receive food packages from relatives or friends, usually former Aryan in-laws, and by the spring of 1943 some 3,000 such packages a month were flowing into the town. At about the same time, the SS also began allowing Jewish organizations with representatives in Geneva, such as the World Jewish Congress, the Joint Distribution Committee, and Hijet, an organization of orthodox rabbis, to send food to Theresienstadt through the International Red Cross. Before the year was out, the IRC had shipped nearly 12,000 pounds of condensed milk, dried prunes, and other foodstuffs to the community along with 86 crates of medicine. Arrangements were also made for sending individual packages of sardines from Portugal.

The packages arriving in Theresienstadt bolstered not only the ghetto residents' physical health but their mental well being as well, for they reassured them that the outside world had not forgotten them. The foreign minister of the London-based Czechoslovakian government-in-exile reported to his colleagues, "These shipments are an expression of sympathy by the Czechs for the Jews."(6)

In the meantime, the Nazis were moving forward in making Theresienstadt seem more like a normal community. In the summer of 1942 they decided to set up a ghetto bank, with every resident to receive a fixed amount of money depending on which of five categories he/she belonged to: member of the Council of Elders, *Prominente*, heavy worker, regular worker, or nonworker. The bank would employ 50 to 60 people and issue 53 million crowns in notes of 1-to-100-crown denominations.

Designed by ghetto artists, these ghetto crowns bore Edelstein's signature and displayed a picture of Moses holding the Ten Commandments. The notes did not actually arrive until the spring of 1943, for Heydrich felt the initial designs made Moses appear too Aryan. The final version, therefore, showed a hooked-nose, kinky-haired Moses whose arm, possibly intentionally, was obscuring the commandment, "Thou shalt not kill."

The Nazis also began authorizing outlets for spending the new currency. Thus, in the fall of 1942, a few stores opened up along with a lending library. Ghetto crowns were also to be used for showers and laundry. Then, on December 8, a coffeehouse was opened where, for two ghetto crowns, residents could sit for two hours over a cup of substitute coffee. With its opening, the Nazis relaxed their ban on music, which they had not rigidly enforced in any case, and allowed--indeed ordered--a band to play.

The band, under the baton of an engineer who was an amateur trumpet player, called itself "The Ghetto Swingers." It was certainly a most unusual swing band since it included three violinists but no pianist, no suitable keyboard instrument then being available. Its regular vocalists were three young women who sang in the style of the Andrew sisters, a then famed American singing trio whose films the women had apparently seen before the war. Various instrumental and vocal soloists also performed. Thus, the coffeehouse had no trouble keeping its tables full from 10:30 A.M. when it opened to its closing at 7:00 P.M.

With such features as these, one can understand the later comment of one woman who ended up in Theresienstadt after a stay in Auschwitz. "It was a city for prisoners and you could walk freely wearing a star. It was heaven." Edelstein himself, when authorized in October 1942 to write a letter to Fritz Ullmann, the Jewish Agency representative in Geneva, hastened to assure "Dear Ully," that "you need not worry about us. We are alive and well." Edelstein told Ullmann how his wife Miriam, for example, after performing her household chores, "works in the garden, an activity she is good at and enjoys." He then went on to describe the various achievements of the ghetto, praising especially the accomplishments of Dr. Erich Munk, who headed the health services.

To be sure, this letter was written under Nazi supervision, but a month later, in a more private communication to some of his associates, the Theresienstadt elder said, "If I were to review the past year, I would have to admit that all the things I really wanted and which were worth fighting for have gradually been realized . . . a beneficent destiny has fashioned our lives better than I had imagined or feared."

When Edelstein wrote his anniversary letter expressing satisfaction with the way things were going, he was still Theresienstadt's Jewish administrator. But already the influx of German and Austrian Jews was weakening his hold over the community. At the beginning of October the Nazis removed six or half of the members of the all-Czech Council of Elders and replaced them with four German and two Austrian Jews. They also removed Zucker as Deputy Elder and installed a former executive director of the Berlin Gemeinde, Heinrich Stahl, in his place. When Stahl died a few weeks later, they named Desider Friedmann, a former president of the Vienna Gemeinde and one of their Austrian appointees to the Elder Council, to replace him. (The other Austrian appointee on the council was former Zionist leader Robert Stricker.)

Edelstein still reigned as Elder and Zucker remained, in fact if not in title, his second in command. But on January 27 a telegram arrived for Seidl from Berlin saying, "Important (Jewish) functionaries leave this morning for Theresienstadt." This would create more critical consequences for Edelstein and for the community he headed.

Among those arriving the next day from Berlin were Leo Baeck and Paul Eppstein. Arriving the following day from Vienna was Benjamin Murmelstein.

Baeck posed no threat to Edelstein's leadership, for the courageous rabbi had frequently incurred the Nazis' displeasure. Once, for example, when summoned to Gestapo headquarters on a Saturday, he had declined, saying, "On the Sabbath I go to services." (Baeck, it should be noted, had no fear of death, having faced it repeatedly as a chaplain to German Jewish soldiers in the trenches of World War I.) Because of his international prestige, the Nazis had taken no action against Baeck; indeed, they had retained him as president of the National Association of German Jews (RVE), an organization they had created to help administer Jewish affairs. But on his arrival at Theresienstadt, he was given no special title or treatment and, in fact, was assigned work as a common laborer.

But with Paul Eppstein, who had served as executive director of the organization which Baeck headed, it was a different story.

Born in Mannheim in 1901 and thus two years older than Edelstein, he had become a docent or assistant professor of sociology at a local university at the comparatively young age of 25. He had also been active in Zionist affairs. When he lost his academic position following the Nazi takeover, he moved to Berlin and went to work for the RVE. His abilities as an administrator, plus the departure or death of the other functionaries, allowed him to move up, eventually assuming the post of executive director.

Eppstein was a meticulous man--one survivor characterizes him as a "buttoned-down type"--and something of an aesthete as well. He loved music and played the piano. But he had at one time spent four months in a Gestapo prison where, reportedly, he was frequently tortured. This, in the words of another observer, left him "frightened and compliant," a shadow of his former self. Could he be called a collaborator? Certainly, he worked with the Nazis, but so did nearly all Jewish leaders including Baeck himself. In any case, Eppstein was not the Nazis' first choice for executive director of the RVE; they had appointed him only when Baeck threatened to resign as president if they insisted on their number one candidate, a rank opportunist named George Kareski. Baeck apparently found Eppstein's activities in the position at least acceptable if not always applaudable.

Eppstein himself, though industrious and ambitious, displayed a somewhat beaten-down demeanor. He even walked with a slight stoop as if he felt unequal to the burden he bore. Lacking Edelstein's optimism and elan, Eppstein's mien often expressed sadness and fear. Since his imprisonment he had kept cyanide with him at all times, telling an associate, "I know the time will come when I'll no longer be able to say yes. . . ."

This was the man the Nazis now decided to appoint as Theresien-stadt's new elder. As stated in a memo issued after a meeting between the Jewish functionaries and the SS officials, "For the time being, Theresienstadt will be run by a board of 13, with Dr. Eppstein at its head."

Why the Nazis replaced Edelstein with Eppstein remains unknown. Perhaps they preferred to deal with an urbane German Jew than with an unpolished Galician whose accent and manner betrayed his humble origins. Quite possibly they felt the educated Eppstein would make a better figurehead for show purposes, for the former professor not only spoke a pure German but also a fairly fluent English, and the Nazis may have been planning to use him for overseas broadcasts. (There is some hint of this in later documents.) Also, they may have feared Edelstein's popularity and thought Eppstein would more faithfully execute their wishes. But all this is speculation. The fact remains that Eppstein was now Theresienstadt's Jewish administrator while Edelstein was his deputy.

The Nazis did attempt to soften the blow. According to the memo issued by Edelstein and Zucker after the meeting, "Herr SSOSBF [SS Obersturmbannfuehrer or Lieutenant Colonel], Eichmann extends to the Jewish elder, Edelstein, his expressed acknowledgment of his activities and wishes that the announcement . . . will not be interpreted as a demotion. The creation of a new ghetto similar to Theresienstadt is being considered, and it is well possible that Edelstein will be entrusted with the leadership of this new ghetto. However, no decision has been made on this matter." Far from assuaged, Edelstein could not resist pointing out that "after 14 months of constructive work I can hardly accept this decision with a feeling of satisfaction." Moreover, "I scarcely feel physically strong enough to take on the task of organizing a new ghetto." Edelstein, in fact, tendered his resignation from the Council of Elders and asked for assignment as an ordinary laborer.

Eichmann, however, wanted to keep him as Deputy Elder, and when Edelstein's Czech followers urged him to accept the number two position, he did so. The Czechs still conidered him their leader and came to him, not Eppstein, with their concerns.(7)

Although Eppstein expressed some discomfort over displacing Edelstein, whom he acknowledged as having done all the preparatory and foundation work for the ghetto, he showed little zeal for sharing power with him. Their contrasting backgrounds, tastes, and life styles alone argued against any close cooperation. Soon he stopped taking Edelstein with him to his daily meetings with Seidl. When friends pointed out that he might want a witness to what Seidl ordered or did not order him to do, Eppstein replied scornfully that he did not want to have anything to do with this "union secretary." (Edelstein had once been secretary to the Czech branch of Poale Zion, a Zionist labor organization.) Edelstein, for his part, showed little enthusiasm for assisting the seemingly stuck-up Prussian Jew who had replaced him.

But Eppstein was not the only newcomer to shake up Theresienstadt's Jewish hierarchy. There was also Benjamin Murmelstein.

The rabbi who arrived in Theresienstadt a day or two after Eppstein did not receive a warm welcome. Edelstein and Zucker's memo points out that they had received no orders to give special treatment to the functionaries arriving the next day, and adds, "This observation is expressly valid for Dr. Murmelstein." The memo also states that Seidl had made it clear that "he would be compelled to intervene if any person such as Dr. Murmelstein should attempt to make difficulties for the new leadership because their own aspirations had not been satisfied." So Murmelstein received no extra food allowance, no preferred housing, and no prestigious position. But this changed the following day when word arrived that Joseph Loewenherz, who had headed the Viennese Gemeinde and whose arrival had been anticipated, would not be coming after all. At the last moment, Eichmann had decided to keep Loewenherz in Vienna.

The SS had originally intended to install Loewenherz as the third member of a Jewish "triumvirate" which would administer Theresienstadt. They now installed Murmelstein instead.

Although Murmelstein was to represent the Austrian Jews in Theresienstadt, he enjoyed little favor or support from them. In Vienna, as Loewenherz's deputy in charge of deportation, he had become known for his ruthless efficiency. Once ordered by the Nazis to prepare a list of 1,000 Jews for deportation, he had proudly announced that he had 2,000 ready to be shipped out. Few of his fellow functionaries in the Vienna Gemeinde liked or trusted him.

His appearance and manner also argued against him. An obese man with small, sunken, unrevealing eyes--"pig's eyes" was the way some characterized him--he had become known for his abrasive, often abusive, manner in dealing with his fellow Jews. No one disputed his brilliance, for he had written not only well-regarded scholarly articles on religious matters but also semipopular books on Jewish history and Zionism, although he was not much of a Zionist. But most believed that the able theologian had become an all-too-able, and all-too-ambitious, administrator.

As the number-three man in the Jewish administration, Murmelstein now had to be given special treatment and assigned some executive responsibilities. But since neither Eppstein nor Edelstein liked him, they assigned him an office in a former potato cellar and appointed him overseer of the Health and Technical departments, a post where his lack of professional expertise in these areas would limit his decision-making power. He was also made head of the Hebrew library, which, although a pet project of Eichmann, carried little real weight in Theresienstadt's overall operations.

Although Murmelstein would later claim to have written most of Seidl's Ph.D. thesis when both were in Vienna, Seidl showed no desire to support him in any way and rarely called him to his office. Nevertheless, Murmelstein's appointment injected a further discordant note into the Jewish administration. The "triumvirate" consisted of three men, none of whom liked or felt any real allegiance to the other two. This would hardly help the community confront the problems which were already plaguing it, and which would plague it still more in the future.

---

4. All told, over 300 Luxembourg jews, or more than 10 percent of those remaining in the Duchy, would be sent to Theresienstadt. This was double the percentage of Dutch Jews who would be so favored, while no French Jews other than the Mayer family and no Belgian Jews at all would be shipped there. Just why so many Luxembourg Jews were selected for the model ghetto remains a mystery.

5. The patients traveled on mattresses in freight cars while the others were allowed to ride in passenger cars. The following day the leaders of the Munich, Wuerzberg, and Bamberg Jewish communities, whom the Gestapo had imprisoned three months earlier for having given their lists of deported Jews to a Christian charitable organization which had requested them, were dispatched to Theresienstadt. Some 820 employees of Jewish organizations in Salonika, Greece were not so fortunate. Told that they too were going to "the new Jewish republic, the new Israel," their train took them in mid-June directly to the Auschwitz gas chambers.

Despite the massive deportations from Germany, there were still over 15,000 Jews left in Berlin, with a small staff working under a Council of Elders to administer their affairs. A similar setup was operating in vienna, which had 5,000 Jews. Vienna's Gemeinde had been dissolved the previous January.

6. The memos and letters of the exiled Czech government displays a deep and sincere concern for the welfare of the Theresienstadt's new inhabitants, whom they seemed to have looked upon simply as Czechs and not primarily as Czech Jews.

7. The memo also notes that "Herr Camp Commandant Captain Dr. Seidl stresses that he will energetically intervene in the event that this change of personnel creates any unrest in the camp." It is interesting that his memo, which the SS of course had to approve, refers at this point to Seidl as "Camp Commandant" and to Theresienstadt itself as a "camp."

CHAPTER 3
"A JOKE HATCHED IN HELL"

By late spring 1943, Herr Gottsche, the SS *Referent* for Jewish emigration in Hamburg, had become curious about the model ghetto in Bohemia where he had been sending his city's more prominent Jews. So on June 6 he decided to join a Theresienstadt-bound deportation train to see it for himself. Arriving at the Bauschowitz train station, he noticed in the distance the ivy-covered embankments of the former fortress town with the church steeple rising above them. The town did look quite picturesque. But when he announced his plans to the superior SS officer on the platform, he was asked to go first to Prague. There he was directed to return to Hamburg forthwith.

In the confusion and commotion at the railroad station, Gottsche became separated from two young aides who had accompanied him. They, meanwhile, had marched on to Theresienstadt. On arriving at the town gate and announcing their mission, they were hustled along a fenced-off perimeter street to Seidl's office. There the commandant told them to clear off immediately. They were unable to retrieve their handbags which on leaving Hamburg they had tossed into the baggage car with the luggage of the deported Jews.

What made the SS so sensitive to such impromptu visits even from its own people? If Herr Gottsche could have accompanied one of his own deportees, Kaethe Starke, he would soon have seen why. Starke, on entering the privileged community, almost fainted from the combined stench generated by the delousing station, the latrines, the potato cellars, and numerous other odiferous facilities. The dust from the town's unpaved streets, which the embankments tended to trap, further added to her discomfort.

Teenager Ditta Jedlinksy from Vienna also found the stench overpowering. But, on reaching her new quarters, she was overpowered by the sights as she observed a dead body being dragged down the stairs, while at the top of the steps she saw the rear end of a woman defecating.

Gerty Spies, a middle-aged writer and poet from Munich, recoiled in horror at the sight of ragged figures lying on multitiered bunks and even on floors. "Where was the old people's home, the living quarters about which we have been told?" she wondered. "Where were the clean houses where each would have his or her own room?"

One way or another, entering Theresienstadt for the first time was a jolt to most of its new residents. As Elsie Dornitzer put it, "Upon our arrival in Theresienstadt, my husband and I suffered the typical admission shock which paralyzed one's whole being. My husband was never able to recover. . . ."

From the very beginning of its existence it was evident that Theresienstadt would be a far cry from the paradise ghetto which the Nazis had depicted. The first work detail on November 21 had no sooner alighted from the train in Bauschowitz than they found themselves encircled by Czech gendarmes who henceforth guarded their every move. They could not even go out on the street in the evening, much less return to Prague for Sunday visits. Nor could they send or receive mail.

Lodged in barracks where they slept on the floor, they did not at first have a shelf on which to put their belongings or even a nail to hang a coat. When the food they had brought with them ran out, they received only the skimpiest of rations, and worked with constant hunger pains. When one of them developed acute appendicitis and the doctor who had come with them asked for the patient's transfer to a hospital, Seidl not only refused but threatened to punish the physician if he made any further such requests. The patient, a young man, died in agony six days later.

For subsequent deportees the trauma of Theresienstadt began when they received their deportation notice, giving them only three days in which to wind up their affairs and ordering them to pack no more than 110 pounds of belongings per person. In practice, most ended up taking far less, for the healthy adults had to carry the bags of elderly parents, sick relatives, and children, and sometimes the children themselves. The use of Jewish orderlies rather than storm troopers may have somewhat softened the deportation process, but for those from Prague it meant dealing with Robert Mandler, a former travel agent who oversaw departures for the SS at the city train station. Dressed in black coat and black boots, he looked and often acted like an SS man and he even intimidated the Czech gendarmes by insisting that they address him only in German.

The trip to Bauschowitz took two to three hours from Prague and often two or more days from Germany. On arriving at the town depot, the deportees were herded into four rows and, carrying their belongings and sometimes their children, they had to march the two miles to Theresienstadt. While many of the Czech gendarmes who supervised them showed sympathy, a few behaved harshly, beating them on the arms whenever they slowed down.

The elderly and infirm were loaded onto trucks but were jammed together so tightly that even disabled veterans on crutches had to stand. Once a young SS driver took a curve too sharply, catapulting all 27 of his elderly passengers into a ditch. At least ten were killed outright while the others either died a day or two later or were permanently crippled.

Once in Theresienstadt the new arrivals were marched through ghostlike streets--everyone in the town was ordered to stay indoors with window shades drawn when a group of deportees arrived--to whatever building had been designated as the intake center, which soon became known as the *Schleuse* or sluicegate. Here they filled out lengthy forms and underwent interrogation and examination. Some had to strip for body searches which understandably most upset the women since the searchers were men. (There was no sexual molestation, however.) All their valuables except wedding rings, but including sanitary napkins, were seized.(8)

Confusion was common and hysteria was not rare. But in the words of one deportee, "What was most unbearable was the crying of the children. What could these small innocent creatures know about the penalties of having been born Jews? The children's shrieking continued, for the adults could not console them enough to end it."

The arrivees might spend as long as five days in the *Schleuse*, during which time they bedded down on the ground or floor or, if truly lucky, in a bunk. One woman recalls sleeping in a bunk with an unknown man, both remaining fully dressed. No residents could visit the *Schleuse* to greet or assist family members or friends who might be among the new arrivals, although this rule would later not be strictly enforced. Those who had not brought their own food suffered greatly during this time, as they received little from the authorities. Spies says her group got some bread the day after their arrival, and though it was supposed to last for three days, they had to throw it away on the second day for it had already become rotten.

Emerging from the *Schleuse* brought further surprises and shocks. Until the evacuation of the town's Gentile population, the deportees were housed in army barracks where they were separated by sex, with the women and children in one building and the men and adolescent boys in another. Contact between the two groups was strictly forbidden except on Sundays when the children would be marched under gendarme supervision to spend two hours visiting their fathers.

The women rebelled at this arrangement and stormed Edelstein's office in protest. When he told them that the SS order had to be obeyed, they insisted that he try to change it. Finally, he agreed and left the room, ostensibly to go to Seidl, only to return a half hour later saying Seidl had refused to see him. In reality, he had not left the building; indeed, like the others, he was forbidden to do so.

During Theresienstadt's first six months, this segregation decree was strictly enforced. Six men who left a work detail to talk to their wives were given ten strokes of the cane, while another man, a 40-year-old with a doctor's degree who had spoken a few words to his wife and daughter but later denied it, received 25 strokes.

Punishments for other offenses were similarly severe. One could receive ten or more strokes plus jail time for leaving quarters without authorization, for failing to lift one's hat to a passing SS man or gendarme, for using an electric cooker, or for addressing an SS man or gendarme except on an official matter. For collective punishment the Nazis would sometimes cut off all electricity to a barracks after 6:00 P.M.

The Nazis were especially concerned with isolating the Jews from all unmonitored contact with non-Jews. They forbade them not only from making purchases or talking with townspeople, but even from walking on the sidewalks. Many of the town's Gentiles, however, felt sorry for the Jews and helped them secretly by providing food and posting letters.

The SS regarded the latter as an especially egregious offense. Although they were planning to allow the Jews to assure Gentile friends and relatives, such as half-Jewish children or former Aryan in-laws, that they were still alive--the ghetto itself was designed in part for this purpose--such contacts should take place only under strict supervision. Clandestine letters would defeat this aim by revealing the terrible truth of the paradise ghetto. When the SS learned in mid-December that a local glazier who frequently worked in Prague had been posting letters for Jews, they took forceful action.

Seidl and his number-two man Karl Bergel called an assembly to announce that a Czech Aryan had been caught with smuggled letters, but if the guilty persons confessed, they would not be punished. Two admitted their guilt and were promptly arrested. The investigation continued and on January 9 Seidl told Edelstein that nine men had been sentenced to death. Most of them had committed other offenses besides sending secret mail. One, for example, had removed his Jewish star in order to buy a cookie at a local store; another had once turned around quickly and without realizing that an SS man was behind him, had accidentally poked the Nazi with his elbow.

Seidl gave orders for the Ghetto Watch to carry out the executions and for the Council of Elders to observe them. Edelstein relayed the orders, but no one in the Ghetto Watch was willing to serve as executioner. Finally, a short, stocky man who had been an assistant to the executioner of Prague agreed to do so.

At 10:00 A.M. the nine men, clad only in shirts and pants in the freezing weather, and escorted by 15 gendarmes, were marched to the execution site. When a 17-year-old youth cried out, "All I did was write a note to my grandmother," the other eight shouted, "Keep quiet and don't damage our honor." At the gallows, one called out to the SS men, "You can do this but you still won't win the war." And when an SS man said to one of the prisoners, "Come here, you cowardly dog," the man replied, "I'm not a coward but I am innocent," and he placed the rope around his neck himself. A third yelled, "We are not afraid and in any case you will not win the war." Still another sang a Czech battle song.

Despite the early hour, most of the SS men present seemed half drunk. The Czech gendarmes, however, watched in stony silence, some with tears in their eyes. Edelstein and his fellow elders were, of course, horrified. That night Kaddish, the Jewish prayer for the dead, was recited throughout the men's barracks.

A further execution took place six weeks later, but this time Edelstein refused to attend and offered his resignation as Elder. The Nazis rejected the resignation and allowed him and the other Council members to stay away. The SS staged no further executions in Theresienstadt itself. They found other, though scarcely less harsh, ways of handling such "major offenders."(9)

The evacuation of the Czech townspeople brought a relaxation of many of the rules governing Theresienstadt's new residents. Men and women could now visit each other's barracks after work, while children could roam about fairly freely. Walking on the sidewalks was also allowed.

But removal of the town's regular residents opened the gates to the arrival of German and Austrian Jews as well as additional Jews from Czechoslovakia. This only aggravated an already aggravating problem: the shortage of space.

The population had increased 50 percent in June, but in the following month it doubled. The influx continued during August and September, and by mid-September over 58,000 people were living in an area little more than seven football fields long and five football fields wide. No other Jewish ghetto approached this degree of congestion, while comparisons with normal urban living densities seem bizarre. If Berlin, for example, had had the same population density as Theresienstadt had in that month, the German capital would have contained nearly 100 million people or more than the combined populations of Germany and Austria!

As *total* living area shrank to less than 18 square feet per person, the Jewish administration, which had not anticipated the Nazis' plan to send non-Czech Jews to their ghetto, worked frantically to exploit every inch of available space. New arrivals were jammed into attics or cellars, even though such quarters were often without windows, plumbing, heat and, in the case of cellars, floors. Rooms that had once housed three or four people now had to shelter up to 60. Triple-tiered bunks, each tier sleeping two persons, were placed almost cheek-by-jowl, leaving barely enough room for climbing in and out. Vertically, the tiers themselves were so close together that an occupant had to lean forward to avoid bumping his or her head. To sit in a chair was a luxury.

Yet those with bunks were actually the luckier ones, for over one-third did not even have a bunk during Theresienstadt's first year. They huddled on the floor or ground. Sam Berger recalls wandering after arrival from one men's quarters to another seeing "everywhere the same sight: the building jammed from cellar to roof with people. . . Healthy persons lay alongside sick ones, mobile individuals next to those who could no longer move. There was no in-between space and people had to crawl over one another when they wanted to go anywhere."

Conditions for women were no better. "I was not given much of a welcome," Clara Eisenkraft later recalled, "for the room was already overcrowded. My neighbors to the left and right complained bitterly when they had to make room for me. . . Every morning there was a lot of bickering when beds were made. 'You pushed your mattress onto my space,' was the general complaint. 'These five centimeters belong to me.'" If she stretched her legs in her sleep, she would get a rough kick that woke her and then would not be able to get back to sleep. "That's when I cried."

The town's plumbing facilities were primitive to begin with, for flush toilets and running water had only been installed a few years earlier. Under the pressure of the new population, they quickly became swamped. Each toilet now had to serve over 50 and sometimes as many as 100 people. Most had no lights and this, plus their constant use, made them almost impossible to keep clean. Water taps were not only few in number, but because of the town's limited water mains their use had to be restricted to three one-hour periods a day. A resident could reckon on getting a shower at the central bath house only once every two months and on using the central laundry once every three or four months. Furthermore, anyone having his/her bedding laundered could scarcely get anything else washed, since strict limits governed how much could be sent.

Such conditions naturally favored the growth of vermin and battling them soon became, in Baeck's words, "a war waged hour by hour, day and night." One woman remembers killing 103 bugs at night and then finding 40 to 50 on the walls the next morning. Physicians removing a plaster-of-paris cast often found a swarm of bugs crawling on the injured limb.

The most feared form of vermin were lice which could spread typhus epidemics, the chief non-Nazi scourge of all ghettos and concentration camps. With SS approval, since the Nazis feared typhus themselves, the administration kept a delousing station in nearly constant operation. Delousing squads equipped with gas masks also made regular trips to living quarters, and after ordering everyone out and sealing up the windows, would spray Zyklon-B, the same gas used in the Auschwitz gas chambers. But all these efforts achieved only minimal results. A few days after delousing, a room and its inhabitants would usually be infested again.

Many other factors contributed to making Theresienstadt's shelter situation a source of torment. A constant shortage of coal caused most residents to shiver all winter--some actually froze to death--while the lack of ventilation caused those in the attics to nearly suffocate during the summer. Also, families remained separated for the most part, and this only increased with the establishment of children's houses. Now, father, mother, sons, and daughters would typically find themselves all living in different places, with a grandparent in still another location. On the other hand, a few found themselves living too close to family or former family members. For example, Victor Ullmann, a brilliant Czech musician, who had conducted opera in Prague at the age of 22, came to Theresienstadt with his third wife only to find himself living almost next door to his two former wives.

For these as well as other reasons, such as the constant search for additional space or the takeover of one's own space for other purposes, Theresienstadters moved frequently. One woman claims to have changed her quarters 17 times during her stay there. For women, such moves could be especially onerous, since they usually needed the help of men to move their mattresses, etc., and unrelated men expected to be compensated, usually with food.

Finally, there was the constant commotion, especially during the early evening visiting hours, and a lack of privacy and solitude which prevailed at all hours. "There was no place in camp where one could withdraw to meditate or to be for one hour a separate individual," writes Heinrich Liebrecht. "There was no private conversation which was not necessarily overheard by someone else. . . When one whistled a tune, someone always chimed in, especially if it was by Dvorak or Smetana. . . . "

Horrendous as Theresienstadt housing conditions may have been during these early years, they were not the residents' chief source of daily suffering. Food, or the lack of it, weighed on them much more heavily.

The Nazis claimed originally that the ghetto residents would receive a per capita food ration equivalent to that of the Protectorate. This may even have been their intention for, as we have seen, Theresienstadt was designed *in part* for people whom the Nazis wanted to keep alive, at least until they won the war. But whatever their intentions, most residents never enjoyed anywhere near the food rations of the Czechs outside their walls, who were themselves none too well supplied.

The menu consisted chiefly of bread, potatoes, and a watery soup. Some margarine and sugar--about two ounces per week of the former and less than one and one-half ounces of the latter--were sometimes included. The residents were also to receive up to four ounces of meat, mostly horseflesh, and up to eight ounces of skim milk a week, though many a week would see less or none of these foodstuffs available. No fruits were ever officially distributed, and turnips were the only vegetable to show up with any regularity.

Estimates of total per capita calories provided daily ranged from 1300 or less, to 1800, with the lower figure being more frequently mentioned. This should be compared with the "Special Regime" given the worst offenders in the Soviet labor camps which provided about 2,000 calories.

The shortage of kitchen facilities added to the problem by forcing people to stand in line for long periods, sometimes in rain or snow, to get their meager portions. Distributing lunch, the main meal of the day, could take five hours and the food was frequently cold by the time it was consumed. Though this situation gradually improved, it never quite cleared up.

Food, as penologists well know, assumes great importance in any group sealed off from the outside world, and given the restricted rations at Theresienstadt, it soon became an obsession. No other internal matter was more thought about or discussed. Most would do anything to acquire additional food, and those who had managed to smuggle in watches, jewelry, or other valuables, quickly traded them away for an extra potato or slice of bread. Even badly needed clothes would often change hands for a few additional mouthfuls. Many, after spooning down their soup, would not just lick their bowls but would scrape the bowls with their sleeves and then lick their sleeves to squeeze out an extra bit of nourishment. "After three months in Theresienstadt," writes Emma Fuchs, "there was only one feeling left in my body: hunger."

Jobs which brought a person into contact with food became a blessing, since they offered opportunities to gain an extra morsel or two. Many outfitted themselves with special pockets for smuggling food, and others found still more ways of secreting it. For example, teenager Alisha Shek, who worked on the SS farm, would hide an egg every day in her brassiere. A 12-year-old girl who worked on the farm once brought home a single cherry to share with her delighted parents. (Her father, former chief of medical services at Prague's Jewish hospital, carefully trisected the cherry into equal portions.) In the health services, doctors and nurses frequently found glucose ampules broken into and their contents emptied.

What about the food parcels and bulk shipments from abroad? The food parcels certainly helped, but the majority did not receive any during the first 18 months of the camp's existence. Even if the parcels had been uniformly distributed, they would have come to less than one per resident per year. As for the bulk shipments from Switzerland, they were apparently confiscated by the SS for their own purposes. No survivor recalls getting any additional food.

Theresienstadt's inhabitants could not refrain from talking about meals they had eaten or prepared in their former lives. Writes Gerda Haas, "We'd rub our stomachs while imaginary feasts rose before us and would call our game *magenonamie* (stomach masturbation)." Some wrote poems about food; others managed to make jokes. One popular expression was "without a bite (to eat), one goes to bed and with a thousand bites (from fleas, etc.) one gets up."(10)

Predictably, the ghetto's living conditions exposed its population to a slew of illnesses. Most rampant during the first year was enteritis. It claimed at least 4,000 lives and to some degree affected almost everyone, including, according to his later account, Seidl himself. The misery it imposed was compounded by the lack of toilet facilities which forced long, agonizing waits in line.

Conjunctivitis was the second most common illness. It, along with the frequent flare-ups of night blindness, was attributed to the lack of dietary vitamin A. Other vitamin deficiency diseases, such as scurvy and pellagra, were also common. There were also numerous other illnesses, including heart and lung problems, hepatitis, and typhoid. The latter, oddly enough, was considered by some to be a blessing, since it caused no pain while it enabled the sufferer to spend several days in bed.

At times, almost as many people were sick as were working. One February day in 1943 over 30 percent of the entire population were reported ill.

Such indices of illness, along with the general stresses and strains of daily existence, caused the death rate to spiral. While high almost from the very beginning, it started to soar with the arrival of the generally older German and Austrian Jews in the summer of 1942. The average daily death toll reached 32 in July, 75 in August, and 131 in September. It then began to back off, but Theresienstadt's total death count of 24,000 for the entire year was 23 times that of a normal central European city.

Given the congestion, corpses lay everywhere. One often had to step over them when going up or down the stairs. Once an exhausted young woman sat down on a rolled-up carpet only to find, when the carpet slightly unrolled, a naked body inside it. A nurse reports regularly finding five or six dead patients every night as she made her rounds. Furthermore, "since the toilet was on the other side of the barracks, one had to go in wind and rain over the yard to empty and clean the bucket, and often there was a dead person on the commode who had expired from hunger and weakness. . . ."

The task of coping with so much disability and death frequently led to errors which in another context might seem humorous. One overworked and undertrained nurse, believing a somnolent patient to be dead, had him transferred to the mortuary where the man woke up to find himself in a pile of dead bodies. A hard-pressed doctor, hurriedly scribbling a death certificate, failed to note that the piece of paper he had grabbed was the back of an envelope addressed to someone other than the deceased. As a result, the addressee's name was substituted for that of the deceased, and the error was not discovered until the addressee himself died.

The four-man death squads charged with removing the bodies were similarly overworked. Spies speaks of such a squad transporting a dead man down the stairs. "The four are so emaciated that they cannot carry him but have to drag him, so that the corpse's head goes bump, bump against the steps."

The bodies were borne to the mortuary in formerly horse-drawn but now man-drawn hearses taken from former Jewish funeral societies. As the men pulled the hearses along the street, an arm or leg would dangle out.

At the mortuary the dead were initially put into crude coffins and stacked. The names were read and Kaddish was recited. In the ghetto's early days, the rabbis would often give a short eulogy but the SS banned such talks when one rabbi went too far in bemoaning the fate of his people. Certain hours were allocated to the Catholic and Protestant congregations for their own funeral services.

After the services, trucks transported the dead to a swampy field just outside the town. Mourners were permitted to accompany the trucks as far as the town gate. One young man joined a burial detail so that he could accompany his mother's body to its grave.

At first, the dead were buried individually, but as their numbers mounted they were dumped into mass graves. Another problem soon arose when the high water level started pushing the bodies up to the surface. This was resolved in September 1942 with the opening of a crematorium, which could dispose of four bodies at one time. Many at first regarded it as too large for the community's needs, but the 4,000 people who died that month soon convinced them otherwise.

Among those who perished during the ghetto's early days was 51-year-old Trude Herzl Neuman. Baeck conducted her funeral service and observed in his eulogy, "If we had listened to the words of the father of this unfortunate woman, we would not all be here today."

Except for cases of medically certified illness, the rigors of ghetto life provided no unauthorized exemption from work. All able-bodied and even partially disabled men, as well as most women, from 16 to 60 were required to work unconditionally. For example, the gardening which Edelstein told Ullmann that his wife was doing and "enjoyed" was actually work on the SS farm and the fruits of her labors went to the SS, not to the Edelsteins.

Those from 14 to 16 and from 60 to 65 were assigned work conditionally, that is, at jobs deemed suitable for their age. Men over 60, for example, were usually employed in cleaning streets or pulling wagons. Even those from 65 to 70 were expected to work part time. Leo Baeck, who had not quite reached 70 when he arrived, worked for a few months pulling one of the hearses which were used not only for hauling bodies but also for other tasks such as delivering bread or removing garbage.

Those employed in "productive" enterprises, such as the ghetto workshops or in construction and maintenance, labored 52 hours a week, those with office jobs worked 57 hours. But compulsory overtime was quite common. When in May 1942 the Czech resistance assassinated Heydrich, the Nazis virtually exterminated the Czech town of Lidice in reprisal and then dispatched a detail of Theresienstadt men to bury the Lidice dead. They toiled 36 straight hours, returning half dead themselves to find their worried comrades saying Kaddish for them.

Women did not normally work in construction and maintenance but put in long hours in workshops, health and welfare services, kitchens, administrative offices, and on cleaning squads. By mid-1943 they outnumbered male workers by almost 50 percent.

But despite such efforts, the ghetto never realized Edelstein's hope of becoming economically viable, let alone militarily valuable to the Nazi regime. Although the Nazis spent less per capita on the residents of the "privileged" ghetto than they did on the inmates of Buchenwald, the ghetto at no time paid for itself. The nearest it came to doing so was in April 1942 when it produced enough to cover 84 percent of its cost, but even this figure included valuables confiscated from new arrivals. The infusion of largely elderly deportees from the Reich the following summer sank the figure to below 46 percent, and although the percentage later rose, it never reached much more than 60 percent.

There were many reasons to explain and underscore this failure. For one thing, the Nazis, or at least the SS, were not all that interested in creating an economically useful ghetto. (If they really wanted to exploit Jewish productivity, they would never have launched the Holocaust.) Also, the SS were terribly inefficient. For example, they ordered 900 sewing machines with the idea of setting up a large clothing factory but never got around to taking the machines out of their cartons. The only items whose production really interested the SS men were articles for their own ease and enjoyment. In so doing, notes Adler, "The corrupt and luxury-loving SS helped weaken the war economy and hastened Germany's downfall."

The Jewish administration itself tolerated, and in some respects even encouraged, such inefficiency by allowing many administrative offices and certain other facilities to be overstaffed. (We will see some of their reasons for this in the next chapter.) Thus, while many in Theresienstadt worked long and hard, others did not. Some jobs required only two hours of actual work a day.

But the major cause for Theresienstadt's inability to cover its costs lay in the character of its population. With so many elderly, sick, and disabled, and with a fair number of children including some 600 infants, there were simply not enough workers. By September 1942 the work force dropped to less than 30 percent of the population, and while the proportion of workers rose steadily thereafter, it had reached only about 58 percent by July 1943. Even then, all too many were employed in taking care of the other 42 percent. Theresienstadt had essentially become a custodial community and would remain so for the rest of its existence.

The privations of the privileged ghetto affected and afflicted nearly everyone. Young, previously healthy people suffered from vitamin deficiency diseases and digestive complaints, including flatulence and incontinence. Those who did not have to empty their bladder several times a night were continuously awakened by those who did. Many women stopped menstruating after arriving, although most resumed after several months to a year.

Though the Jewish administration exerted special efforts to protect children, they too frequently succumbed to malnourishment and disease. One woman who came to Theresienstadt with her husband and year-old baby girl brought no clothes for herself, nothing but the dress she was wearing, in order to bring all of her baby's things. She washed the child's clothes intensively and bargained away anything of value she and her husband had in order to provide for the child. Yet the baby weakened for lack of fresh food and died.

But if all groups suffered, one group suffered by far the most: the elderly. Their special ordeal began at the *Schleuse*, or intake station, where they were more easily robbed of their valuables and could less easily cope with the rigors of the intake process. Then came the mandatory stop at the delousing station which also took a heavy toll. "We received on a winter evening seven elderly people, four of whom died in the night and the other three the next day," writes a nurse. "All had gone through the horrible delousing procedure--hot showers followed by an hour-long wait in a cold room with only a light towel while their clothing was deloused. All of them had developed lung inflammations."

The nurse complained to the Jewish administration, pointing out, "We are still human beings and not the SS." The administration responded by setting up a special room for the sick and frail. The mortality rate receded somewhat, yet many still died.

Those older persons who survived the delousing process then had to contend with Theresienstadt's housing situation. Because most could not manage triple-tiered bunks, they were lodged largely in attics, lofts, and cellars which, as we have seen, frequently lacked air circulation, regular heat, and, in the case of cellars, even floors. And then there were the vermin. "In the quarters of the fragile, life was most unbearable," writes Adler. "Hardly had the lights been put out when the bedbugs swarmed over them and they could not sleep no matter how many they killed."

Understandably, the digestive systems of the elderly adapted less well to the Theresienstadt regime and severe enteritis or similar ailments affected almost all of them. In the long waits for the scarce lavatories they commonly, to their great discomfort and shame, defiled themselves. Emile Utitz recalls a former multimillionaire, who had once owned one of Europe's most renowned stables, saying to him, "Look at me now. An old, louse-ridden, decrepit Jew."

Bad as these conditions were, a decision by Edelstein and the Council of Elders six months after the ghetto came into existence made them still worse. It had become apparent that an even distribution of the food supply would not enable the ghetto to survive. Those doing heavy work needed more than those doing normal work, and the latter needed more than nonworkers. In addition, children required extra rations, for they represented the Jewish future and without a future, why struggle to maintain the ghetto at all?

"The dilemma," writes Bondy, "remained almost until the end of the war: how to manage justice in a regime of injustice, how to distribute the starvation rations so that at least some of the inmates would preserve their strength? After all, few of the elderly were likely to survive in any case, even if they remained at Theresienstadt, and only the young could ensure the continued existence of the Jewish people."

Thus, heavy workers, including doctors and nurses who, it was felt, needed extra nourishment to resist disease, now began to receive a little over 2,000 calories of food a day. Children were to get 1800 and normal workers a little over 1500. But the daily intake for nonworkers, which included most of the elderly, fell to less than 1,000 calories.

"When anybody died of hunger in Theresienstadt, it was the aged," writes Ota Klein. "This was . . . dictated by utter necessity. There was no other way but to cut the rations of the old if children and working people were to receive the minimum to stay alive."

This decision, coming on top of all the other deprivations inflicted on them, thinned the ranks of the elderly and transformed many of those remaining into nearly ghostlike figures. "We were often unable to recognize people from our native city who came to visit us--emaciated skeletons with dull, fixed stares, broken people," writes Dormitzer, while Emma Fuchs says that "many bore no resemblance to the grandmothers we knew . . . they were fleshless, formless, hungry, dirty human beings. We were alarmed."

The decision also transformed many of the elderly into scavengers and beggars. After devouring their scanty rations, they roamed through the town begging, sometimes successfully, bread or soup from others. They would also pounce on any morsel of food such as a pile of potato skins, food considered fit only for pigs. Then they would continue what Zdenek Lederer called "their aimless pilgrimage, dragging along their emaciated bodies, their hands trembling, and their clothes soiled."

Most heavily affected by these horrors were the elderly from Germany and Austria, especially the former. They rarely had younger relatives or friends in the camp to help them and they could not speak Czech, the unofficial ghetto language. What's more, they arrived totally unprepared, both materially and mentally, for what would confront them. Having been told that they were going to a resort town, and urged to pack and dress accordingly, they came with fine clothes and useless mementos. Many did not even bring a soup bowl or spoon, the indispensable elements of Theresienstadt existence.

Their arrival in Theresienstadt was not only a shock for them but for those charged with their welfare. One physician speaks of the gruesome irony of seeing elderly Jewish women clad in fine lingerie while lying in filth. Another, Karel Fleischmann, writes, "I see them, the first people from Cologne, leaning against the wall, dead tired, with tormented faces, old men with well-trimmed white beards and mustaches, white-haired women with black hats, dresses, and gloves, walking sticks with silvery crooks, elegant suitcases as if they had come to a spa. . . But everything was horribly crippled, deformed, dirty, and stank of human filth . . . a vision of old age, misery, gloom, dimly lit by a few candles, with nurses running to and fro bearing improvised commodes."

Yet despite their distress, most of them still sought to maintain some shreds of self-respect. In his testimony at the Eichmann trial, Mordechai Anbacher noted that "Particularly the Jews from Germany were the ones who died like flies because they couldn't adapt to the conditions." He went on to say, "But it is interesting to note how they helped one another, with what pride, with what sense of honor. Most of them died of starvation and dysentery, and when they swooped on the remnants of food, very often one heard, 'Excuse me, Herr Sanitatsrat. Excuse me, Herr Doctor, you were the first. Oh, I'm sorry, Mrs. M. . . .' Yet in spite of their efforts at dignity, they were really nearly pushing one another. They couldn't help it."

Sometimes this drive for dignity reached perverse proportions. A former highly decorated Austrian army colonel walked through the town daily with a blanket wrapped tightly around him. Only when he caught pneumonia and was brought to an infirmary was it discovered that under the blanket he had not a stitch of clothing.

More successful in maintaining his dignity was Leo Baeck, three of whose sisters had died in the camp before his arrival. (The fourth died soon after.) Though he initially received no special treatment and shed 50 pounds, he continued to wear a suit, vest, and tie and to keep his beard and hair trimmed. Said Baeck, "I had only one thought: Never give in to rudeness, never to become a mere number, and always to keep my self-respect."

But what about all the facilities the Nazis had created supposedly to make life pleasant for their privileged Jews? What about the stores and the post office, the bank and the coffeehouse?

The stores, which eventually numbered 14 in all, sold mostly those goods which the Nazis had originally confiscated from the residents and later found they didn't need or want. The useless mementos of the German and Austrian Jews made up much of their stock. One store sold only suitcases, hardly an everyday necessity for a Theresienstadt inhabitant. There was a foodshop, but it sold only mustard and an acrid-tasting paste of uncertain composition and often did not have even these goods available. On occasion, one could make a useful purchase, but here again irony abounds. Ditta Jedlinsky recalls returning from a shopping trip jubilant at having been able to buy a desirable blouse. But her pleasure was somewhat spoiled when her bunkmate, on seeing it, exclaimed, "But that's my blouse." It had been taken from the girl in the *Schleuse*. In one instance, a man bought back what had once been his own suit.

The bank was usually willing to advance credit for such purchases but rarely found customers. Most of the time the residents had more ghetto money than they needed, for not only were worthwhile goods rarely available but access to the showers, the laundry, and the coffeehouse was so restricted that their usage consumed few crowns. The ghetto crowns were mostly used like Monopoly money in playing cards and other games. Still, the bank staff kept themselves busy balancing their books, and auditors arrived regularly from Berlin to ensure the accuracy of the bank's essentially fictitious accounts.

The post office did function after a fashion, and mail to and from the Reich normally arrived. After all, an Aryan friend, sponsor, or former in-law might make inconvenient inquiries if no word from their Theresienstadt connection ever reached them. Even a half-Aryan son or daughter could create problems by appealing to an Aryan relative. (Some *Mischlings* or half-breeds had Aryan uncles or grandfathers who were well-established Nazi party members. This was the basic reason why half-Jews were usually exempted from deportation.) Even a certain amount of correspondence abroad was allowed. A noted professor of geography was authorized, and indeed ordered, to carry on a fairly extensive, though strictly censored, correspondence with a distinguished Swedish colleague whose friendship to the Reich the Nazis wished to foster.

But most residents could send only one 30-word postal card, printed in block letters, per month and even some of these never reached their destination, especially if they were addressed to someone in the Protectorate. Moreover, while ghetto residents could receive food packages, all money sent them was confiscated by the Nazis, who gave the intended recipients near useless ghetto crowns in exchange.

Finally, while the coffeehouse did provide an occasional brief respite for the elderly, many younger people paid it little heed, finding its seating too limited, its "coffee" too bitter, and its general atmosphere too gloomy to bother with. Adler describes it as "the saddest coffee-house in the world."

As is now painfully obvious, the privileged ghetto represented a far, far cry from what the Czech Jews had hoped to fashion and what the German Jews had hoped to find. One wonders not only whether it was a privileged ghetto, but whether it was a ghetto at all. Would not the term "concentration camp" be more exact?

Certainly, the Nazis referred to it publicly as a ghetto and, in fact, would sometimes intimidate Jews trying to avoid deportation to Theresienstadt by threatening to send them to a concentration camp instead. Yet Theresienstadt's many similarities to the latter institution are indeed striking.

A ghetto, first of all, is part of a larger community and inevitably has some contact with it. This was true of the Polish ghettos even under the Nazi regime. Concentration camps, on the other hand, were self-

contained units, physically cut off from other communities. Theresienstadt obviously falls into the latter category.

All the Polish ghettos also had a residence base. Though tens of
thousands of Jews were dumped into them, they represented additions
to an existing Jewish community. Concentration camps, however, were
created out of whole cloth. Here again Theresienstadt, except for its
basic physical infrastructure, seems to suit the latter category.

In ghettos, families could usually live together; in concentration
camps they usually could not. While some families in Theresienstadt
managed to live together, most, especially during its first year and a
half, did not.

Finally, the Nazis themselves seemed to have looked upon it as a
concentration camp in reality. The SS's Economics Division classified
it as such and the Jewish administration, in its daily bulletins to the
population, continually referred to Theresienstadt as a *Lager* (camp) and
to Seidl as *Lagerkommandant*. These notices, to be sure, were drafted
and issued by the Jewish leadership, but they were of necessity approved
by Seidl and more generally by his superiors in Prague and Berlin.
None of them during this phase of Theresienstadt's existence seems to
have objected to the term.

But if Theresienstadt was a concentration camp, it was a concentration camp of a special kind. To begin with, it was the only camp
designed solely and exclusively for Jews. Then, despite its many
perverse peculiarities, it was a better, certainly less brutal, camp than
most others. Finally, it did enjoy, if that is the correct word, a measure
of self-administration. Thus Theresienstadt can perhaps best be
regarded as a peculiar Nazi hybrid, a cross between a concentration
camp and a ghetto. Both terms will be used interchangeably to refer to
it in the chapters that follow, as will the terms "residents" and "inmates"
to describe its inhabitants.

Still more complex, even contradictory, were its purposes. It was
designed, as we have seen, to divert attention from, and provide a
coverup for, the holocaust. Indeed, the plans for a "privileged ghetto"
and for the holocaust arose almost simultaneously. At the infamous
Wannsee Conference on January 20, 1942, Heydrich, in disclosing the
government's scheme to systematically exterminate the Jews, also
disclosed that Theresienstadt would serve to house those Jews whose
prominence might occasion anxious inquiries or adverse comment
should they suddenly disappear. As Eichmann later put it in a talk to
his subordinates, "Theresienstadt will allow us to preserve our appearance abroad." (*Nach aussen das Gesicht zu wahren.*)

A second purpose of Theresienstadt was to appease the German army, which felt that anyone who had ever honorably worn its uniform should receive a modicum of respect. Hence Theresienstadt's role in providing a supposed haven for highly decorated or severely disabled Jewish war veterans.

Another group needing mollification were those Aryans, especially influential ones, who had Jewish in-laws or friends whom they wished to protect. As Himmler, with great exasperation, once observed, every SS man seems to have his pet Jew who he feels is different and so should be spared the fate of the others. Deporting such favored Jews to Theresienstadt should eliminate or at least ease this problem.

Then there were the elderly German and Austrian Jews to be dealt with. Since they obviously posed no peril to the Reich, deporting them to the East would raise eyebrows not only abroad but in the Reich itself. The deportation process alone would be messy and Eichmann spoke of wanting to spare the Gestapo the "disagreeable task of dragging off elderly people" to the collection centers. Furthermore, the home purchase scheme would enable the SS, and not the German government proper, to acquire their assets. (Although the Nazis firmly controlled the German government, the SS was constantly striving to expand its own role within it.)

All these purposes were in many respects related or at least reasonably consistent. But Theresienstadt was also designed for another purpose which was quite different.

At two conferences with his close subordinates in Prague in October 1941, Heydrich noted how "there are difficulties with the evacuation of the Jews from the Protectorate." The difficulties could be largely overcome, he claimed, with the establishment of a "temporary concentration camp." Theresienstadt would serve as such a "temporary" camp.

Consequently, while most Jews sent to Theresienstadt would almost certainly have found the phrase "a joke hatched in Hell" to be suitably descriptive of its conditions and operation, many have since referred to it as "the anteroom to Hell."

In the next chapter we shall see why.(11)

---

8. According to Troller, those concealing things in body cavities were frequently discovered. However, many still managed to elude discovery. Paper money, for example, was sometimes successfully hidden in cans of baby powder, bread loaves, and even rolled up into fountain pens.

9. We shall examine the other expedients employed by the Nazis in the next chapter. However, another reason for doing away with the practice in Theresienstadt itself may have been that pictures of the first execution eventually appeared in the Swiss press. They had been taken by Czech gendarme who had secretly operated a camera with his foot. He gave the pictures to a priest in Prague, who later smuggled them to the Vatican, which in turn sent them on to Switzerland.

Seidl told allied interrogators after the war that rather than execute the men, he had wanted to hold them in prison as hostages against further letter smuggling, but that Guenther, who was being accused by his Gestapo colleagues of being too soft on the Jews, had overruled him. Seidl also said that in one instance the rope broke and he told Guenther that under Austrian law the prisoner would be pardoned. Guenther snapped back that no such law existed in Germany.

10. The camp's orthodox rabbis met and decided to waive all restrictions against eating nonkosher meat. Nevertheless, about 20 orthodox Jews still refused to consume it and instead traded their scanty meat portions for other foods.

11. The phrase "a joke hatched in Hell" is taken from Joseph Conrad's novel *Lord Jim* where it is, of course, used to describe something entirely different. I think most readers will agree, however, to its suitability as the title for the chapter they have just read.

CHAPTER 4
THE ANTEROOM

Most of the 141,000 Jews who would come to Theresienstadt would not remain there. Where would they go?

Some 31 went back into German society having proved, almost always with the help of Aryan connections, that they were not Jews under the Nuremburg laws. Among them was the Viennese countess mentioned earlier.(12)

A slightly larger number, some 37 in all, made their way to freedom by fleeing. This was not too difficult to do, especially during the early days when Czech civilians were still living in the town and the town gate remained unguarded. A resident could simply remove the Jewish star and board the bus to Prague. Moreover, many were allowed to go outside on errands for the camp or to work elsewhere. Jewish farm workers tilling the fields and tending the livestock at the SS farm outside the town walls were frequently unsupervised. In going to their jobs they crossed over the Prague-Dresden highway which ran alongside the town.

But if going away from the camp was relatively easy, staying away was not. Their short haircuts, lack of identification papers and, in some cases, their Semitic features all too easily gave them away. One young couple who went to Bauschowitz and boarded the train to Prague were caught when gendarmes spotted the transportation numbers they had forgotten to remove from their luggage.

The area's geography also discouraged escape. Fleeing in one direction brought the fugitive almost immediately into the Reich. Fleeing in the other direction brought him into flat and open Czech farmland with no real woods or mountains in which to hide.

Still another deterrent were the consequences to an escapee's family and friends. His family would be deported from Theresienstadt, while the rest of the camp would be given a collective punishment. This usually took the form of a 6:00 P.M. curfew and *Lichtsperre* or lights-out order.

Although the camp's 37 escapees included three women and a 61-year-old man, most were young males. Two who managed to avoid capture have left written accounts of their experiences.

One simply went over the fence at night with three companions. The four then split up and the writer of this account survived by finding a Czech farmer who sheltered him until the end of the war.

The other left with two brothers, all of them shinnying down a rope from a painter's scaffolding at the same fence. (The fence ran along a perimeter street which only the SS were supposed to use.) This group also separated, for the two brothers did not look Jewish and did not want to be seen with this escapee who did. However, the writer made his way through the countryside, fell upon a German sentry at a bridge, and after strangling him with his bare hands seized his rifle and ammunition and fled into adjoining Slovakia. There he joined a partisan gang and took part in the Slovakian uprising toward the end of the war. Though severely wounded and permanently crippled, he survived to tell his tale.

Both men point out that all those who fled with them, including the non-Jewish-looking brothers, were caught. This was the fate of nearly all who tried to flee the privileged ghetto.

Some arrested escapees were sent to the Little Fortress, the former Czech prison now being used by the Gestapo. There they joined the 400-500 other Jews who would be sent to this prison during the war. About half of all Jewish prisoners in the Little Fortress would come from Theresienstadt, most of them sent directly from the camp. For after the second round of hangings in the winter of 1942, the SS decided that executions in Theresienstadt itself were too unsettling for its inmates and too potentially damaging for its image as a privileged ghetto. So the Nazis began using the Little Fortress to punish those guilty of such crimes as smuggling, sending unauthorized letters, or smoking illegal tobacco. (The ban on tobacco was more rigorously enforced in Theresienstadt than in most other concentration camps.) Generally, they were not formally executed in the prison; instead they were subjected to privations and punishments so severe as to cause most of them either to die or to kill themselves.

The Jewish prisoners in the Little Fortress were segregated from the Czech prisoners and much more harshly treated. Crowded into cells which afforded only three feet of space per person, they could not stretch out but had to sleep sitting on their heels on concrete floors, often with snow and rain coming in through the roof. Each morning found several dead.

Their nourishment consisted of 12 ounces of bread twice a week and a watery soup daily. As a result, many died from malnutrition, and instances of cannibalism occurred as the living sometimes devoured the flesh of the dead. But the greatest horrors came from their daily work routine.

Two surviving Christian prisoners, a Czech priest named Jan Merril, and Milos Bic, a Protestant minister, both of them former theology professors imprisoned for anti-Nazi activity, have described the treatment of Jewish prisoners which they witnessed.

After responding at roll call with *Stinkjude* or *Saujude* (Jewish pig) when their names were read, the Jewish prisoners might be forced to push wheelbarrows filled with rocks up a slope and then push them down again. Those unable to push fully loaded wheelbarrows were beaten senseless and dumped into ice-cold water until they died. On other occasions they would be ordered to lick pig dung from their shovels. Those who flinched at doing so would have their heads pushed against their shovels until they suffocated or choked to death. The Rev. Mr. Bic once saw an SS guard order a Jewish prisoner to load a wheelbarrow with his mouth.

Once an SS guard, annoyed that work on pulling down a wall was not going fast enough, ordered ten Jews to undermine the wall from the bottom while the rest worked on the top. Then, in Father Merril's words, "there was an explosion as the falling brickwork and mortar buried these poor souls in the pit. It was indeed a terrible sight! There were the groans of the buried and the laughter and shouting of the SS men whose main concern was to save not the victims but the pick-axes and shovels." Those still alive were thrown crosswise into wheelbarrows "so that their heads knocked against the ground as they were transported to their cells. Thus everyone of them died because their heads had been broken before they reached their cells."

A favorite SS sport was getting the Jews to kill one another. Father Merril recalls seeing several Jewish prisoners being driven into the ditch below the morgue, given sticks and pitchforks and ordered to fight for their lives "while Joeckl [the prison commandant] and his crew observed the scene with laughter from a bridge above."

Transfer to the Little Fortress, however, accounts for only a tiny fraction of the Theresienstadt residents who were removed from the model ghetto. Yet, as we will now see, most of the others would share the same ultimate fate.

On January 5, 1942, less than a month after the first Jewish families had arrived in Theresienstadt, the Jewish administration, acting on orders from the SS, ordered a deportation of 1,000 to Riga. The announcement fell on the camp like a thunderbolt, shattering whatever sense of security the residents still retained. Virtually all of them, from Edelstein on down, had believed that however harsh their life in the camp might become, they would at least remain there. Now even this hope had suddenly vanished.

The deportation was scheduled for January 9 and those selected were ordered to assemble at 3:00 A.M. For three hours they waited in the freezing cold before being marched to the Bauschowitz train station. An eyewitness account portrays a "tragic picture of people wading through the snow with knapsacks on their backs and holding their children by the hand. When they arrived at the station one and one-half hours later, they were packed into unheated cattle cars. The cars are sealed but there is another wait of several hours before the train finally leaves."

Back in Theresienstadt the Jewish administration posted a new Order of the Day shortly before dinner time. It contained only one sentence: "Transport O departed for Riga at 2:40 P.M."

Transport O was followed by 39 more transports during the next 13 months, carrying some 50,000 to the East. No more official announcements were issued as to destinations, but up to early summer the deportees were taken to Minsk and Lublim. Then, in late July, Treblinka began operation and this extermination camp became the terminus for all Theresienstadt deportations until October 21, when the first group of Theresienstadters arrived in Auschwitz. Auschwitz or its branch camp Birkenau would be the destination of all Theresienstadt deportees from then on.

Those deported from Theresienstadt generally suffered the same fate as other Jews sent to the East. Ironically, more survived in Auschwitz than any place else thanks to a work selection which some managed to pass. In addition, twins were sometimes spared for Dr. Mengele's infamous experiments. Most of those sent to Minsk, however, were taken into the woods and shot while nearly all those sent to Lublim either died there or were sent on to Treblinka. The only survivors from one early deportation were two young men who jumped from the train. (They eventually joined Russian partisans and later returned to Czechoslovakia as soldiers in the Red army.)

Theresienstadt's Jews knew nothing of the fate that awaited the deported, and some went when they could have stayed behind. This was the case with Ruth Elias's family which was listed for one of the earlier transports. Because Ruth was under 21 and ill at the time, they could have avoided the trip, but her father suffered from lung disease and was having difficulty breathing in a room crowded with 40 other men. Thinking the air would be better in the East, he declined to seek exemption and left with his wife and other daughter. He urged Ruth to go with them, but she took advantage of her illness to stay behind.

Most of those who left voluntarily, however, did so to accompany a loved one. In one instance, a young man listed for deportation became upset as the hour for his departure neared and his fiancee had not shown up to say goodby. Suddenly she walked in beaming with joy; she had gotten herself included on his transport. The couple decided to leave as man and wife, so a hastily summoned rabbi married them in a corridor while friends held over them an impromptu *chupa* (canopy) fashioned from a prayer shawl. A kindly cook provided two cups of watery soup which they quickly spooned down, little realizing that their "wedding feast" was also their last meal.

Illness, as we saw in Ruth Elias's case, provided an exemption from deportation and this reassured many residents that those being shipped out were leaving to work, not to die. So did the ban on elderly deportees, for everyone over 65 was excused from the earlier transports. Families--husbands, wives, and young children--also were not split so that anyone married to an exemptee benefitted from the spouse's exemption.

If the initial exclusion of the elderly and the ill was reassuring, some of the other exemptions were not. They included those classified as Prominenten, those with foreign citizenship from countries not occupied by Germany, and those who had had valid Aryan marriages, especially if such marriages had produced children. Most war veterans were also exempt, as were the families of those sent on work assignments outside the camp. Such categorizations only strengthened the notion that the right to remain in Theresienstadt was a privilege not to be lightly foregone.

More impressive in shaping the residents' view of deportation was its use as a punishment. Under SS orders, those who had been found guilty of even the most minor crimes, such as finding a lost food card and using it to get an extra meal, were put at the top of the next transport list. This made the mild punishments of the ghetto court much more severe than they seemed. Moreover, even those whose offenses had not brought them before the bar of ghetto justice, such as pregnant women who had not reported their condition--the SS had ordered all pregnancies originating in Theresienstadt to be aborted, but many women wanted to bear their children--became prime candidates for deportation. Similarly, the rabbi who had spoken out too strongly at a funeral service, thereby prompting the SS to ban all eulogies, was shipped out on the next transport. Rabbis, it should be noted, were not generally spared unless, like Murmelstein and Baeck, there were other grounds for doing so.

Other unsettling factors about the deportations included the absence of mail, other than an initial and occasional postcard on arrival from those who had already gone and the known hostility of the Poles to Jews. Consequently, while a few went cheerfully and even voluntarily to the collection center, most did all they could to stay behind.

These fears did not diminish when, in the fall of 1942, the SS suddenly reversed its policy regarding the elderly. The arrival of large numbers of older German and Austrian Jews during the summer and into the fall, plus the previous deportations of younger Czech Jews, was overtaxing the camp's facilities and staff and threatening to undermine its existence. Elderly Jews were also more susceptible to and thereby more likely to spread infectious diseases. Furthermore, the overcrowding they were causing could destroy the notion of Theresienstadt as a privileged ghetto. So in early September the SS began ordering the Council of Elders to prepare transports of older Jews who were not otherwise exempt.

During the next seven weeks nearly 13,500 people, all over 61, were sent off, along with over 2,000 younger people, many of them voluntarily accompanying their aged parents or other loved ones. But deporting the elderly proved troublesome, for many had become senile from lack of nourishment and other privations and wandered about the streets with little idea of what was happening. Many were also physically weak and had to be assisted or carried to the collection center. "It was a frightful sight," recalls one resident, "to see the diseased, undernourished people on the streets and paths to the *Kaseine* where the registration was to take place."

The elderly first had to stand in line for hours to be registered and then had to march to Bauschowitz. The ordeal proved too much for many, who died on the way. Their corpses were nevertheless loaded on the train so that the body count would match the prescribed figure. The dead may have been luckier than the living who, according to one observer, "were loaded onto the cattle cars with much screaming and shouting by the SS who mercilessly beat the elderly people."

Though the deportation of the elderly created more uneasiness about the fate of deportees, few if any believed that they were earmarked for extermination. The SS insisted they were being sent to another "welfare ghetto" in Silesia where "conditions were as good as those in Theresienstadt." Emma Fuchs says her 75-year-old aunt, who was being carried to the collection center on a stretcher, made one last request of her. "I lost my handbag. If you find it, bring it home to me."

In accordance with what had become standard Nazi practice, the SS left the task of selecting deportees to the Council of Elders. Of course, the Council had to work within the prescribed guidelines. They were required to include "criminals" and to exclude those in certain categories such as Prominenten, war veterans, mischlings, etc.

As we have seen, the SS would frequently add to or change these guidelines. It not only ordered the deportation of the hitherto protected elderly in the fall of 1942, but on another occasion it forbade the Council from deporting the 300-400 patients in the camp's mental hospital. (If the Council's desire to send off these unfortunates seems cruel, one must remember that their places would have to be filled by others.) Once the SS halted a train that was leaving and removed a group of young women to work in the beet fields.

The SS would also intervene in individual cases. When Jiri Lauscher, a recently arrived carpenter from Prague, found himself and his family on the deportation list, he showed the SS a toy dog he had invented. It would stand up whenever someone pulled its tail. Thinking his invention would make a great plaything for the children of the Reich, the SS removed him and his family from the list and put him to work producing the toy.(13)

In addition to the exemptions stipulated by the Nazis, the Council of Elders created an exemption list of its own. On it were the members of the first two work details who had helped prepare the camp for settlement; the leaders of certain camp factions, such as the Zionists and the communists; the heads of various departments and subdepartments within the camp administration, along with members of the ghetto police, fire service, and the transport administration itself, since it was needed to dispatch the others. (One camp wisecrack had it that in the end only Eppstein, Edelstein, and the transport commission would be left. The latter was sarcastically referred to as the "Poland commission" and its director, a man named Kantor, was dubbed "Poland Kantor.")

Other individuals and groups whose work was considered vital to the camp's operation and who could not easily be replaced were also spared. This included employees of the Hebrew library, women splitting feldspar, and most engineers and skilled craftsmen. Finally, the Council exempted outstanding artists, musicians, and other camp favorites.

As a result of all these exemptions, the Council had to cull its deportation lists from hardly more than one-third of the camp's population. In deciding who was to go, the Elders used certain guidelines of their own.

Those considered most eligible for evacuation, aside from those who had come into conflict with the ghetto's judicial system, were recent arrivals. Since they usually had not yet established a niche for themselves, either occupationally or socially, they could be sent off with a minimum of trouble. Max Mannheimer, who arrived in January 1943, recalls spending only one night in the Schleuse before being sent on to Auschwitz with his six-member family. (He was the family's sole survivor.)

Others who placed near the top of the eligibility list were those whose work was considered less vital to the camp's operation or whose work performance was considered wanting. All department heads submitted lists of their employees grouped into four categories: indispensable, relatively indispensable, relatively dispensable, and dispensable. Even the order of the names within each group reflected the relative rating of those listed.

The use of such lists spurred many into seeking work. As a result, the unemployment office was flooded with applications following the first deportation. It also encouraged most to perform their work with diligence, if not always with zeal. Employees also sought to cultivate the favor of their bosses in other ways, such as through obsequiousness or flattery. Many, for example, would compose poems of praise for their boss on his birthday. (Nearly all such bosses were men.) Even foremen and other low-level supervisors received such tributes, since their recommendations customarily carried weight with their superiors.

Since spouses of those exempted were themselves exempted, the early deportations also inspired a wave of hasty marriages. Applications submitted before noon, if in order, enabled a couple to wed at 3:00 P.M. Occasionally, however, divorce became a device for avoiding deportation since a man targeted for transport could sometimes spare his wife by divorcing her.

It was sometimes possible to bribe one's way off a deportation list by offering valuables or, in the case of attractive women, becoming someone's mistress. But such efforts, says Adler, did not happen often and succeeded only occasionally. Moreover, they did not furnish permanent protection. The rescued individual might be shipped out on the next transport.

Avoiding deportation by going into hiding without the cooperation of the Jewish administration was nearly impossible. As soon as anyone's name appeared on the transport list, he or she had to surrender his/her food ration card. Also, the camp was so congested that hiding required the cooperation and complicity of many others, and anyone helping another to avoid deportation became immediately subject to deportation himself. What's more, a "reserve" was provided for each transport and its members would be on the lookout for any hideaways, since they, the reservists, would have to fill the missing places.

Despite these obstacles, some 120 scheduled deportees refused to appear for one transport and sought instead to secrete themselves in the camp. They were quickly rounded up and jailed. Edelstein eventually persuaded Seidl to release them and to not automatically include them on the next transport. Still, most did leave on the next transport and a five-day curfew and a 6:00 P.M. *Lichtsperre* were imposed on the camp.

In another instance, some scheduled deportees persuaded a doctor and a nurse to inoculate them with typhus to keep them from having to go. This ruse too was discovered and the deportees were dispatched to the East. The doctor and nurse had a shorter journey. They were taken to the Little Fortress and killed.

Deportations usually came in bunches, with a pause in between. From October 26, 1942, when the last of the elderly transports stopped, to January 20, 1943, a period of nearly three months, no trains left for the East. But then, in a period of about two weeks, 7,000 people or more than one out of eight residents, were dispatched to Auschwitz.

Each pause made the more optimistic hopeful that the deportations had ceased. But the appearance at the camp of high SS officials, such as Eichmann, or an offhand remark by an indiscrete SS man, would eventually start the rumors circulating. Although the optimists would spread counterrumors, claiming the Germans needed the trains for troop movement or that Allied bombings had made the tracks impassable, the rumors of further deportations almost inevitably proved true.

The Jewish administration would officially announce the transport before it had put together the list. Then the Council of Elders would meet and, with the Ghetto Watch guarding the door, would decide who would go and who would not. Despite its numerous guidelines, the Council deliberations usually lasted through the night and well into the next morning.

In an attempt to reduce the haggling and logrolling over individual cases, Edelstein proposed allowing each Council member to automatically exempt 30 residents exclusive of his own family. The Council eagerly adopted the idea, but since most wanted to exclude far more, the haggling and logrolling continued.

Finally, a list would emerge, but it was only provisional. Anyone on it could appeal and most did so. This necessitated further deliberations, during which, says Bondy, "The members, red-eyed from lack of sleep and ashen-faced with weariness, weighed every appeal. Each list was compiled again and again following appeals and last-minute changes; some names were removed, others added and new appeals submitted."

Some appeals succeeded and sometimes people were removed from the collection center and, on one or two occasions, from the train itself. But most such efforts proved fruitless, for the quota had to be met and the removal of one person required the delivery of another.

The case of a young farmer named Romoald illustrates this dilemma. Romoald had observed how Miriam Edelstein and a few other women working with her on the SS farm had secreted some food in their clothing. He had also noticed that a Czech gendarme, known to be hostile to the Jews, had become suspicious of them. He therefore warned the women who promptly discarded the food and so escaped punishment.

When Romoald's name subsequently appeared on a deportation list, his fiancee went to see Edelstein. She managed to corral the Jewish Elder around midnight in the corridor of his barracks. Telling him of what her fiancee had done for Edelstein's wife, she sought his exemption. Edelstein replied, "All right, I'll do it. Just tell me whom I should send in his place." When she faltered in coming up with a name, the conversation ended.(14)

Understandably, tension at the camp reached its height during the time the Council was compiling its lists. Consequently, the list was revealed as soon as it was completed. Reports one householder, "When I entered the room with the list in my hand and turned on the light, everyone immediately awoke and stared at me with anxious eyes, in each of which I read the question, 'Am I on it?' Then began the worst part: informing someone that he was to go. Confusion, complaints, and crying--especially when, as often happened, elders were split from children or siblings from one another." The prohibition against separation of families, it should be pointed out, governed only young children.

Those selected were given certain last-minute privileges, such as having laundry done and the use of the internal mail service to send messages to friends and family members within the camp. The SS also allowed them to take along most of their belongings, since this would allow the Nazis to seize more easily goods that otherwise would be given away to those left behind. But what the deportees couldn't take, such as a wall shelf, or didn't want to take, such as ghetto money, they customarily gave to others. An often valuable gift was a proxy enabling the recipient to collect the deportee's mail, including food packages.

Some individuals went shamelessly about the camp collecting such proxies, but most, relieved that they were not on the list, would assist those who were going with packing, running errands, and offering consolation and encouragement. The latter was especially difficult to do. Conversations with those destined for deportation were, as Lustig puts it, "Strange, like someone going out into the rain without clothes on and making believe it wasn't raining, something like that."

The end of the deportation produced an abrupt break in the tension. As one camp physician noted, "Once the deportees had departed, the miracle happened. Everyone began to breathe easier. What's gone is gone. To be sure, here cries a young woman whose parents have been sent away; there weeps another whose son was shipped out. But life in Theresienstadt goes on. . . ."

For some, life actually improved, for deportations often opened up more desirable jobs or promotional opportunities in one's existing job. Kaethe Starke, after initial service on the cleaning squad, found a position in the camp library. With no training or experience, she was the lowliest member of a staff of 19. But as a result of deportations as well as deaths, some eight months later she had become the library's deputy director.

The departures also opened up more desirable sleeping spaces or positions in various leisure-time activities. A defensive back on the soccer team who wanted to play goalee might get his chance if the current goalee was on the list. Then there were the mail proxies, the wall shelves and hooks, and the left-behind belongings which the deportees customarily bestowed on family and friends.

But these benefits and bounties were greatly overshadowed by the burdens which the transports produced. They tore gaps into the camp's work units, stalling and sometimes stifling important projects. They ruptured relationships, often leaving those remaining not only emotionally distraught but materially impoverished, since they might have relied on the deported person for assistance of various kinds. They even generated fierce arguments at soccer games over who was to play and who was to sit on the bench, for, says Lustig, "No one wants to be left out because no one is sure that he will be here for the next match."

The effect of the transports on life in Theresienstadt can scarcely be overstated. "The ever-present threat of deportation to the East dominated life in Theresienstadt; it hung over everybody day and night," writes Lederer. Ruth Schwertfeger, who has combed through numerous written accounts of Theresienstadt women, comes to the same conclusion. "Fear of the transports," she writes, "pervades every single memoir."

The stresses of camp life which the deportations only intensified produced much disagreeable and disheartening behavior. "The prisoners showed less emotional restraint than people living in a normal city," says Lederer. "Such small comforts as a place near the stove in the billet assumed disproportionate importance." Adler says young men who lacked normal outlets for their energies became especially prone to irresponsible, immoral, and impolite actions. "It was not pleasant to visit their quarters. Unprovoked, one became subject to their coarse and rude deportment."

But if conditions in the camp made some testy and aggressive, it made others despondent and resigned. Those most severely affected opted for suicide.

The official records list 271 suicides during the camp's existence, over half of them occurring during the first year. This figure greatly understates the actual number since many simply allowed themselves to waste away. One middle-aged woman who was in generally sound condition declined to accept any food. Brought to the hospital, she died in eight days, having resolutely refused to touch even a drop of water.

Hospital personnel not only tried to prevent suicide but to disguise it when it did occur for, ironically, the Nazis strictly prohibited a Jew from taking his or her own life, and would punish the crime by deporting the suicide's family. The medical department's often successful efforts to cover up suicide makes the official count still more of an understatement.

A more common and far less drastic form of escape was to retreat into the past. Old pictures were lovingly looked at and proudly displayed. Past events were recalled with tender joy. In doing so, the residents would often exaggerate not only how they lived but what they had accomplished. In this way, a small shopkeeper became a department store proprietor, an elementary school teacher became a university professor, and one former mime from Germany became the most famous comedian in central Europe.

Some sought to compensate for camp conditions by bearing children. In so doing, they defied the rule requiring all pregnancies originating in the camp to be terminated. Although many would be deported, others would somehow succeed in having and keeping their child. Some 207 children would be born in Theresienstadt, as opposed to 350 official abortions.

The fairly numerous pregnancies tell us something more about life in Theresienstadt, namely, that despite segregation of the sexes, and despite overwork and undernourishment, sexual activity was by no means absent.

In the camp's earliest days, when only cleaning and supply crews, along with corpse and garbage collectors, could enter the women's barracks, desperate husbands would give money to members of these crews for the chance to take their places. "It was a common sight," writes Toller, "to see columns of longing husbands with their milk cans or coal sacks waiting in front of the barracks gate to be let in by the gatekeeper. Barely inside there was a lightning delivery of the goods they brought to cellar or kitchen. They then took their wives, who were waiting for them, and disappeared into cubicles, storerooms, and coal bins. They did so rapidly because in 20 to 30 minutes they had to reassemble."

When early evening visits between the barracks became permissible, some wives would occasionally ignore the curfew and spend the night with their husbands. The latter would move to a top bunk and there, under a blanket, the couple could once again be man and wife. One woman recalls doing this in a room where there were 36 other men.

Sexual contacts were not limited to married couples. Indeed, love affairs of all kinds flourished in the camp. To carry on such activities, Theresienstadters became adept at finding or creating *Kumbals* (cubbyholes or hiding places) under stairways, in storage bins and other places. Sometimes a workshop or office could be used after hours. So despite the camp's congestion, couples who wanted to be alone together could usually find a way.

As might be expected, adultery was not rare. One woman, childless in 12 years of marriage, became pregnant in the camp. While her delighted husband did not want the child aborted, she told Edelstein that another man was the father. In some instances, people who had conducted clandestine extramarital affairs before coming to Theresienstadt now had to be more open about such liaisons. The impact on their marriages was predictable. Although only 20 divorces officially occurred in the camp, Murmelstein says this figure greatly understates the number of dissolved unions.

Not all sexual activity involved romantic love. "Sexual morality relaxed thoroughly," says Adler, "especially among leading officials, those who had access to desirable commodities such as food, coarse individuals, and young men." Some women became mistresses of influential men to protect themselves and/or their loved ones from deportation. Others pursued young men from the first two construction details, AKI and AKII, in the hope of making a Ghetto marriage that would spare them from the transports.

A few women simply broke down under the stresses of camp life and became almost indiscriminate. One was a nurse who slept with numerous doctors, including the head of the Health Service. Finally, a few others became full-time prostitutes. Lustig recalls visiting one of them, a young, beautiful half-Jewish girl who had once been an admired horseback rider in Germany. Her fee was 10 grams of margarine or 100 grams of sugar. On one occasion she was invited to the room of a group of young men who were being deported and who had decided that none of them should leave as a virgin. The young woman climbed up to a top bunk and had sex with each of the youths in turn. (Some of them had to be prodded into taking part.) In return, they gave her everything they could not take with them.(15)

Despite its lapses in conventional morality, Theresienstadt was no Sodom or Gemorrah. Although Adler claims that some things which occurred would almost indicate a "bordello economy," he admits that most reports of sexual excesses were widely exaggerated and that "discussions involving sex were not part of everyday conversation." Moreover, while weak marriages collapsed, strong marriages became stronger. As Norbert Fryd puts it, "Marriages that were not stable internally fell immediately into ruin. . . Marriages that withstood Theresienstadt were genuine marriages." Even among the unmarried, most sexual contact took place between couples committed to each other. The prevailing attitude toward sex is perhaps best described by Elias, who married her fiance in Theresienstadt.

We seized at everything that came along for we lived only for the moment. We never knew what tomorrow would bring or when we could be together again, and therefore we drank every draft of life to the end. It was amazing how, despite undernourishment, one yearned to give oneself to love. Love meant life and we continually wanted to feel and wanted to prove to ourselves that we still lived. . . It was as if we sensed the end that stood before us. We wanted to surrender nothing but instead to seize with both hands the little beauty that we could find in the ghetto, hold it fast and not let go.

As the summer of 1943 approached, the mood of the camp began to brighten. Conditions had begun to improve; in some respects, markedly so.

The camp's population, for one thing, seems to have stabilized at around 45,000. While this still made the town six times as congested as a normal European city, it represented a vast improvement over the previous fall. Moreover, by putting up some new buildings for workshops, the Jewish administration had freed some existing buildings for living space.

The camp also seemed to be getting a grip on many of its other problems. Work squads had laid over seven *miles* of water mains and pipes, more than quadrupling the amount of available water. All buildings were now hooked up to the central water system, whereas nearly a quarter of them had not had plumbing when the Jews arrived. The camp now had over 1,000 commodes, nearly two-thirds of them flush toilets. The electricity capacity had increased by 50 percent.

Other accomplishments include the crematorium, mentioned earlier, a delousing station which in April had been enlarged and upgraded, an increasingly improved central laundry, and a substantial expansion of cooking facilities. The latter included a tripling of kettle space and the establishment of a noodle factory. Making these accomplishments all the more impressive was the fact that they were achieved by work crews who not only lacked training and experience but who often had to make do with scrap materials.

The most ambitious project was the construction of a railroad spur from Theresienstadt to the Bauschowitz station. In a little over nine months, some 300 workers had moved 20,000 yards of earth and laid nearly two miles of track. Its official opening on June 1 was a celebrated event.

While the railroad spur did little to improve conditions within the camp itself, other than give the inmates a sense of achievement, most of the other accomplishments had made life more livable. The water system now delivered four gallons per resident per day. Though only one-fifth of the minimum considered necessary for clean and healthy living, this was still far more than the amount supplied earlier. The increased electricity enabled the wiring of attics and other previously unelectrified areas. The improved delousing station along with the increased efficiency of the fumigation squads enabled the camp to gain some control over the vermin. Finally, the improved kitchen facilities, while they did nothing to increase the supply of food, had managed to shorten the waiting lines. Moreover, work crews had built eaves on the buildings to shelter those who did have to wait.

As is evident, many Jews were developing abilities they never knew they had. The cooks, mostly males with little or no previous kitchen experience, were baking better bread than that previously brought in from outside. They had also created a pudding which even some Nazis were consuming with gusto. Others had learned to make or remodel clothes, fashion baby carriages out of wood, create a Theresienstadt version of Monopoly, and brew an alcoholic drink using the camp's grain "coffee" as a base.

That some could make contraband liquor and get away with it, points to still another development that was making ghetto life less onerous. The Nazis were becoming less energetic in enforcing many of their own regulations and prohibitions. They had unofficially relaxed the rule on separation of the sexes, thereby making it possible for a few couples who were not Prominenten to live together. (Nevertheless, with up to 10 or 12 couples sharing a room, there was still little privacy.)

The Nazis continued to vigorously enforce the ban on tobacco. They also kept a close eye on sports, forbidding gymnastics or any other kind of activity specifically designed to foster physical strength. Yet they allowed soccer and handball, and numerous teams of those sports had sprung up.

Soccer was especially popular. Games were at first played in stray corners at opportune moments, but in the spring of 1943 a league was formed with two adult and one juvenile division. Most adult teams were organized around work stations, such as the Ghetto Watch, the bakery, the medical service, etc. Lack of space limited the teams to seven instead eleven players, but games were regularly scheduled and formally refereed. In May, the Zionists commemorated the first 18 months of the ghetto's existence, as well as Herzl's 83rd birthday, by organizing a *Hechalutz* day complete with soccer matches, speeches, and a *hora* dance.

Women formed volleyball teams and, since the Nazis worried less about female physical capacity, a former physical education teacher conducted a daily gymnastics hour in the courtyard of the Hamburg barracks. "It was astonishing," writes Elias, "how many women, despite hunger and deprivation, took part each day in this activity."

As significant as these improvements were in daily life, however, two other factors did still more to raise the camp's spirits. The first was the apparent stoppage of deportations. There had been no transports since the first few days of February, and while pauses had occurred before, this was the longest yet. As June turned into July with no rumors circulating and no high SS officials in sight, hopes increasingly rose that the deportations had ended once and for all.

The second factor raising the camp's morale was the course of the war. The year had opened with the shattering German defeat at Stalingrad, followed by consistent, persistent German retreats on the Russian front. These were matched by similar defeats in Africa, where in May the remaining German armies had surrendered.

Through their secret radio, smuggled-in newspapers and tips from friendly gendarmes, the inmates were avidly following the Allied successes. Indeed, the Theresienstadt rumor mill worked overtime to embellish and spread such reports, as well as to create nonexisting ones. If you entered a barracks and voiced a new rumor, says Utitz, and then went to another barracks 15 minutes later, someone would rush up to you to repeat the rumor you had spread in the first barracks. There was even a joke that the course of the war was following the camp's rumor mill. In this fashion Africa was liberated while the battle of Tobruk was still being waged and the Russians were entering Poland while the battle of Stalingrad was still underway.

The Nazis' behavior only fueled such hopes, for the apparent end to the deportations and the easing of some restrictions indicated to Theresienstadters that their captors were becoming fearful. At one time, the SS had posted copies of a German newspaper published in Prague on the camp bulletin board. With the defeat at Stalingrad, they had stopped doing so.

The residents had long felt confident that the Allies would win. Now they began to see victory on the immediate horizon. One man traded his warm clothing for food, believing he would be home before the cold weather. Optimists generally felt the war would end in six weeks or so, while pessimists, who were in the minority, thought it might take as long as six months. Hardly any believed it would take almost two more years for the Allies to defeat the Germans, and that most of them would not be alive to see it happen.

---

12. The Nuremberg racial laws were quite complex. For example, a half-Jew lost his or her "Mischling" status if he or she had married, and refused to divorce, a Jewish spouse. Also, despite the thoroughness with which the Nazis examined such cases, errors invariably occurred. In fact, at least three non-Jews are believed to have ended up in the camp, two by mistake and one through a false denunciation.

13. Lauscher and his daughter Michela demonstrated the toy dog to me in their Prague apartment in the winter of 1989, saying, "This saved our lives."

14. Romoald was later removed from the list, presumably through the intercession of the German farm manager.

15. The young woman mentioned by Lustig may be the same person interviewed years later by Baker, but not identified. Baker describes her as a lovely young woman from a Berlin family, who could not adjust to camp conditions and so became a prostitute "to get an extra scrap of food, a feeling of warmth...."

PART II

SHORTCOMINGS AND SUCCESSES

CHAPTER 5
THE GOVERNORS AND THE GOVERNED

Like most Nazis involved in Eichmann's operations, Siegfried Seidl was an Austrian. And like many of them, he was also fairly young. Barely 30 on assuming command of Theresienstadt, he was a year younger than his superior, Hans Guenther, and only six years younger than Eichmann himself.

He was, however, more educated than the typical SS officer even though his Ph.D. in philosophy may have been obtained with Murmelstein's help. Most likely his Ph.D. influenced Eichmann's decision to pick him to head a camp designed at least in part for highly educated and cultured Jews.

Seidl certainly seemed to fit the part. He spoke high German easily, dressed immaculately, and rode his horse majestically through the streets of the privileged ghetto, his favorite German police dog trotting faithfully at his side. That he was only a 1st Lieutenant when he took over the camp in no way detracted from his aura of authority, for the SS often gave substantial responsibility to lower-ranking officers. Eichmann himself would never rise beyond the rank of Lieutenant Colonel.

As noted earlier, Seidl seemed to get along quite well with Edelstein and frequently yielded to the Jewish Elders' pleas for concessions. Yet the camp commandant remained an avowed anti-Semite nonetheless. He kept a caricature of a Jew on his desk bearing the caption, "Don't get upset; just smile." When the camp's high death rate of September 1942 was reported to him, Seidl smilingly replied, "The clock is ticking right on time."

He could also manifest such sentiments in more direct ways. On one occasion he noticed, while going over a list of new arrivals, the name of a former Viennese real estate agent who he felt had improperly handled the sale of a piece of property belonging to the Seidl family. Seidl immediately clapped the now aged man in jail and kept him there in darkness and on starvation rations until he died. On another occasion, he was riding through the town when he noticed a camp teacher named Teitelbaum out walking with his pupils. Seidl suddenly ordered the teacher to start running and then he and his police dog chased him until the young man dropped to the ground exhausted. He then put Teitelbaum in jail and deported him on the next transport.(16)

Seidl's behavior, brutal though it could be, seemed almost mild compared to that of his second-in-command, a former hairdresser from Dortmund named Karl Bergel. The latter's short, squat figure and low forehead set over bulging eyes gave him, in the view of one inmate, the look of an enraged bulldog. His actions frequently matched his appearance. During an interrogation over a smuggled letter he beat upon a sick prisoner who was being carried on a stretcher. When he once went to strike another resident, and the victim lifted his arm to protect his face, Bergel ordered him executed. (The victim was apparently one of those who were hung during the second and final batch of executions within the camp.)

Bergel became almost as well known for his stupidity as for his brutality. He had ordered the Jewish administration to prepare a wall chart showing the daily death rate. When the death rate began to fall after reaching its zenith in September 1942, he complained to Edelstein that the line was going down. So the statistical department replaced it with a chart showing the cumulative total, and since some deaths occurred every day in the camp, the line once again began moving up. Bergel was now satisfied.

Brutality and terrorism also characterized the inmates' contacts with other members of the camp's SS garrison. The younger SS men were especially cruel, and the elderly, who frequently wandered about in a confused state, were often their victims. One 22-year-old SS man once struck an elderly man on the street for failing to salute him. When the man tried to protect himself against a possible second blow, his tormenter promptly pulled out his gun and shot him. On another occasion, an elderly woman crossing the street suddenly saw a tractor bearing down on her. Paralyzed with fright, she remained rooted on the spot while the tractor ran over her and continued on its way. (The driver was well known in the camp for his penchant for trying to run down Jews, so most jumped out of the way whenever they saw him coming.)

As was the case with other concentration camps, the ill and infirm were not spared. One disabled war veteran liked to hobble through the streets on his crutches with his *Pour le Merite*, Germany's highest award for valor, proudly pinned to his chest. One day a young SS man suddenly came up to him and, after badgering him with questions, pushed him down and kicked him. Another of the camp's Nazi overseers liked to inspect the hospitals at night, waking up patients and forcing them to stand naked in open doorways while he made his rounds.

Incidents of on-the-spot violence were not always acts of impulse. In some situations at least, such behavior was officially sanctioned and even required. An Order of the Day dated August 28, 1942 notes how corn had been stolen from the cornfield. "The guards are instructed to make use of their firearms if they come across any such incident." Another bulletin posted the next day says, "Herr Camp Inspector SS 2nd Lt. Bergel strongly complains that ghetto residents can still be seen on the street at night. Herr Camp Inspector SS 2nd Lt. Bergel expressly warns that he will use his firearms against anyone who, without a valid reason, is found on the street after midnight."

Mindful of the strict Nazi laws against "racial pollution," the SS men generally refrained from sexually molesting the town's women. These laws did not prohibit ogling, however, and Seidl himself frequently found a reason to visit the bath house when younger women were showering. A lieutenant from the Lodz Ghetto, who visited the camp from time to time, went further. He would seize attractive women on the street, take them to the bath house, and make them bathe before him, sometimes pinching them before or after.

While Theresienstadt's SS garrison included no women, three SS women from Leitmeritz came regularly to search the women's quarters for contraband goods. Escorted by gendarmes, they would ransack every room seizing anything of value. They sometimes searched men's quarters as well, for Berger remembers having once gulped down three cigarettes when he heard them at the door. If they didn't find anything worth taking, they would out of frustration break or destroy anything else they found and leave the room in a state of total disorder. When Seidl learned that they were keeping much of the loot for themselves instead of turning it over to the SS, he had them prosecuted. They received prison terms of 18 months and no further visits from SS women occurred.

It should be noted that non-SS Germans involved with the ghetto behaved quite differently. The head of the electrical works treated his workers quite fairly, while the German in charge of the farm became known for his kindness. He would go out of the room, purposely leaving his cigarettes on the table. On some occasions he would even post letters for his employees. When two of his workers married, he set up a one-room cottage so that they could live together.

In similar fashion, the German doctor in Leitmeritz, to whom the SS referred all the medical department's requests, almost always approved them. The SS eventually became suspicious and would not allow him to confer with a ghetto doctor without an SS man being present. At a

later time, some ghetto men were assigned to building a rifle range for
the German army in Leitmeritz. The German soldiers who supervised
them also behaved well for the most part, often posting their letters and
sometimes even supplying the stamps.

The Nazi presence in the camp became less noticeable as camp
conditions somewhat stabilized and the Jews' own administrative
apparatus developed. The SS had taken over a few buildings in the
main square, one of them the town's only hotel, and there behind a
cordon of fences and barbed wire they spent much of their time. Their
activities included a great deal of drinking, which occasionally ended in
pistol shots. The Nazis had also fenced off a street leading to the main
gate so that they could come and go without encountering any Jews.
Still, Theresienstadters sometimes encountered one of them sauntering
or, after a drinking bout, staggering down the street. They would
invariably give him a wide berth.

The Nazis did rely on the residents for a host of goods and services.
Jewish artists painted pictures, most of them portraits, as well as murals;
Jewish artisans made furniture for their homes along with trinkets and
toys for their families; and Jewish tailors and seamstresses outfitted their
wives and children. Although they had their own doctors in nearby
Leitmeritz, many continued to follow the good Austrian custom of
cursing the Jews but running to a Jewish physician at the first sign of
illness. On occasion they even called on Jewish medical personnel to
perform abortions on their wives and mistresses, a medical procedure
which, though required for Jewish women, was illegal for Aryans. While
their SS patients were invariably courteous, even affable, during their
visits, the Jewish doctors and dentists treating them sweated with fear
lest they make a mistake and pay heavily for it.

The Jewish administration generally managed to meet even their
captors' most challenging demands. Bergel once gave them a large
assortment of stamps with instructions to have the stamps classified,
arranged, and placed into an album by the next day. The Jewish
administration, after consulting its files, rounded up the camp's
philatelists. The latter, working through the night without a catalog or
other research materials, classified the stamps, put them on separate
sheets, and had the sheets bound. The album was delivered, as directed,
the next morning.

Seidl once ordered them to draw up his family tree, going back 13
generations. When they pointed out that its 8,000 branches would

require eight yards of space, Seidl told them to make it pocket-sized. The Jews solved the problem by putting it into folding sections.

Once the SS ordered a library to be set up in their main lounge. The Jewish librarians carefully selected works they thought would appeal to the Nazis. An inspection after the war indicated that not one of the books had ever been taken off the shelves.

Since most of the SS were Austrians or South Germans, they were presumably Catholic. Yet they showed no interest in religion. They kept the town's single Catholic church locked up, neither using it themselves nor allowing the Catholic Jews to use it. The only Jew allowed to enter the building was a clocksmith, who daily adjusted the clock in the belfry.

Finally, and most importantly, while they made full use of their privileges and perks, they generally eschewed the more mundane tasks of governance. In running Theresienstadt, they exhibited more Austrian *Schlamperei* (sloppiness) than German *Tuchtigkeit* (efficiency). They frequently ordered buildings erected but then did not use them and, in some cases, even had them torn down. While they ordered hundreds of sewing machines to produce uniforms for the German army, they failed to order needles, thread, and other materials for their use. The machines were found after the war rusting away in their cases. When some German army officers visited the camp to see how the assembly of tank kits was going, the SS found itself with no kits on hand to assemble. So they hurriedly had some finished ones disassembled so that they could show the visitors a scene of Jews busily assembling new ones.

This lack of efficiency in some respects eased the plight of the Jews. Life in Theresienstadt, it should be stressed, was smothered in rules; virtually everything not expressly allowed was forbidden. Moreover, as we have seen, the punishments for infractions could be severe. Spitting on the street was a heinous offense, and smoking could cost someone his life. But thanks to irregular and generally lax supervision, women got to spend nights in their husband's barracks, Zionist organizations and a communist network managed to function, and underground cabarets entertained their guests with anti-Nazi humor. Occasionally, Czech relatives or in-laws came to the camp and got to speak to inmates through holes in the perimeter fence. In one instance, a German half-Jew came to visit his 83-year-old grandmother, and though he never got to see her, he did get as far as Seidl's office before being ejected.

As mentioned earlier, this laxity seemed to increase as the first 18 months of the ghetto's existence drew to an end. Still, the residents remained well aware of their captors' essential malignancy and might. As Adler puts it, "One perceived their power without being able to gauge it correctly. . . They seemed like evil spirits which now and then burst on the scene, perpetrated their misdeeds, and then disappeared until their next appearance." And, adds Adler, "That next appearance could come at any time."

Theresienstadt's SS garrison, at least during this first phase, never numbered more than 20 regular SS men plus a handful of employees. How did a corps of about two dozen rather slack and slothful men rule a community of up to 58,000?

One answer lies in the Czech gendarmes, whose exact number is not known, but appears to have ranged from 120 to 150. Outfitted in green uniforms topped with knights' helmets and armed with rifles topped with bayonets, they supervised the work details, guarded the SS jail, patrolled the streets and, with the help of the Ghetto Watch, kept the residents in line. All Theresienstadters were required to salute them as well as the SS.

The gendarmes were headed by a police lieutenant named Theodor Janetschek, a somewhat grotesque-looking man whose giant head and spindly legs earned him the secret nickname of "Cauliflower." Though a Czech, he had been born and raised in Vienna; as a result, he spoke German better than Czech and addressed his men in that language. Janetschek's origins also apparently influenced his attitude toward Jews, for he treated them as ruthlessly as did the SS itself. He brought even the slightest infractions to the attention of his Nazi superiors and zealously saw that whatever punishments resulted were faithfully carried out. Theresienstadt's inmates feared him as much as they feared the SS itself.

His men also feared him for he would denounce them as readily as he would the Jews. This, in addition to his insistence on speaking German, not only alienated his men but probably helped make many of them more favorably disposed toward those they guarded and governed.

But other factors also drew the gendarmes closer to their captives. While some had been policemen before the German occupation, others had been more or less forced into the service and loathed it. Nearly all of them despised the SS who treated them as inferiors and forced them to speak their language. That the Nazis, despite the formal facade of "Protectorate," dealt with their country as a conquered nation, and increased their harshness toward it considerably after Heydrich's assassination, also helped. So while the gendarmes did the devil's work, they were not, for the most part, the devil's disciples. Only a dozen or so shared the virulent anti-Semitism of their commander and the SS; the rest behaved quite decently toward the Jews and some went out of their way to help them.

The most conspicuous of these sympathizers was a sergeant named Karel Salada. In addition to taking photos of the first executions and smuggling them out of the ghetto, he also smuggled out letters and even smuggled in a radio. Other gendarmes also smuggled out mail and brought in contraband, chiefly food and newspapers. In many instances, the inmates paid them to do so but often the Czech policemen did this on their own. In supervising work details, they would frequently allow a relaxed pace. As one gendarme once told a group of men working on a construction project in mid-winter, "Work just hard enough to keep from freezing."

Some who helped Jews got into trouble for doing so. During the ghetto's existence, 14 in all would be arrested and sent to the "Little Fortress." While six were eventually released, the other eight remained there until the end of the war, one of them dying three days before liberation. Others received lesser punishments. One who wrote a letter to a relative describing conditions at the camp and expressing sympathy for the Jews, was confined to quarters for 15 days. Salada, though repeatedly interrogated and finally transferred, was never fully found out.

The friendly gendarmes did more than just ease the privations of overwork and undernourishment. They provided the residents with a link to the outside world and helped them feel they were not abandoned and forgotten. They shared with them the joys of Nazi defeats in Russia and Africa and the hopes of a speedy end to their nightmare. As one Theresienstadt woman later recalled in speaking of the gendarmes, "If there had not been a group of decent men among them, no Jew would ever have survived."

As is known, mental patients sometimes suffer delusions of grandeur. In one such patient at Theresienstadt's mental hospital, however, such delusions took an unusual turn. This man did not believe he was Napoleon or Julius Caesar, but a member of a Council of Elders. As such, he demanded total deference to his wishes and unconditional obedience to his commands.

One's first reaction may be to regard this poor fellow as doubly unbalanced since the role model he had chosen seemed ill suited to instil a sense of greatness or power. The Council of Elders was essentially a tool of the SS who could and would overturn any of its decisions as well as appoint or remove any of its members. In the camp's early days, Seidl deported one member who had obtained some vegetables for his family from the outside. He did this purposely, he later said, to show that they had to obey the rules like everyone else.

Like the camp's other inmates, councilmen had to salute any SS man they encountered on the street. Edelstein never wore a hat even on cold days, so that he would not have to raise it to his Nazi overseers. Council members also had to salute the Czech gendarmes, whose authority over them was nearly as absolute as that of the SS.

Yet, a closer look makes the mental patient's choice of a power figure to personify seem less bizarre. Subservient though they were to the Nazi rulers and the Czechs in their employ, the elders of Theresienstadt nonetheless wielded life and death powers over the community's inhabitants. This power was manifested most openly and directly during deportations. As earlier noted, each member could place 30 people, in addition to his own family, on the exemption list. But in making up the deportation list, he could usually shelter many others as well.

Council members could also protect their favorites or promote their interests in numerous other ways. An Elder's recommendation would help greatly in securing a better job, improved living space, or some other benefit. Such benefits could not only improve the beneficiary's life but even save it, for a job handling food might enable him or her to avoid, or recover from, a fatal illness while a job deemed vital to the camp's operation could offer protection from deportation.

Council members also enjoyed numerous personal privileges. They could live with their families, write more frequently and fully to friends and relatives outside, and visit places inside Theresienstadt sealed off to others, such as the Schleuse. They could also bring their musical instruments to the camp. The Nazis had even brought Eppstein's grand piano down the river on a barge.

Initially, the SS had offered the Elders still more privileges, including their own kitchen and dining room. Edelstein had at first rejected such offers, warning his co-workers that the Nazis wanted them "to forget that we are representatives of the Jews." During the camp's first few days he and his staff lived together in barracks like other residents. But when Seidl accused him of "communist practices," he reluctantly relented and accepted family housing for himself and other top administrators. He did not, however, accept a separate dining room.

Despite his efforts at keeping a modest profile, Edelstein's seemingly powerful position as Elder naturally placed him on a pinnacle, if not a pedestal, and induced others to treat him with exaggerated respect. One camp musician used the first letters of his name, EDE, as the musical notes for the theme of a string quartet which he composed and dedicated to Edelstein.

This glorification of the camp Elder reached an apogee under Eppstein who became something of a royal personage. His granting of a brief audience was viewed as a great favor, his words were listened to and heeded with near reverence, and his appearance at any activity transformed it into a major event. His birthday produced a torrent of speeches, poems, musical compositions, and various objets d'art created by inmates. The Central Supply Division once presented him with over 70 pounds of food so that he could observe his birthday in a fittingly festive manner.

The food was quickly consumed by the mock royal court that had collected around him. This entourage consisted of various high officials of the camp administration along with a bevy of courtiers. The group held musical evenings, parties, and even balls. Adler claims they once held a masked ball on the eve of a deportation.

The extent to which Eppstein actively encouraged such practices is unclear. He remained in Theresienstadt essentially what he had been in Berlin, a hard-working, somewhat aloof German bureaucrat seeking to carry out his assigned duties in a diligent manner. Still, he apparently did little to discourage the development of an influential inner circle with himself at its center. Utitz, in noting how Eppstein had once been a cultivated and respected scholar, observed sadly, "The situation was simply stronger than he was."(17)

The deification of the Jewish Elder, who, after all, was the only man who met regularly with the camp commandant, produced a commensurate diminution in the power of the Council over which he presided. This process was further abetted by the Council's gradual, if unofficial, enlargement for those removed from the Council, such as the six Czechs whom Seidl had replaced with Germans and Austrians, continued to come to meetings and to be allowed their say. Such a large, and largely disunited group--even the Czechs on the Council were split between Zionists, assimilationists, and one communist--was forced to rely increasingly on its head. Moreover, the latter could usually gain the members' approval for what he wished to do by simply saying or implying that he was carrying out the commandant's commands or at least his desires.

The elevation of the chief Elder's power began under Edelstein but accelerated under Eppstein. As Murmelstein somewhat snidely remarks,

"Edelstein did it more cleverly; Eppstein did it more clearly." Both
men also used the Council as a screen to escape responsibility and
personal opprobrium for doing unpopular things which had to be done.
To quote Murmelstein again, "The Council of Elders served as a cover
for necessary but unpopular measures and, on occasion, for dealing with
influential people to whom one did not want, on one's own responsibility, to say no." (American city managers and school superintendents
often use similar methods in dealing with school committees and city
councils.)

By 1943 the Council had ceased to play an important role in camp
decision making. Even the camp's formal procedures recognized this
fact. Decrees once issued in the name of the Council of Elders now
simply emanated from the "Jewish Self-Administration." Yet Council
members retained their privileges and perquisites, and if their power to
shape policy had largely disappeared, their power to help or, in some
instances, to harm individuals still remained.

Beneath the Jewish Elder and his Council stretched an elaborate and
elongated hierarchy. It included department heads, division heads,
section heads, and other supervisors. It also included block elders,
house elders, and even room elders. (The Nazis favored the term
"elder" because they did not want to give any Jew a title implying real
power.) All told, nearly a quarter of the work force had managerial
authority.

As with most organizations, an informal network had arisen which
supplemented, and in some instances supplanted, the formal one. For
example, Kurt Schliesser, the former salesman who headed the camp's
economic department, wielded an influence far exceeding his rank on
the organizational ladder thanks largely to his capability and craftiness.
Adler, in fact, regards him as "perhaps the strongest man in the ghetto."

Schliesser's department was outnumbered in size by the camp's
medical service, but the latter was exceeded by the camp's internal
administrative apparatus which employed close to one-third of Theresienstadt's workforce. The various security services alone employed some
769, while the leisure-time activities division had an employee roster of
276.

Why so many?

For one thing, possibly to justify their own jobs to their superiors as
well as to promote the illusion of Theresienstadt being a self-governing
community, the Nazis authorized numerous officers, issued constant
commands, and demanded continual reports. The central registry, for

example, had to report the camp's statistics every day. These statistics included deaths, deportations, and the status of the existing population broken down into various categories, such as country of origin, work status, and age. Since age was reckoned not by year but by date of birth, with a tolerance of three days, the office had to prepare a new age table every three days. Each night some employees worked into the small hours preparing the morning report.

The camp administration sought not only to supply the asked-for information but to add to it. In this way they wanted to impress their supervisors and, if possible, influence them in the right direction. Furthermore, since the Nazis seemed to like visual material, the camp's numerous artists were kept busy drawing up charts and graphs.

Another factor which encouraged the swelling of the administrative workforce was the malnourished and weakened state of its workers. This made it necessary to use three people to do the work of two or even one. The antiquated typewriters and generally poor office equipment also made additional labor necessary. Then there was the perceived need to provide work for those untrained or otherwise unqualified for more technical and directly productive work. As Ansbacher has testified, "Sometimes in a particular office, tens of people would be working although actually the work could be done by four persons, but the attempt was made to distribute work so that everybody should feel essential." Joblessness, it should be remembered, not only reduced an inmate's food ration but made him or her more vulnerable to deportation.

But over and above all these factors was simply the tendency to expand that seems inherent in all organizations unconstrained by such things as the need to make a profit. Supervisors generally love to increase the number of their subordinates, while the latter like to add to their span of control as well. So, while responding to the Nazis' requests and the inmates' needs was responsible for much of the ghetto government's growth, the needs of its own administrative apparatus played a by no means insignificant role.

Administrative growth led to the issuance of more and more rules and regulations, as well as to increased paperwork. By 1943 the camp was consuming over 100,000 sheets of paper a month. When the Jewish administration, in a frantic move to halt this growth, required all future requests to be fully documented, the problem only intensified. Now requests came in accompanied by numerous sheets of facts and figures.

"German red tape ran wild," says Lederer as he notes that the particulars of each resident were entered on 12 index cards and other records. One former employee of the Central Registry gives the number of file entries on each resident as 17, and adds, "Quite possibly German *Grundlichkeit* (thoroughness) and systematic paperwork never celebrated a greater triumph than in the concentration camp of Theresienstadt." To Adler it represented "a monstrous spinning of wheels or running in place as officials competed with each other and overran each others' territory." The administrative mechanism, he says, "became an end in itself."

This helped to transform life for the resident into a seemingly endless paper chase. There were constantly forms to fill out, officials to see, and matters to straighten out. To move required approval from four separate offices, even when the move was only temporary such as to allow for fumigation. Getting a shoe repaired or a lost button replaced became a major undertaking. It was said that one could have launched a small business in prewar Prague with the energy and effort required to procure a shoelace in Theresienstadt. To be sure, the Nazis provided the basis for such a situation, but the Jewish administration seems to have contributed more than its share. As one resident wryly observed, "Theresienstadt was a concentration camp made more severe through self-administration."

The camp had also developed a complex social hierarchy which in some instances paralleled but in other cases diverged from its political power structure. The most conspicuous example of such divergence were the *Prominenten*, who enjoyed various privileges but who generally wielded little political influence. The Prominenten, who with their families numbered about 200, were divided into two classes, A and B. The A's had received their special status from the SS; the B's had received theirs from the ghetto administration.

As might be expected, the A's enjoyed the most benefits. They did not live in barracks but had a whole room for themselves and their families, plus extra food and additional mail privileges. They were not required to work, although some did so voluntarily. Their most important privilege, however, was their general exemption from deportation.(18)

Most class A Prominenten had held important positions or attained high status in pre-Nazi days, or had received high decorations while serving as top-level officers in World War I, or had formed close ties to the Nazis either through previous marriage or friendship or through serving as informers or collaborators. But there were exceptions. One widow, whose husband had been an Aryan, had merely operated a small restaurant. The mayor of her city liked to dine there, however, and so had recommended her for special consideration.

Aside from their not always certain exemption from deportation, class B Prominenten enjoyed fewer favors. They received somewhat better housing, but little else.

The privileges of the Prominenten, whether A or B, should not be exaggerated. Many were lodged in the small rooms of the town's former poorhouse. Nor did the Nazis go out of their way to protect them. When Mandler, the former Prague travel agent who so ruthlessly had helped deport his fellow Jews, arrived at the camp, the SS rewarded him with Prominenten A status. But when some young Czech Jews gave him a beating for his previous activities, the SS made no serious effort to locate and prosecute them.

Some Prominenten still sought to cling to their former eminence. Kaethe Starke, who came from a prominent but not internationally known or connected Hamburg family, soon experienced this. Like most women, she was initially assigned to a cleaning squad and while cleaning one Prominenten house, she attempted to discuss some mutual acquaintances with one of its residents. He was Dr. Emil Klein, the 70-year-old founder of Germany's natural health food movement. Klein, however, quickly cut her off, saying, "I don't carry on conversations with servants." Although at first mortified by his rude response, she soon found it a cause for amusement, as did her cleaning-squad colleagues.

The rest of the camp population were divided, according to Adler, into two groups: workers and beggars. But this greatly oversimplifies the situation, for a pecking order had arisen which, when compared to that found in a normal modern society, almost seems like a hierarchy standing on its head.

Among the professions and trades, engineers, technicians, and artisans enjoyed superior status. Physicians, along with professionally recognized musicians and artists, managed to maintain roughly the status they had enjoyed in civilian life. (One should remember that the position of physician in Europe is not so highly esteemed as in the United States.) But bankers, industrialists, merchants, attorneys, and professors without special claims to eminence, fell to the bottom. Many a former millionaire pulled a garbage wagon, while his former tailor and shoemaker enjoyed much more prestige and far more perquisites.

Some businessmen ended up working for their former employees. Many were happy to do so. Kurt Schliesser, for example, appointed his former boss to head the bakery, one of the camp's prized positions.

All jobs that facilitated contact with food conferred special status. One Theresienstadt poet wrote a poem describing how he had had a "beautiful dream" in which everyone loved him, couldn't do enough for him, and continually solicited his attention. In the poem's last line he reveals the reason. "I dreamed I was the head of the kitchen." Utitz recalls hearing an older man, who was acting as matchmaker for a young woman, ask her if she would like a bank director, an attorney, or a professor. When she said no to all three, the matchmaker became exasperated and exclaimed, "What's the matter with you? Did you think I could get you a cook?"

Another group who enjoyed special status were the members of the first two work details who had prepared the camp. For the most part, they continued to live together and the Council of Elders exempted them and their families from deportation. As the camp's pioneers and groundbreakers, they felt superior to those who came later, while the latter felt superior to those who came after them. As in most organizations, longevity in Theresienstadt itself apparently conferred a distinction of its own.

The often reverse nature of the camp's social order, reverse at least when compared to the outside world, affected family relationships as well. Young people who would otherwise be living at home while attending a university or high school frequently found themselves caring for their weakened, ill, or simply demoralized parents. Since women generally endured the physical and emotional shocks of the camp better than men, they frequently became their husbands' providers and protectors. In these as in many other respects the privileged ghetto seemed like a normal world turned upside down.

The political and social hierarchies which transected the camp were overlain, and in many respects overshadowed, by still other divisions. Ideological, religious, and, most of all, ethnic differences also sundered the inmates, frequently causing disunity and disruption.

Ideological differences first manifested themselves in the split between the Zionists and non-Zionists. "The enmity between the Czechs [sic] and Zionists conditioned the development of the camp from its initial days," says Adler. "Feuds repeatedly flared up in the executive branch as well as among the rank and file." Still, these disputes gradually grew less pronounced as the Zionists, who included not only Edelstein but most of the younger Czechs, became increasingly prominent and eventually predominant. Two factors, other than Edelstein's position as camp Elder, fostered their rise: a higher death and illness rate among the non-Zionists, who tended to be older; and Hitler's racial policies, which were making a Jewish state seem not only desirable but necessary.

The third basic Czech faction, the communists, numbered, as noted earlier, only about 100, and generally sought to work with the Zionists. Because the Nazis would have immediately deported them or even sent them to the Little Fortress had their political affiliations become known, they kept a low profile. Yet, thanks to their cohesiveness and commitment, their influence, says Fryd, "was felt everywhere."

Religious differences played only a minor role in camp life. Most Theresienstadters were at best "three-day-a-year Jews" when it came to attending religious services and in any case strict adherence to religious commandments, such as keeping kosher and devoting the Sabbath to prayer, was impossible. The small group of deeply religious Jews who sought to maintain as far as possible their religious commitments created little disruption and incurred little disfavor.

The Christian Jews did arouse some animosity. It was directed not at those who had been raised Christian, but at those who, as adults, had converted. Camp residents were often openly scornful and contemptuous of such Christians, branding them as renegades and opportunists. Goldschmidt, the Protestant leader who had been raised a Christian and so was shielded from such scorn himself, sought to have the date of confirmation eliminated from the records of later arrivals so as to protect them from possible abuse. Nevertheless, the unpleasantness continued and some Jewish Christians eventually enrolled themselves as Jews or as *konfessionslos*.

The situation was not helped by those few baptized German Jews who, along with quite a few half-Jews, clung so fiercely to their German identity that they refused to have anything to do with the regular residents, especially the Czechs. Some maintained that "the Jews [sic!] are responsible for everything that happened," and one or two even insisted that "if the Fuehrer only knew what was happening here, then everything would be different. He would not tolerate such goings on."

All these differences, however, paled into insignificance compared to what was certainly the most disruptive division within the camp: the animosity between the Czechs and the Germans. The Czechs looked upon Theresienstadt as their camp. They had built it and had put it into operation. Then suddenly hordes of Germans poured in, dressed as if going to a resort, speaking only the hated language of their captors and, for the most part, unable to make any useful contribution to the camp. Housing and feeding them greatly lowered the living conditions which the Czechs had been struggling, with some success, to raise to a halfway decent level.

To make matters worse, the SS tended to treat German Jews a bit better than Czech Jews. Most of those selected for Prominenten A status were Germans or Austrians and this had probably led the Council of Elders to set up a second level of Prominenten consisting largely of Czechs. The replacement of Edelstein with Eppstein was seen by the Czechs as an especially bitter blow.

The continual deportation of younger Czechs during the summer of 1942, while train loads of German Jews were arriving and being settled in the camp, only increased the ire of the Czechs. It seemed that Czechs were being shipped out to make room for Germans. Thus, when the first deportation of the elderly in September took away German Jews for the first time, some Czechs even expressed a degree of pleasure. "Now the Germans will learn what 'transport' means," they said. A few crude and coarse individuals behaved especially badly, verbally taunting the elderly German Jews as they proceeded to the Schleuse. But the following month the SS began deporting the Czech elderly, thereby enabling the German Jews to experience a measure of *Schadenfreude* (joy at another's misfortune).

The German Jews were shocked and dismayed at the attitude of the Czechs to their arrival. "We had thought that in Czechoslovakia we could find a land of friendship to unite with us in our hate of Hitler," said one. "What a disappointment! . . . They did not see in us fellow sufferers but only Germans whom they hated." One 80-year-old German woman recalls how a relative of hers was introduced to a group of Czech women as "a nice lady even though she is a German," while a Czech rabbi recalls how his middle-aged nephew and niece, in planning their daughter's wedding, argued bitterly over every detail except one: not a word of German was to be spoken and therefore not one German was to be invited.

The German Jews themselves, it must be added, did little to help matters. Aside from Eppstein, few were Zionists. Moreover, although the Czechs continued to hold most camp offices, even the younger German Jews showed little interest in learning Czech or in familiarizing themselves with Czech customs and culture. The German Jews had long been known for their passionate patriotism, and in Theresienstadt they continued to a great extent to think and act like Germans.(19)

Acting like a German meant, at least in those days, faithfully following the rules and deferring to authority. This hardly helped their relations with the Czechs, who constantly strived to get around the rules and to subtly defy the Nazis. As one Czech later remarked, "A great number of leading German Jews always wanted to prove that they were loyal to the SS camp leaders and followed their orders exactly. And because of that, they often did more than they would have had to do."

Eppstein seemed to personify this tendency and thereby perpetuated and exacerbated the Czech/German antagonisms. The Germans generally liked and admired him. He not only appeared to act like a model, high-level Prussian civil servant but spoke a cultured and at times even eloquent German. If he diligently, almost zealously, sought to execute the wishes of the SS, then they, as well as perhaps Eppstein himself, thought that doing so would impress the Nazis and induce them to treat the camp with   more consideration.

Eppstein himself made little effort to learn any Czech and for a while even kept Czech books out of the camp library. He expressed annoyance when he attended an event where Czech was the predominant language. His distant manner and officious behavior further displeased the Czechs, as did his faithfulness in following Nazi orders. Their leader, Edelstein, had often managed to wheedle concessions, albeit minor ones, from Seidl; Eppstein, it seemed, never even tried to do this. Finally, Eppstein's seemingly royal lifestyle, complete with musical soirees and masked balls, stirred up further scorn. The arrival of his grand piano created adverse comment throughout the camp.

The antagonism between the Czech and German Jews did not greatly affect the Austrian Jews who managed largely to escape the Czech's disfavor. For one thing, many of the older Austrian Jews had originally come from Czechoslovakia. Among them were Stricker and Friedmann, the two Austrian members of the Council of Elders. For another, Austria like Czechoslovakia had been taken over by the Germans and thus the Austrians could be considered fellow victims like themselves. Then, the Austrians were relatively few in number, at least compared to the Germans, who as a group were nearly three times as large.

But perhaps the biggest reason why the Austrian Jews proved more acceptable to the Czechs than the Germans lay in their demeanor and deportment. If the German Jews displayed the uprightness and rigidity so characteristic of Germans, the Austrians manifested the flexibility and adaptability characteristic of Austrians and therefore adjusted much more easily to camp conditions. They picked up some of the camp's argot when they did not speak Czech itself, and in true Viennese tradition often succeeded in ingratiating themselves.

This does not mean that all Austrians fared well in the camp. Some of the later arrivals were considered informers and collaborators, for

Vienna had a JUPO or Jewish police known for its ruthlessness. (It only contained, however, six members.) Those suspected of such activities were beaten by some of the younger Czechs. Nevertheless, most Austrians got along fairly well not only with the Czechs but with the German Jews and even the SS, many of whom, it will be recalled, were Austrians themselves.

One final, ironic note about the Austrian Jews. Nearly all came from Vienna where they had experienced a Jew hatred far more virulent than that suffered by the Germans and, of course, that suffered by the Czechs. In German cities and towns, for example, most Gentiles watched in uneasy silence as trucks carted off their local Jews to a collection center. In Vienna, however, Gentiles often cheered when witnessing such a sight. Yet no group of Theresienstadters missed their native city more intensely or spoke of it more longingly than did the Viennese Jews.(20)

The political, social, and ethnic divisions which fissured and fragmented the camp contributed to, if they did not actually create, one of its most pervasive and disheartening aspects. This is what Norbert Troller calls its "galloping corruption."

To be sure, Theresienstadt in this respect was hardly unique. Corruption *in the conventional sense* was the way of life in virtually all concentration camps and Nazi-created ghettos. In Theresienstadt it most often took the form of what its residents called *schleusen*, for it was in the intake centers that it first arose or, at least, first became apparent.

Those who came to the camp during its early days found the transportation commission personnel, who operated the Schleuse or intake centers to be correct and often helpful. But when swarms of German and Austrian Jews began arriving in the summer of 1942, things changed. Before, new arrivals only had to worry about the SS confiscating their possessions; now they had to worry about the transportation personnel doing so as well.

The practice of appropriating desirable goods from new arrivals grew and eventually jumped ethnic lines as the intake center employees began filching things from their later-arriving fellow Czechs. In this way, there arose the term *schleusen*, a verb created out of the noun *Schleuse*.

"Sluicegating" could take some bizarre turns. Soon after her arrival in the camp, Starke was awakened one night by the sound of a motor starting and stopping. She looked out the window to see a tractor pulling up and coming to a halt at the door of the Magdeburg barracks. Since the driver left the engine running, the tractor, an old one, began vibrating wildly. The vibrations almost immediately caused parcels and other objects it was carrying to start falling to the ground. As they fell, shadowy figures darted out of the darkness, picked the objects up, and then disappeared back into the darkness. The scene was repeated several times. Gradually she realized that the tractor was bringing goods from the Schleuse that had been brought in by new arrivals. These goods would obviously end up in other hands.

Retrieving such goods or anything else that got "lost" in the Schleuse proved difficult and even dangerous. A younger German woman found the mattress which she had brought with her and which bore her nametag in the courtyard of a building. As she approached it, two young Czechs approached her. In German she wished them good day and in friendly fashion pointed out that the mattress on the ground was hers. They did not reply but gave her a hostile, indeed an indignant, look and then returned to their work of building a bed frame.

The practice of sluicegating soon spread, affecting more and more areas of camp life. The camp postal employees were required, under supervision of the gendarmes, to inspect all parcels and remove all contraband goods. After a while, they began removing other goods as well. Again, it was the non-Czechs who bore the brunt of this brigandage. When Rabbi Baeck opened his first parcel from Germany, he found only an empty box.

Cruder, more common forms of stealing, also occurred. Utitz recalls finding his suspenders stolen and for a while scarcely dared to go out on the street. The dead and even the dying were frequent victims, and all too often the family of a dead person would show up to claim the deceased's goods, only to find them gone. Still, most stealing was directed not against individuals but against the community as a whole, and its main target was food.

Some 1300 residents were employed in handling food, and most of them used their positions to advantage. Potato peeling, for example, was one of the more arduous jobs in the camp. The peelers, all women, sat around a circle on crude boards and peeled until their hands were red. Yet, such positions were eagerly sought, for the peelers usually managed to stash away a potato or two for their own use. Many a peeler who arrived for work in the morning looking quite thin would leave at night with a well-rounded figure, thanks to the potatoes secreted under her clothes. Although all were examined by other women as they left, many had become adept at finding ways of eluding discovery or in arranging with their examiners to let them pass.

Other kitchen employees also became quite clever at carrying on such games. Once an employee showed up for work in heavy rubber boots and kept them on despite the fierce heat from the stoves. Afterward, he boasted how he had stuffed them with 20 pounds of yeast dough. Another stashed some food in a bucket, covered it with burning coals, and then holding up the bucket and yelling "Fire! Fire!" dashed out of the building past the guard.

When the women in the typing pool would be called out to unload potatoes, one woman, who owned a pair of gym pants, would quickly change into them. The pants closed at the ankle and thus enabled her to slip a potato or two down her leg.

Those not directly involved in food handling tried to benefit from those who were. A later-arriving Dutch woman remarked on her daughter's good fortune in finding a kitchen job. "She is the queen and we feel ourselves as the royal family. All our acquacintances want to know from which window she gives out food." Some even trained their children to steal, and those whose children proved especially skillful at this were envied. One resident recalls seeing a mother poke her little boy through a hole in the wall of a potato shed and then pull him out. The youngster emerged with a potato in each fist and a triumphant smile on his face.

Though food served as the most frequent object of sluice-gating, other goods and services also fell into the camp's complex web of corruption. Carpenters, tailors, seamstresses, and others performed extra services or simply extra-fast services for payoffs. Their materials were also in demand. A job in the carpentry shop was almost as good as one in the kitchen, for an extra bit of wood had great value, while a nail had even more. "If one had a friend in the carpentry shop, it was a great bit of luck," says Elias, "for one might get a nail or two to hammer in the wall to hang clothes on." A laundry worker could arrange for someone's wash to be done out of turn, while a house Elder who had told a would-be lodger that no more spaces were available would suddenly find one when a few cigarettes were deposited in his palm. One survivor reports purchasing a job in the bakery by giving one hundred cigarettes to an influential chain smoker.

All kinds of things could be used for barter and bribery, such as jewelry, clothes and, in a very few instances, one's body. Money was also used, including German marks, Czech crowns, and even American dollars. But the two biggest mediums of exchange were bread and cigarettes. There were, of course, no community stores of cigarettes to schleusen; they had to be smuggled in from the outside, usually through the Czech gendarmes or through those few other Czechs or Germans who visited the camp on business. Their price would vary. Usually cigarette prices were at their highest after an SS raid on a supplier or dealer, but they were never cheap or easily obtainable and a smoker could rarely procure more than one or two a day. Frequently, a group would share one, passing it around until the last smoker burned his fingers. But despite the high cost and the high risk involved, Theresienstadt smokers continued to puff away whenever they could. Some inmates even took up smoking in Theresienstadt.

Other delicacies and delights, including fruit and even wine, were also available, for black marketeering flourished. This led to still further divisions within the camp's population. "On one side there was deprivation to the point of hunger," says Berger, "while on the other side there was a group, and they were not few in number, who suffered no deprivation but actually had more than they needed."

The epidemic of corruption which engulfed the camp did not infect everyone. One who remained immune from the contagion was Leo Baeck. Given responsibility for the welfare of the elderly, he worked tirelessly and sometimes successfully to ease their plight. Once he complained to the head of the housing office about the abysmal crowding in a particular building and pointed out how a few modest changes could alleviate it. When the official, after saying he would correct it, failed to follow through, Baeck seized him by the scruff of the neck and forced him up the building stairs to see the situation for himself. Soon thereafter the desired changes were made. One can well understand why Adler calls Baeck the most revered man in the camp.

Another camp hero was the Austrian Zionist leader Robert Stricker. Though a semi-invalid, the result of a previous stay in Dachau, he used his training as an engineer and his position as head of the Council of Elders technical committee to work continuously in improving the camp's stoves. He and his wife Paula gave away all of the few possessions they could spare, even sharing the small parcels of food they occasionally received. They also used his position to obtain clothing for the poorest and oldest residents. Remarks one who knew them in Theresienstadt, "No language has words to describe the grandeur of their conduct."

There were also incorruptibles among the camp's rank and file. For example, one tall, thin and tubercular-looking man was seen leading his 8-year-old daughter by the hand to return a big potato the little girl had schleused and brought to her mother. As she restored it to the potato shed, her father gave her a brief and kindly talk on the importance of respecting the common good.

Numerous other instances of incorruptibility emerged from the records and reports on life in Theresienstadt.   Still, they remain exceptions. The norm was otherwise. Why?

Studies of organizational behavior show that those below take their cues from those above. If the leadership acts in a certain way, the rank and file will follow suit. The real leadership in Theresienstadt came, of course, from the SS, who were thoroughly corrupt. Therefore, although their Jewish captives did not like or even respect them, they tended in some ways at least to behave like them. The fact that the SS stole everything of value which they could get their hands on, and indulged themselves to the limit, only encouraged the Jews to do likewise.

The SS even directly encouraged and participated in corruption among the residents themselves. One reason, perhaps the main one, for the strict prohibition against smoking was that SS men were apparently involved in the tobacco smuggling trade. For a while, they would allow or even assist the inflow of tobacco into the camp, and then, when the camp's dealers got too rich, or when the increasing supplies drove down the price of cigarettes, they would stage a raid. This would not only allow them to rob the dealers but would drive up the price again, increasing the profit on subsequent inflows. They certainly provided a poor role model for the rest of the camp, including the administration.

The Jewish administration under Edelstein did make some efforts to curb such abuses. When it became apparent, a few months after the camp was launched, that mattresses were being unfairly distributed, the administration set up a special *Referat* to try to correct the situation. Henceforth no one would be allowed to take mattresses when moving, and unused mattresses had to be handed in. When the postal employees gave themselves and their friends a lavish New Year's banquet, Edelstein launched an investigation which resulted in the removal of the post office's director along with many others. The ghetto court followed up by sentencing them to jail for up to three months. When this produced only modest improvement and continued complaints, the administration then required all parcels to be inspected only in the presence of the recipients.(21)

Food stealing proved the most pervasive and pernicious crime. Sam Berger tells of how, in working at the bakery, he found out that a supply of dough had been set aside to be baked into buns at night for a select group which included the head of the bakery. (He was, it will be recalled, Schliesser's former boss.)   Outraged, Berger enlisted the support of three other bakers, one of them a Christian Jew, and together they marched to Edelstein's office. Edelstein heard them out but seemed somewhat noncommittal about what he would do. On leaving his office, the quartet encountered Zucker in the hall and told him of the planned escapade, but he seemed even less interested. Nevertheless, on the scheduled night, extra ghetto police showed up and stopped the action. Those involved, including the bakery head, lost their positions although none suffered any additional punishment.

Food stealing proved so rampant and uncontrollable that eventually the administration allocated the cooks an extra allotment of food in an effort to cut down the flagrant misappropriations. Nevertheless, the thefts continued. Indeed, the administration officially acknowledged this by customarily giving a ghetto worker who had recovered from a debilitating illness a new job that involved handling food. In this way, the reassigned worker could better restore his or her health. As to Edelstein himself, it apparently could be said of him what a doctor in the Lodz ghetto said of that ghetto's Elder, "He himself was incorruptible but he could not control the corruption around him."

The situation worsened under Eppstein, for he kept himself more remote from the rank and file, receiving people in his office only from 4 to 5 P.M. and maintaining a lifestyle hardly designed to encourage others to accept deprivation. He and his chief functionaries, for example, consumed most of the limited supply of seltzer water which was supposed to be reserved for hospitals and clinics. Edelstein's flat, on the other hand, has been said to have resembled a railroad station, with people continually coming and going.

The corruption issue eventually led to the camp's fiercest power struggle. It did not pit Eppstein against Edelstein; rather, it pitted Eppstein against a half-Jew named Lowenstein.

As indicated earlier, German half-Jews who ended up in Theresienstadt were special cases. Lowenstein's case, however, was more special than most.

Before World War I Lowenstein had been a close friend and naval aide to Germany's crown prince. During the war itself he had served aboard ship, winning numerous decorations for bravery. As might be expected, he had formed many close connections with high-ranking military officers. As a *Mischling* he would in all probability have escaped any appreciable hardship, but his involvement with a group of Protestant dissidents in Germany had brought him into conflict with the Gestapo, who eventually deported him to the Minsk ghetto. His friends had not abandoned him, however, and a high-ranking German general secured his release to Theresienstadt in late spring of 1942. (The German military had been told, and generally believed, that Theresienstadt provided near-idyllic living conditions for its fortunate Jews.)

The SS at Theresienstadt did not know at first what to do with Lowenstein, so they put him in jail while at the same time treating him almost royally, supplying him not just with necessities but even luxuries. In September, possibly in response to further pressures from his high-level contacts, they released him and created a new organizational unit for him to run. Called the Security Department, it grouped all the ghetto's police, investigative, and fire services under his command.

Lowenstein plunged into his new assignment with true Prussian fervor and efficiency and his efforts soon began bearing fruit. He got many punishments revoked, including caning, and numerous jail sentences reduced. When he observed SS men bullying and abusing the elderly during a deportation, he tactfully remarked to their commander that such practices were not worthy of a German officer. The mistreatment ceased.

The Ghetto Watch at the time of his takeover was at a low point. The previous spring the SS had found some of its members, along with a few gendarmes, engaged in smuggling. The gendarmes had been sent to the Little Fortress, the Ghetto Watch members deported, and the Watch itself had become demoralized. Lowenstein took it in hand, appointed former German and Austrian military officers as commanders, and rebuilt it into a paramilitary organization using the Prussian drill order including the famous "goose step." It was he who increased its membership to over 400 and initiated the oath of allegiance to the camp Elder, Edelstein.

But Lowenstein did not stop there. He was horrified at what he saw as the camp's widespread corruption and moved forcefully to eradicate it. He used his influence with the SS to procure better measuring devices for allocating food. The sugar ration, for instance, was now carefully weighed and put into separate paper bags. When he found the kitchen personnel consuming 12 dumplings each, he managed to get their consumption cut to seven. He also arranged for left-over soup to be given to the elderly.

But the more energetically he moved, the more enemies he made. Although their morale improved, the young Czech Zionists who made up the Ghetto Watch did not always appreciate his Germanistic, and Germanizing, efforts. The Czech non-Zionists who ran the economics division found themselves frequently fighting off his attacks. So did the 1300 residents who worked in the kitchens.

His brisk, curt, and rather officious manner did not help, nor did the tactics he sometimes employed. Eric Munk, who ran the medical service, personally disavowed corrupt practices. He had even posted a sign on his office door warning "I recognize friendship but not favorit-ism." But when Lowenstein, acting on the complaint of another physician, planted a female operative disguised as a nurse to investigate wrong doing in the hospitals, Munk protested, saying he did not want "informers" in his organization.

Increasingly, Lowenstein became a thorn in the side of the Jewish administration. Edelstein began finding him bothersome, while Eppstein viewed him more and more as a threat to his own position. When Lowenstein issued an official request that heavy laborers forego their extra lunch portion one day a week in behalf of the elderly, Eppstein sharply rebuked him for overstepping his authority.

In this way Eppstein and Lowenstein, two highly Germanic Jews, became locked in battle, and given the large number of enemies Lowenstein had accumulated, it is no wonder that he lost. He was eventually accused of having several food ration cards and, after being tried by the ghetto court, was jailed. He was released soon thereafter and given Prominenten status, but his days of influence were over.

His aggressive anti-corruption efforts do not appear to have altered Eppstein's attitude toward the problem. If anything, the Jewish Elder became more defensive on this issue and more suspicious of those who sought to correct it. Sometime after Lowenstein's eclipse, a member of the detective bureau sent Eppstein a lengthy report on camp corruption and its many ramifications. As far as is known, no action resulted from this report. However, its author, along with his family, was put on the list of the next transport to Auschwitz.

The attitude of the Jewish leadership toward corruption, especially under Eppstein, only aided and abetted its growth. And grow it did, encompassing in one form or another almost all aspects of camp life. One Theresienstadt joke had it that vitamins B and P were the two ingredients most necessary for surviving at the camp. B stood for *Beziehung* or connection; P for *Protektion* or pull. And woe to anyone who lacked them, for, as Utitz remarks, "Without connections or pull, every errand became a path of thorns."

But other factors also helped corruption to flourish. We can see some of them by taking another look at the intake process where, at least on an aggressive and extended scale, it first arose.

The SS, as noted, confiscated anything they wished from the new arrivals. This provided a rationale for the intake processors to do the same. They argued, said Lederer, "that rather than leave the cream to the Germans, they would skim it for themselves." And he adds, "This philosophy served as a justification for many abuses."

The German and Austrian Jews, who began arriving in the summer of 1942, decked out in their Sunday-best as if going to a resort and speaking only the hated language of the Nazis, elicited little sympathy from the Czech Jews who processed them through the Schleuse. Moreover, they arrived in such numbers that the Czech intake workers had to work overtime. Adler dates the start of sluice-gating from a period in July when the intake personnel had to work 36 hours at a stretch in processing German and Austrian Jews.

Late arrivals to Theresienstadt were also considered to have enjoyed a privileged existence. They were suspected of having had special connections or to have been informers or collaborators. Such suspicions, which in some cases were certainly correct, gave the intake crews an excuse to steal not only from German and Austrian Jews but also from later-arriving Czech Jews. At the same time, it left the late arrivals with a desire for revenge and with the notion that such stealing was standard camp practice, which indeed it was rapidly becoming.(22)

Two other elements that provided a basis for corruption should also be mentioned. It has been said in discussions of government expenditures that everybody's money is nobody's money. In like manner, one can say that everybody's food is nobody's food. To take a potato or two from a large pile or a spoonful or two from a kettle doesn't *seem* to hurt anyone. Consequently, it does not appear to be wrong.

Even Theresienstadt's religious residents succumbed to this way of thinking. Brumlik-Marcus, the woman who slid a couple of potatoes down the leg of her gym pants, was an observant Jew, while Rabbi Richard Feder, in describing the wedding lunch of his grandniece, cheerfully notes how "the bridegroom had taken the potatoes from the cellar without asking anybody's permission while the thickening of the soup had been brought from the kitchen by one of the cooks." Three rabbis, including Chief Rabbi Unger, together with three cantors, officiated at the wedding. Apparently none of them expressed any concern or felt any compunction about how the food was procured.

The second element that encouraged corruption was simply the proliferation of rules. Since it was impossible to survive if one obeyed all of them, breaking them became an everyday affair. Says Bondy, "Since all life's pleasures, from a moment stolen with one's family to playing the harmonica, were prohibited, existence became a series of attempts to get around rules and regulations." In making lawbreakers of virtually the entire population, the Nazis and, to some degree, the Jewish administration which added so many restrictions of its own, blurred the line between the legal and the morally objectionable, making it all too easy to cross from one to another. As Adler puts it, "In reality, nothing was actually allowed, but almost everything was tolerated." This in turn, he says, destroyed any feeling of community cohesion, making personal needs and desires the dominant force.

Although no admirer of either Edelstein or Eppstein, Adler admits that "The Jewish leadership faced an unutterably hard situation. Even the greatest integrity could not have prevented the sum total of their decisions from ultimately becoming bad." They could and certainly should have tried harder to contain corruption but, he concedes, "If the Jewish administration had truly tried to counteract all the camp's many evils, it would only have succeeded in destroying itself."(23)

---

16. Just why Seidl reacted so savagely is not clear but Starke, who witnessed the scene, believes it may have been Teitelbaum's ginger hair and general Aryan appearance. It was apparently a source of considerable annoyance to the SS men, most of them south Germans if not Austrians, that so many Theresienstadt Jews looked more Aryan than they did.

17. The wives of Edelstein and Eppstein were both somewhat self-effacing, and to the extent the camp had a "First lady," it was Zucker's wife Fritzi. Attractive, vivacious, and outgoing, she showed up on special occasions at children's homes and women's gatherings. She was almost universally loved.

18. When Kurt Phillipson, a 78-year-old former professor of geography from the University of Bonn, arrived at Theresienstadt, he was handed a letter from a Swedish colleague named Sven Hedin and was ordered to reply to it in full on the spot. Hedin, a well-known explorer as well as geographer, was an influential figure in Sweden and the Nazis wanted to keep him friendly to the Reich. Hedin, on his part, feared for his elderly colleague's future and so wrote frequently to Phillipson, who allowed and even required to respond fully.

19. When the first German Jews arrived in Israel after Hitler's assumption of power, they asked for German schools for their children. They expected to return to Germany as soon as Hitler, whom they regarded as a fluke, disappeared.

20. Those believing I have exaggerated this discrepancy between German and Austrian anti-semitism, or desiring more details and documentation regarding it, may wish to consult my book, *vienna and Its Jews: The Tragedy of Success*, which discusses this paradox at considerable length. Louis Lowy is my source for the homesickness of Austrian Jews in Theresienstadt.

21. This report by Adler on post office corruption is rigorously repudiated by Ernest Seinfeld, who worked in the post office for a short time after coming

to Theresienstadt. According to Seinfeld, much if not most of the problem stemmed from faulty packaging by senders and careless handling by overworked post office crews.

22. One should note at this point hat not all corruption was due to self-interest. For example, a sell-known Czech writer named Karel Polacek was given extra food portions even though he didn't seek them; the young Czechs in the kitchen crews simply admired his work. Actor Kurt Gerron received double portions because of his physical stature--he was a heavily built man over six feet in height--and also because of his prewar celebrity status as a stage and screen actor.

23. Conditions at other camps and ghettos were much the same. Thus a Jewish physician in the Lodz ghetto wrote, "In a short tine the people of the ghetto became imbued with a new morality that might be compared to that of convicted animals... Under ghetto conditions most people forgot the value of collective welfare."

CHAPTER 6
PROTECTING THE FUTURE

Probably no community in history ever demonstrated such devotion to its young as did the Theresienstadt ghetto. Its children, of whom there were approximately 3,200 under 15 years of age by mid-1943, were considered and treated as its most precious treasure.

A Theresienstadt child regularly received more food and double as much living space as a normal adult. In addition, stray food parcels, such as those addressed to dead or deported people who had not assigned their proxies, were automatically passed on to their special kitchens. The Jewish administration made every effort to spare younger children from deportations and during the camp's first eighteen months had generally managed to do so. Many adults gladly gave of their scarce time and energy to help teach, entertain, and build things for the youngsters. Says Adler, "Very rarely did anyone seek to benefit himself at the expense of the children; most willingly made sacrifices for them."

The reason for the ghetto's intensely pro-child policies and practices are not difficult to discern. To begin with, Jewish tradition, especially perhaps in the Diaspora, has always made the care and protection of children a prime priority. During the 19th century, for example, Europe's Jewish population grew twice as fast as its non-Jewish population. This occurred not because of a higher birth rate but because of a substantially lower infant death rate. While many factors figured into such a development, including lower Jewish rates of illegitimacy and alcoholism, one underlying cause was the Jewish community's greater concern for child welfare.

Such a concern became still more pronounced in Theresienstadt for, among other things, it provided a rationale for working with the Nazis to keep the camp in existence. As Edelstein observed, "If we can only save the young . . . the Jewish people will have biological continuity." Edelstein, it should be noted, defined young people broadly as all those under 35. Since he was 38, he excluded himself from this priority group.

Zionism added still greater emphasis to this goal, for the Zionists believed such biological continuity would lead to, and find fulfillment in, a Jewish state. Notes Lederer, "The Zionists felt it urgent to preserve as many children as possible in as good a condition as possible in order to build the promised land."

But beyond such ideological or rational reasons, more emotional forces were at work. Children represented an affirmation of life itself, and conditions in Theresienstadt made any affirmation of life something to be avidly seized and vigorously supported.

In terms of organization, the youth welfare division started out as a branch of the camp's welfare department, but given the priority assigned to its mission, it soon became a department of its own. When the resident Czech townspeople departed in the summer of 1942, the department took over the community's former schoolhouse and converted it into a home for Czech boys. Soon thereafter it created a second home for Czech girls and a third one for older boys working as apprentices. Separate houses for German-speaking children, convalescent children, and maladjusted children soon followed. It also set up a special children's kitchen and later established a second one for infants and toddlers.

In 1943 the administration created a special court for juveniles so that their cases would not have to be reported to the SS. Presided over by psychologists and social workers as well as jurists, it most often issued only reprimands. Yet it sometimes imposed harsher penalties, such as loss of certain privileges or confinement to quarters for a period of time.

The ghetto's probate court, which handled foster care and adoption cases, played a more important role in youth welfare since quite a few of the ghetto's children, perhaps 10 percent of the total, were orphans or strays. The parents of most of these youngsters had died or been deported, in many instances before the youngsters themselves had come to the camp. Others were of mixed parentage who for one reason or another had fallen into the net of the Nuremberg Laws.(24)

The probate court generally experienced little trouble in finding suitable adults to assume responsibility for a child since many were eager to do so. When Gerda Brumlik, an orthodox Czech Jew, saw the name of the 12-year-old *Mischling* Liselotte Neuhaus on the transport list, she "rushed to take her." An 8-month old baby from Vienna named Jonas Spegal was quickly snapped up and warmly cared for. As Murmelstein, who cared little for the ghetto's many lawyers and jurists, remarks, "Arranging adoptions was one of the few ways the ghetto court proved itself useful."

Such arrangements for the most part worked out strikingly well. I. Lauscherova, a children's matron, says, "There was not much difference between children with or without parents; childless families or single women took charge of the orphans. Thus the orphan had somewhere to go in the evening . . . there was a mother who made a cake for them from her ration of buns, synthetic coffee (from grain), and margarine.

They, too, had someone to give a small present to, a little drawing, a bookmark, and someone to invite to the party in the children's home."

On occasion the drive to nurture could get out of hand. Liebrecht reports how the woman who looked after his baby daughter would sometimes leave the little girl sleeping in an improvised carriage outside only to return and find her gone. She would then have to scour the women's quarters to find the missing child.

Egon Redlich, a 24-year-old former law school student and former vice-principal of the Youth Aliyah school in Prague, headed the youth welfare department from its very inception. Though reserved and somewhat inhibited, he possessed a lively intelligence and good organizational skills. With the helpful support of his wife, who was as expansive and effervescent as he was retiring, he organized and oversaw the community's youth program.

A much more conspicuous youth leader was a former physical education teacher in his late twenties named Fredy Hirsch. Born and raised in Germany, Hirsch had fled to Czechoslovakia in 1935 and spoke Czech reasonably well. Virtually all the camp's young people worshipped him.

Hirsch was tall, handsome, and erect and these features, along with his short leather jacket and black boots, made him an impressive figure. He was also a superb athlete. But what most endeared him to Theresienstadt youngsters was his firm commitment to their well being. As head of the camp's physical education program he continually stressed the need for them to prepare themselves physically as well as mentally for building a Jewish state. According to Bondy, he brought to Zionism many of the principles and practices, along with the zeal and elan, of the old German youth movement.

Though fiercely admired by his charges, Hirsch was somewhat disdained by his peers for his supposedly shallow intellect. One recalls how "Hirsch believed blindly that the Fascists would let him lead the young people to Palestine and became angry when I said it was nonsense. He had been raised and educated in Germany and could not believe the SS would commit such dishonorable deceits and crimes." Redlich in his diary likens Hirsch to a "soap which lathers but doesn't wash." While this is certainly an overstatement, possibly motivated in part by jealousy over Hirsch's popularity as well as his good looks-- Redlich was physically unprepossessing--it does contain a germ of truth. There was a weakness or softness in Hirsch which would have significant consequences not only for himself but for many of his young followers.

A third youth leader worthy of note was an Austrian named Aron Menczer. Though only a high school dropout of 20 when the Nazis took over his country in 1938, Menczer, a brilliant young man and an ardent Zionist, soon became Vienna's foremost Jewish youth leader. He also headed up its Youth Aliyah school. He twice succeeded in leaving Vienna, once to escort a group of teenagers to Israel and another time to attend a Zionist conference in Geneva. But each time he returned to his Nazi-ruled city, saying Vienna's Jewish children still needed him. He may well qualify as Vienna's foremost Holocaust hero.(25)

Many of the camp's leading figures also devoted time to the children. Leo Baeck frequently talked to them as did Edelstein, who told them they represented the future of Judaism and often led them in Zionist songs. Zucker's wife Fritzie enjoyed great popularity. "We called Fritzie the second mother of all the children," recalls Ansbacher. "She educated them, she inculcated the basic moral values and tried to imbue us with the spirit of Zionism, love for our country and love for our neighbors. She saw to it that food and goodies were shared equally, at least on festival days."

Then there were the teachers, matrons, and others who worked tirelessly to promote the children's well being. Lauscherova describes what their lives could be like:

> To be a matron in a home meant to be on call for 24 hours a day, to sleep with the children, to get up at night and wake up Rudy to prevent him from wetting his pallet, a half-hour later to wake Charles for the same reason, to rinse Michael's inflamed eyes, to give a pill to Freddy, to change Tommy's compress. There were many sick children in every room. Often the matron had to sit down at the bunk of a restless sleeper and stroke his brow to prevent him from waking and frightening the others with his cries. During the day she had to look after the children's cleanliness, their rations, distribute them, get a voucher for shoe repairs, take a child to the surgery, get hold of some medicines, beg for a little yeast in the bakery since yeast was the best available medicine for sties. . . .

Educating the children presented several formidable challenges. To begin with, teaching was officially banned. Consequently, it necessarily became a clandestine and quite dangerous activity.

Then there was the question of deciding what kind of education to give them. Should it be primarily Czech or Jewish or something else?

Some wanted to exclude German completely, viewing it as the language of the devil. Finally there was the daunting task of procuring materials such as books, paper and pencils, items that would have been difficult to obtain in any case but now became more so because of the need to keep the Nazis in the dark as to why they were needed.

Eventually these problems were more or less resolved. Since the Nazis realized that the children had to be kept busy, the teachers were able to disguise much of their instructional activity through such devices as games, plays, and songs. Geography, for example, was sometimes taught by a game called City and Country whereby the teacher would state the capital city and the pupil would give the country. Ze'ev Shek, one of the Ghetto's few Hebrew teachers, took voice lessons so that he could teach Hebrew through songs.

When more traditional teaching was required, someone would watch at the window. If they spotted an SS man approaching, the group would start singing, dancing, or playing games. If the Nazi entered the room, the teacher would say that she or he was just keeping the youngsters out of trouble.

There were, of course, several close calls. Louis Lowy, who taught German-speaking boys, once staged *Maria Stuart*, a drama by the classic German author Frederich Schiller. To promote the project he had put up posters in the boys' home with quotes from the play, one of which read, "May all the enemies of this island die the way Maria Stuart died." Since the island referred to was Great Britain, he was understandably uneasy when Guenther, the SS captain from Prague, suddenly dropped in. But Guenther, a former salesman, had probably never read the play and in any case ignored the poster.

The issue of whether to teach German resolved itself with the arrival of children from the Reich. But Shek went further and persuaded his fellow Czechs to allow German to be taught to Czech children as well. Some knowledge of German was vitally necessary for ghetto living and, as he pointed out, "It is not the language which is bad, but what you use it for that's bad." Herzl's Zionist manifesto, he reminded them, was written in German.

The question of whether to give them a Jewish education was more easily decided. To quote Shek again, "We were sure we had to give them a Jewish education, a universal but Jewish education, by no means chauvinistic. They were in the ghetto and we wanted to bring them out of the ghetto spiritually and morally sane, so that they would become quite normal people. I call it a positive approach to life."

Predictably, the Jewish education which resulted displayed a more Zionist than a religious orientation. If a matron woke up her youngsters in the morning by singing a Hebrew song, the song was more apt to be about building Palestine than about praising God. If some Hebrew was taught even at the kindergarten level, it was customarily conversational, not biblical. If Friday evening was the highlight of the week, it was observed more as a festive than as a religious occasion.

Still, problems continually arose. Some Czech teachers, especially those from the Sudetenland, actually knew little Czech. Teachers, matrons, and social workers often failed to check with each other, thereby creating confusion and frustrations. There was a constant demand for more Hebrew instruction, a demand which, due to the shortage of Hebrew teachers, the administration could not fulfill.

Then there were the Communists who, having ideas of their own about the future, had decided to focus their energies on educating the young. They succeeded in making Russian instruction available to some of the older children, in getting Russian songs included in nearly all songfests, and in having one children's home named Skid after a much publicized Russian home for vagrant boys. (No names of children's houses appeared on any official records.) More significantly, they succeeded in getting their message across to their pupils. The diary of one student records how "Magda prepares us for the Communist society which must come once the Nazis have been suppressed."

While the Jewish administration generally tolerated the Communists, it occasionally felt constrained to take repressive action. When in May 1943 a Communist youth leader staged a militant May Day observance which could have aroused the ire of the SS, the administration transferred him to another position. Otherwise the Communists were allowed to make their influence felt. The fact that the entire camp was rooting for the Russians and was expecting to be liberated by them made most residents more tolerant.

All of Theresienstadt's teachers worked with a sense of urgency for they were not only trying to ensure a Jewish future, they were also trying to make up for lost time. Thanks to the Nazis' racial policies, most of the students had been deprived of formal education for a year or two before they had arrived at the camp. So using carefully husbanded pencils, wrapping paper for writing, and smuggled-in texts, some passages of which were secretly mimeographed while others were laboriously copied by hand, plus songs, games, and storytelling, they delivered a remarkably well-rounded curriculum. Their students studied not only academic subjects but, when older, such trades as woodworking, metalworking, electricity, and engineering. Surreptitiously the educational division held qualifying exams for apprentices in the manual trades. It also found ways to exempt exceptionally bright 16- to 18-year-olds from work so that they could receive more advanced academic instruction in such subjects as Latin, Russian, and mathematics.

Theresienstadt's teachers often showed considerable imagination and perception in adapting their activities to the unusual conditions which prevailed. One drawing teacher, working with a group of 10- to 12-year-old girls in a doll-making project, noted how "the girls were strongly inhibited, found nothing beautiful, wanted to make all the dolls into princesses, and were unsatisfied with them once they had made them." The teacher suggested that "out of the ugliness of our lives" they should make dolls of a cleaning squad instead. "Soon they were making a water carrier, a toilet scrubber, cooks, and all were in a good mood."

One popular activity was putting out weekly magazines. These were written by hand and then read aloud on Friday evening. The most notable of these one-copy periodicals was *Vedem* (We Lead), which from December 1942 to September 1944 "published" 800 pages. It included poetry, short stories, essays, and reportage which the youngsters had written during the week. An understandable desire for secrecy prompted most of its young authors to sign their works with their initials or nicknames.

Vedem, like the other magazines, also chronicled the week's events. A report in its January 15, 1943 issue lists the cultural program for a previous week:

> Sunday, Jan. 3rd - recital of Wolker's poems in commemoration of the poet's death. We read and discussed some selected lyrics that were new to us. On Monday Misha delivered the first part of his successful lecture on the textile industry. On Tuesday Dr. Zwicker lectured, explaining some economic terms to us. On Wednesday "lights out" came earlier at 8:15 because of Laubi who is seriously ill. Therefore, the second part of Bicz's lecture had to be postponed till Thursday. On Friday Mrs. Klinke came to see us and sang some Hebrew songs for us as well as an aria from The *Bartered Bride* . . . of special importance, for our cultural life is the re-establishment of two study circles (Latin and Russian).

The Friday evening gathering was the high point of the week. It included, besides reports on the week's events and the reading of the oral "magazines," praise for praiseworthy achievements along with friendly admonitions and positively oriented criticism for failures and slip-ups. There were also songs, occasional hora dancing, and as good a meal as could be provided. As one 14-year-old later recalled, "Every Friday there were plenary sessions which began with a song. The young people on Friday had to have everything in irreproachable order, everything clean, clean clothes, a special electric light, the table arranged lengthwise. All this made it seem like a holiday. . . It was all so nice."

Despite a fairly rigorous schedule, the youngsters were allowed free time to visit parents, socialize, and pursue other interests. For boys the main extracurricular hobby was soccer and every boys' home had its own team with its special name, pennant, and even ragtag uniforms. The youths also played ping pong and "button football," a game similar to tiddlywinks. Girls' interests were apparently more varied but generally centered on dressmaking, doll-making, and reading. Those few youngsters who were devout had adequate time to *davan* (pray) and were not criticized or mocked by the others for doing so.

Children, of course, are natural collectors, and since Theresienstadt offered no opportunities to acquire things like stamps or coins, they began collecting the paper wrappings from razor blades. They would approach newly arrived adults with the request, "*Haben Sie Gilleten?*"

In 1943 Hirsch called for volunteers among the older children to give three hours a week of their free time to help the elderly. Some 300 responded and by the end of the year they had made 5,500 visits to the old peoples' quarters. There they beat mattresses, made beds, cleaned living space, sewed patches on clothing, and made themselves generally useful. There was an iron rule against accepting payment of any kind.

The project brought the youngsters face to face with the most grievous aspects of camp life. Ansbacher reports how "We had to bring the old men food, read to them--from novels and religious books; and all these old people were so touched by this that they wept, and very often it happened that in the midst of this reading these sick and old people would die--the boy would sit and read and the old man would die. And then they would be brought to a yard where the corpses were collected."

Some youngsters made substantial sacrifices to aid the elderly. One boy gave his whole sugar ration for ten days to a group of elderly women living in the shop window of a former store. Young children not in the programs sometimes sought to help as well. A Czech girl of seven brought an extra bowl of soup to an old, nearly blind man whose son had worked with her father. "May I call you grandfather?" she asked. "You have no little girl and I have no grandpa." The friendship lasted until the old man's deportation to Auschwitz.

Despite the most earnest efforts of all those involved with their welfare, the children could not be protected from the numerous tribulations and tragedies of ghetto life. If the youngsters ate better than most adults, they still felt hunger pains. If they enjoyed more living space, they still slept two to a bed in triple-tiered bunks. They also contended constantly with dirt and vermin. The diary of one 12-year-old girl records, "I caught six fleas and three bedbugs today. Isn't that a fine hunt . . . a rat slept in my shoe."

Although their survival rate in Theresienstadt itself was better than that of their parents, death and disease were no strangers to their ranks. Not only illnesses such as measles and scarlet fever but also hepatitis and typhoid swept through the children's homes. Cases of diphtheria, polio, and encephalitis were also far from rare. As another child's diary records, "Lilka's sister died, Lilka has typhoid herself. Vera, Olina and Marta went to the infirmary. They transferred Meka to the hospital yesterday; they say she is in her last agony. 'What's the matter, Hanka? Why have you been crying so hard? What! Dasha? and Zorka . . . died!'"

Yet like the adults, their foremost fears and concerns centered on deportation. Their writings, recovered after the war, contained numerous descriptions of the camp's tense atmosphere when a transport was being put together, the frantic efforts of those selected to appeal, and their last-minute but still not completely extinguished hopes of somehow escaping the *Schleuse*. As friends of their families along with relatives including their grandparents were shipped out, they experienced the dread and despair of the deportation process. Moreover, older children and their families were not spared. Thus a 12-year-old's diary speaks of a friend who is being deported along with her parents. "Everyone gave Zdenka something. She's such a poor thing. . . Her father came to pack her things . . . he wept and thanked the children and assistants for the care they had given Zdenka. We all cried. . . ."

The deportation of the elderly in the fall of 1942 especially upset the youngsters. As one diarist noted, "Why do they want to take these defenseless people away. . . How can these old people be dangerous? If they had come here to Theresienstadt, wasn't that enough? Can't they let them die here in peace!" The sight of the oldsters being pulled along in former funeral wagons to the *Schleuse* added to this young author's anguish. "Skinny, hungry, miserable, there they are. Alive in hearses. How many will arrive at their destination? How many will return?"

The various social divisions which beleaguered the camp also affected the youngsters. The Czech children felt superior to their German-speaking cohorts, for not only had their parents built the camp but their nation had opposed Nazism. Unlike those from Germany and Austria, they could stoutly assert their national pride. "Except for football," writes one, "we had nothing to do with the boys and girls in the home for German and Austrian children. We called these children 'Piffkes.'" (Actually a derogatory term traditionally used by Austrians for Germans.) "At our place there were only children from Czechoslovakia." Dita Loewy, then a teenager named Dita Jedlinsky, recalls being asked her name by a flirtatious Czech boy. When she told him he replied scornfully, "What a pity. A beautiful Czech name wasted on a German."

Understandably, the children who suffered most from this nationalistic pecking order were those of mixed parentage. "A crowd of Mischlings have arrived," notes Redlich's diary for March 13-14, 1943. "Many haven't the slightest idea of their Jewishness. They have simply been taken away from parents who are Catholic, Protestant or something. How can these children comprehend the fate of a nation to which they do not belong? What do they have in common with us? Most of them didn't know up to the moment of their arrival that they were Jews."

A young girl from Vienna, who found Theresienstadt to be a "regular Tower of Babel," reports how "next to me is a girl to whom fate has been very cruel. She arrived three weeks ago from Bruenn; her father is Aryan and her mother Jewish. She is completely alone, badly provided for and does not feel right in a Jewish environment. She cries almost all day long. Her father was allowed to accompany her to Prague where there was a terrible leave-taking, according to a girl who came with her."

The camp's extensive network of sluice-gating also affected them. The older children, at least, not only knew about it but contributed to it. One issue of *Vedem* praises a boy for having "obtained ping pong balls for an upcoming tournament," while another issue thanks a youth who "managed" to get "special dinners for four boys who really needed them." Other issues more explicitly endorse sluice-gating. "Ruses or stratagems are not so bad and everybody needs them like food and drink," writes one youth, while another notes how "without Vitamin P [protection or pull] one can hardly get by in Theresienstadt or keep alive. . ."

The teachers made some attempt to deal with this problem. For example, they would have the youngsters discuss such questions as "Should a child who tried to take bread from the supply cart for his sick mother be praised or reproved?" But the fact that such practices had become so deeply ingrained in Theresienstadt's everyday existence handicapped their efforts. The children knew, for example, that the cooks prepared extra helpings of food for themselves and their favorites, so in stealing food for themselves they felt they were not depriving anyone of their regular rations but were only reducing the surplus which the cooks and their cronies consumed. Moreover, the cooks sometimes gave extra food to certain teachers in order to get extra lessons for their own children. This did little to enhance the moral authority of those teachers involved or the moral behavior of their students.

Thus sluice-gating gradually became an acceptable activity. One youth, in reporting how he and his friends would go out at night to steal coal and wood, says "our teachers knew of this but did not oppose it--in fact they praised us when we came back with a full load."

But on one issue the teachers and other youth personnel drew a firm line. Their charges were not to cheat, lie, or steal from other children. This rule was strictly enforced and generally obeyed.

Corruption in the camp tended to deprive its adults of moral authority, but other factors reduced their stature still more in the eyes of the children. Mothers could not care for, and fathers did not support, their children. Indeed, as Adler notes, the adults themselves had descended to the level of children in having become wards--pawns might be a better term--of the arbitrary authority of the Nazis. The situation was not helped by the difficulties the parents experienced in just maintaining their own existence, difficulties which often deprived them of enough time and energy for their offspring. Nor was it helped by the camp's cruel, if excusable or at least understandable, treatment of the elderly.

The physical separation from their parents, as might be expected, affected the youngest children most. At the toddlers' home there was much weeping, bed wetting, interrupted sleep, and unexpected weight loss. Often the children rejected their mothers when they came to visit after work. But older children were also influenced by the disrupted relationships which camp life created. To cite Adler again, "Children especially suffered from the alienation between the generations for their parents enjoyed little authority and the elderly none at all."

Yet Adler, like others who have studied Theresienstadt's youth program, believes it achieved a good deal. In his view, its major accomplishment was to take youngsters who had become "terribly humiliated and fearful through the persecution they had experienced when living in apparent freedom" (i.e., under Nazi rule in their home communities), and to give them "in the relatively protective environment of the children's home the feeling of a certain freedom and security." Others stress the program's success in providing the young people with an education, a sense of group solidarity and self-reliance, and an ability to fend for themselves. But perhaps its most significant impact lay in stripping aside the superficial and thereby deepening the young people's perspectives. As the diary of one teenage girl reports,

> Oh, how stupid I was when I was unhappy over silly little things! For example, that I was unlucky in love, or that I didn't want to get up in the morning. Everything is so petty compared to what we confront here. Here it is a question of life and we have only one life.

---

24. The case of Liselotte Neuhaus, mentioned in the Prelude and soon to be mentioned again, is one example. Another is that of Cornelia Edvarson, the illegitimate 13-old daughter of a half-Jewish mother and an all-Jewish father. Her mother had later married a fully Aryan man with whom she had more children. Cornelia's half-siblings, being only one-quarter Jewish, were spared by Cornelia, being three-quarter Jewish, was deported to Theresienstadt despite efforts of her mother and stepfather to keep her with them.

25. There were, of course, other heroes in vienna, as elsewhere. Robert Stricker had a chance to flee to Hungary when the Nazis took over the country but felt his place was with his people. The Nazis first sent him to Dachau, then brought him back semi-crippled to Vienna, and finally sent him on to Theresienstadt.

CHAPTER 7
THEATRE OF THE ABSURD

The camp's efforts at nurturing its young are today viewed as a success story. "If anything at all positive was achieved in the ghetto of Theresienstadt, it was achieved in this field," wrote the Czech psychologist Ota Klein after the war. Many, however, would go further and credit the camp with two additional areas of achievement: Health and Culture.

A medical department began operating almost as soon as the first families arrived. Initially it lacked even the most basic equipment and medicines. But when the Prague Gemeinde got SS permission to buy straw for mattresses and, with the cooperation of Czech farmers, began flooding the ghetto with it, the problem eased. Concealed in the straw were, among other things, medical supplies from Jewish hospitals.

Soon thereafter the shortage of medicine and medical equipment eased still more, for the SS, fearing epidemics which could spread to its own personnel as well as to the surrounding Czech and German populations, began bringing in supplies from the now closed-down Jewish hospitals. (They also did not investigate too carefully the smuggling in of other medicines, since they were much more concerned with such contraband as cigarettes and mail.) The Nazis also helped the department build a large medical library and even ordered the doctors to hold seminars for each other, allowing Czech doctors to lecture in Czech.

Reacting perhaps to SS concerns as well as to its own priorities, the medical department set up a special division on infectious diseases in late January, only six weeks after its own launching. Two months later it opened a dental clinic, a central medical laboratory, and a rather primitive radiological division. The following month saw the establishment of subdivisions in gynecology, urology, dermatology, neurology, psychiatry, and pulmonary diseases. The fact that medicine, especially in Europe, was by no means as specialized then as it is today, makes this array of specialized services doubly impressive.

Despite the support it received from the SS, the department labored under severe handicaps. It performed its first operation, the amputation of a gangrenous foot, with a carpenter's saw. The arrival of equipment and medicine from the closed Jewish hospitals permitted more standard procedures, but one thermometer still had to serve up to 60 patients and crepe paper frequently had to be used for bandages. A constant shortage of anesthesia forced surgeons to perform some minor procedures without it. Intermittent shortages of water and electricity forced them to interrupt some treatments and, on occasion, to perform delicate surgery by candlelight. Even furniture posed problems; it was easier in many instances to procure laboratory equipment than tables on which to place it.

One shortage the camp's medical service did not suffer was patients. By February, seven weeks after its opening, it was handling 44,000 patient visits a month. Three months later the figure had grown to 66,000 visits. The arrival of transports from Germany and Austria in the summer threatened to swamp its capacities, since these transports brought not only large numbers of elderly people but also disabled war veterans and patients from Jewish hospitals in the Reich. The number of patient visits vaulted to nearly 177,000 in August and soared well past the 200,000 mark in September when the camp's population, as well as its death rate, reached its highest point. During that month the average doctor saw 570 patients.

Fortunately, the German-Austrian influx also brought numerous physicians, some of them Europe's best. By the end of the year Theresienstadt had over 600 doctors, which must have given it the highest proportion of physicians to patients of any community before or since. However, many of these physicians were elderly and only 373 worked actively at their profession with most of the others serving as consultants.

With the German-Austrian doctors came many professional nurses from the Reich's now closed Jewish hospitals. In some respects they were more welcome than the doctors, for the few Jewish hospitals in Czechoslovakia had provided only a handful of such personnel. Still, the heavy demands placed upon the medical department forced it to continue to rely on untrained people for most of its nursing staff.

The pressures on the health service did not lighten in 1943. Despite the high death rate and deportations of the elderly in the previous fall, the daily average number of those reporting sick actually rose in 1943 to over 10,000 a day compared to about 6,500 a day in 1942. Some of the sick may have been suffering from psychosomatic illness and a few undoubtedly were malingerers. But all asked for and received some medical attention. By mid-year the camp's medical department was operating four hospitals as well as a clinic in every barracks and children's home. It was employing close to 20 percent of the camp's working population.

In the face of the formidable conditions they confronted, the doctors and nurses achieved some remarkable results. This is evident in the survival rates of those stricken by the numerous diseases which swept the camp, as shown in the following table:

Illness	No. of Cases	No. of Deaths
Scarlet Fever (up to 7/1/43)	1601	22
Diphtheria (up to 7/1/43	547	31
Encephalitis (1943 complete)	401	0
Poliomyelitis (1943 complete)	25	4

The debilitated state of most of these patients and the advanced age of many of them make these survival rates more impressive still. (An 86-year-old man was among those cured of diphtheria, while a hernioto-my was successfully performed on a 90-year-old.)

The department's most critical challenge during Theresienstadt's first 18 months came in the winter of 1943 when a flare-up of typhus, the most feared disease in all concentration camps, suddenly occurred. From 127 cases in January the figure shot up to 414 in February. Eichmann on a visit to the camp hinted darkly that unless the disease was stamped out, the privileged ghetto might be shut down. Fortunately, the medical service had vaccines, albeit of questionable efficacy, and by quarantining those infected and inoculating most of the rest it managed to contain the contagion. Moreover, most of those who did contract the disease were cured.(26)

Overextended as they were in simply treating the ill, the medical service still found time for preventive work. Whenever they could obtain vaccines, they used them, inoculating all those from 5 to 65 against typhus, those from 1-1/2 to 40 against scarlet fever, and those 1-1/2 to 18 against diphtheria. They also erected signs, sometimes in rhymed couplets, warning residents to take certain preventive measures such as washing their hands after using the toilet and refraining from rummaging in garbage pails. They frequently called on the camp's artists for help. One poster, designed to boost the inoculation program, humorously depicts a man in a white coat holding a huge hypodermic needle while chasing a small boy who is trying to escape from him. One way or another the Health Service got its message across and thereby kept the death rate down.

The medical department's psychiatry division operated the camp's mental hospital located in a former stable on the fringe of the town. This operation brought the service little credit for conditions in the hospital were deplorable even by Theresienstadt standards. The inmates were allowed to walk around a small part of a courtyard for an hour or two a day; the rest of the time they squatted behind barred windows with nothing to do. Teenagers often made coarse jokes about these patients for they regarded Theresienstadt itself as a crazy place, and to be in its mental hospital was in their view to be doubly insane.(27)

Some doctors, however, had become quite sensitive to the psychological toll which the stresses of life in Theresienstadt were placing on its residents and wanted to do something about the situation. One such doctor was Karel Fleischman, a Czech who was a close associate of medical director Munk. (Fleischman's description of the pitiable condition of the German elderly was quoted in Chapter 3.) Another of these doctors was a Viennese named Victor Frankl.

Frankl, who has become the best known of all Theresienstadt's survivors, was working simply as a young general practitioner in a clinic, where one of his surviving nurses remembers him as good-natured, helpful, and intelligent. In her words, "Such a good man."

Fleischmann, who was not a psychiatrist--his prewar specialty had been dermatology--apparently sensed the capacities which Frankl would soon demonstrate and asked him to organize a special unit to help new arrivals overcome the shock of Theresienstadt life. The group, which called itself the *Stosstruppe* or Assault Squad, included many nonmedical personnel. According to Frankl, one of its more influential and important members was Regina Jonas, the camp's only woman rabbi.

The Stosstruppe centered much of its attention on the most vulnerable, such as epileptics, neurotics, the physically sick, and the elderly. Stosstruppe members sought to engage the minds of such people in constructive ways. For example, a despondent philologist who had specialized in English was conversed with in English by a group member having some familiarity with that language. The latter would ask his patient to explain some of the language's peculiarities.

The Stosstruppe's success led Frankl to set up a suicide intelligence service whereby any expression of a suicidal idea or intention would be immediately reported to him. He would then contact the would-be suicide and seek to dissuade him/her. He based his approach on Nietzsche's dictum that "He who has a 'Why' to live can endure any 'How.'" Thus in talking with two men who said they wanted to kill themselves since they could expect nothing from life, Frankl told them that life nevertheless expected something from them. His efforts are a major reason for a steep drop in the suicide rate after the first year.(28)

Frankl also developed a unique way of safeguarding his own sanity. When he had a spare moment, he would march out into a courtyard and, his feet often aching and his teeth chattering from cold, would deliver out loud to an imaginary audience a lecture entitled "Psychotherapeutic Experiences in a Concentration Camp." The young physician little dreamed that one day, as a world-renowned psychiatrist and the founder of Logotherapy, he would be delivering just such a lecture to an international assembly of distinguished colleagues.

The medical department was largely the creation of its director, Eric Munk. Some remember him unfavorably as a generally poor administrator who drove his people mercilessly, delegated poorly, and criticized harshly. He paid little heed to his own mistakes and rarely encouraged suggestions from others.

Yet if he drove others, he also drove himself, often working through the night. "He terrorized himself as well as his subordinates," says Adler, whose wife headed the camp's laboratory. (She was both a physician and a chemist.) If Munk was inaccessible--the door of his one-room lodging bore a sign saying "Here lives but does not hold office hours Dr. Edward Munk"--he was also incorruptible. (His office door, as previously noted, bore the sign, "I recognize friendship but not favoritism.") He often seemed insensitive, yet he almost certainly was consulted and consented to the formation of Frankl's psychological "Assault Squad."

Munk's zealousness and industriousness set the tone for his department, whose personnel often worked to the point of exhaustion. Physicians sometimes served as stretcher bearers and they and the nurses occasionally gave blood. Despite the extra rations they received, their death rate generally matched that of their age group in the camp. Fuchs recalls how one of the camp's best physicians suddenly died of a heart attack only a few hours after he had patted her on the shoulder, saying, "Keep going, keep going."

Medical personnel were by no means exempt from deportation. Once a physician was preparing to operate when a nurse rushed in to tell him he was on the "Polish Transport" which was leaving that night and so must go home and get ready. After a deathlike silence the younger surgeon who was to assist him offered to do the surgery. "No," replied the senior surgeon, "I'm the one who's been treating him and I'm the one who will do the operation." Two weeks later the patient had completely recovered while the doctor was no more.

Of course, not all doctors and nurses behaved heroically or even effectively. Many physicians became slipshod and superficial and most perhaps tended to become somewhat indifferent to those they could do little to help, such as the elderly. As so often happens with professionals, the interesting case frequently aroused more attention than the suffering human being. Some nurses, especially among the nonprofessionals, also lacked dedication as well as skill. They could neglect patients and even exploit them or allow other patients to take advantage of them. As we have seen earlier, corruption tainted the medical department as it did other Theresienstadt operations.

Still, as statistics show, and as numerous memoirs attest, Theresienstadt's medical department performed extraordinarily well under unusually difficult conditions. In the physical near-squalor, social disarray, and psychological strain that characterized so much of the camp's operations, its accomplishments stand out.

Arnost Weiss, a young Prague building contractor and amateur musician, arrived in Theresienstadt two months after it opened. The next day he was standing in the latrine whistling a tune when an elderly man came up alongside him and asked, "Young man, do you know what you are whistling?"

"Certainly," replied Weiss, "Beethoven's' Razumovsky Quartet No. 1.'"

His reply prompted the older man to introduce himself. He was a former concertmaster for a provincial Czech opera company. Then, with both standing side by side in the latrine, the former concertmaster whistled the violin part while Weiss expertly whistled the three remaining voices.

The incident illustrates still another startling aspect of Theresienstadt life: culture could be found everywhere, including the latrines. As Joza Karas, with only a touch of hyperbole, exclaims, "The arrival of the first *Aufbaukommando* [construction detail] signaled the beginning of a cultural life unparalleled in the history of Western civilization."

This explosion of cultural activity began the month after the first Aufbaukommando arrived when the young construction workers obtained Nazi permission to hold a "Comradeship Evening." Cabaret evenings and impromptu musicales soon followed, with the musicales gradually becoming more elaborate and ambitious affairs. The arrival of the German and Austrian transports in the following summer saw the start of lecture series, as well as the beginning of more formal theatre presentations.

In the fall, a leisure-time division came into existence to arrange, coordinate, and support what had become a swelling wave of lectures, concerts, recitals, cabarets, plays, and poetry readings. On one November evening there were 11 different officially announced cultural offerings plus numerous private presentations for small gatherings.

A 69-year-old former fur dealer from Berlin, Phillip Manes, headed the Leisure Time Bureau. He and his 55 helpers, most of them also over 60, energetically and effectively helped provide space, scenery, instruments, furniture, and posters for cultural events. They did not try to steer the camp's cultural life in any particular direction but wisely left it to the participants themselves to decide what they wanted to do. Although instances of favoritism did occur, Manes and his crew ran a highly regarded operation.

The SS at first restricted, but then allowed, and eventually even encouraged this proliferation of cultural activity. It kept the inmates quiet and enhanced the camp's image as a privileged ghetto. The Nazis did keep an eye on lectures and so the leisure-time activities bureau sometimes changed the titles of such offerings to make them seem more innocuous.

SS leniency went so far as to permit the presentation of works by Jews that were barred elsewhere in the Reich. Throughout German-occupied Europe Theresienstadt was the only place where Mendelssohn's music could be played and Heine's poetry read. As Lederer notes, "Theresienstadt was probably the freest town in Europe with respect to culture. . . Words were spoken on Theresienstadt's stage which, outside the ghetto, would have proved the undoing of writers and actors."

The ethnic divisions among the Jews did not appreciably affect this cultural outpouring. Music, of course, speaks an international language. But even in literature, many Czechs, following the example of their most famous writer, Franz Kafka, wrote in German, while those who wrote in Czech could find an ample audience for work worthy of attention. Of course, differences did show up. German theatre groups tended to be more conservative, preferring classical German plays. Czech groups, being younger, were influenced in their presentations by the avant-garde theatre movement in prewar Prague. The Czechs supplied the most talent since their more able artists and artistes had had less opportunity to flee Nazi rule. Still, the Germans held their own, especially in providing popular lecturers.

The Council of Elders cooperated by modestly compensating performers and producers with such tidbits as an extra dab of margarine or a spoonful of beet jam. Even private presentations could bring small bounties. Gerty Spies first read her poetry to a six-member audience in a tiny room whose bunk beds had been pushed against the wall. One of the six, a commissary worker, rewarded her with a slice of sausage and a roll.

Tickets to most officially arranged events cost 5 crowns and connections could help in getting them to the more popular presentations. Still, most residents had more ghetto crowns than they needed, while the more popular presentations were usually repeated several times. So access to the camp's cultural offerings was generally available to all who could get to them.

And get to them they did. Most cultural events took place at 6:00 P.M., and the residents, tired and sweaty though they might be, would rush to them from work. Older adults would crowd the benches, younger adults would stand along the walls and in the aisles, while children would squat down on the floor in front. In warm weather the door would be left open so that those outside could hear.

There was little separation between the participants and their public. This was true socially as well as physically since the audience often included people as distinguished, and sometimes more so, as the performers. Indeed, speakers and performers customarily mingled with their audiences both before and after their presentations.

Occasionally, an audience member weak from hunger and fatigue would doze off, but most of the attendees usually watched and listened with avid attention. Once during a production of a play by Gogol, a deportation was unexpectedly announced following the first act. None of the actors or audience members knew whether they would find their call-up papers waiting for them on their bunks when they returned. Yana Shanova, one of the performers, describes what happened:

> We wanted to interrupt the performance, but the audience would not permit it. The spectators willingly sacrificed two hours of precious, irreplaceable time, in which they could have said goodby to their friends and packed their necessary belongings, to see once more for the last time a theatrical production.

According to Lederer, Theresienstadt's greatest artistic achievements lay in the field of music. Few would dispute him, for the camp virtually bulged with composers, conductors, and concertmasters, along with countless musicians both professional and amateur. It also harbored thousands of music lovers hungry to hear almost anything they had to offer.

This emphasis on music surfaced during the earliest days. Many members of the first construction crews were musicians who, despite the SS ban, brought their instruments with them. One resourceful cellist dismantled his bulky instrument, wrapped the pieces in blankets along with some glue and clamps, and reassembled them after his arrival.

The men would play after work, secretly at first but more openly when it became apparent that the SS did not much care. They made music an important part of their first officially sanctioned "Comradeship Evening" on December 28. A few weeks later they staged a full-scale musical review which offered, for its finale, a new composition called "The Terezin March." The composition's upbeat lyrics ended with the following lines:

Hey! Tomorrow life starts over,
And with it the time is approaching
When we'll fold our knapsacks
And return home again.
Where there is a will, there is a way,
Let us join hands
And one day on the ruins of the ghetto
We shall laugh.

The review was of necessity an all-male production secretly performed in the men's barracks. But on March 12 Theresienstadt's women responded with a review of their own featuring songs, readings, and dances. They performed the program several times in the women's barracks and eventually in the men's barracks as well. In the meantime, string ensembles were springing up and beginning to give informal recitals. Theresienstadt's lively music life was well underway.

The Jewish administration fully supported these endeavors. It gave the more notable musicians jobs allowing them time and energy to pursue their musical activities. Many were assigned to the kitchens or commissaries where they could get extra nourishment, while more talented violinists, including two youths who had demonstrated considerable promise, were assigned light office work to prevent their fingers from losing sensitivity. Eppstein allowed a young pianist to practice on his grand piano and Zucker often loaned out his violin to gifted students.

Though the camp did not lack musical talent or the will to use it, it did suffer from other shortages. The most pressing one at the outset was the lack of a piano. Then the work detail stumbled across a battered and legless piano perched on a table in a building on the edge of town. It was clandestinely brought at night to a more convenient site and gradually put into working order. But it required constant retuning, even between selections during a performance.

The Jewish administration eventually persuaded the SS to bring in a few decent pianos that had been confiscated from Jewish homes. Their arrival added a great fillip to the camp's cultural life. They also supplied some surprises. One performer was deeply engaged in a recital when she heard a woman in the audience exclaim, "Why, that's my piano she's playing."

Reed and brass instruments were also in short supply and since most of the few musicians who had them were more interested in playing jazz than classical music, no real symphony orchestra ever emerged. On one occasion a pianist played a Mozart piano concerto using a lone accordionist to play the orchestral part.

Getting musical scores also proved difficult. Some were brought in by new arrivals, some were procured from the camp administration, and others were smuggled in. Fortunately, Arnost Weiss, who headed a construction crew in the camp, could on occasion go outside to procure materials. On one such occasion he came across a sympathetic Czech woodwind manufacturer who willingly supplied him with several scores. Since virtually all scores required duplication, some recreation bureau employees worked secretly through the night lining stolen paper with musical staffs and then copying musical notation on them.

Not all of Theresienstadt's music was imported for its own bevy of composers were also busy. Karas lists 50 works known to have been composed in the camp. They included operas, quartets, and collections of songs.

The recreation bureau official in charge of music was the Czech composer Hans Krasa, whose first orchestral piece was performed when he was 11 and whose first symphony some 10 years later was premiered in the United States by the Boston Symphony. Theresienstadt's most unusual composer, however, was Karel Schwenk who, though he could not read a note of music, wrote the music as well as the lyrics for "The Terezin March." His composition became the camp's unofficial anthem.

Since violinists were the most numerous of the instrumentalists, and violins the most numerous instruments, string music became the forte of Theresienstadt's musical life. Early in 1942, Egon Ledec, former concertmaster of the Czech Philharmonic, formed a string quartet with three amateur musicians. Known as the Doctors' Quartet, since all members had doctorates though Ledec's was the only one in music, they began giving private recitals in the quarters of one of them who was a member of the Council of Elders. Ledec later formed a quartet with professional musicians, one of whom was an elderly member of Vienna's world-renowned Rose Quartet. Other string ensembles soon followed, culminating in 1943 with the formation of a string orchestra of over 40 members.

Theresienstadt's most outstanding musician, however, was Bernhard Kaff, a Czech pianist who had given recitals throughout prewar Europe. There were several other prominent pianists, most of them women. One was Juliet Aranyi who had been appearing on concert stages since she was 6 years old. (She was 30 when she came to Theresienstadt.) Pianists generally enjoyed more favorable conditions than other musicians since they needed no accompaniment to perform. Also, many of them could play a great deal of music from memory.

Predictably, vocal music elicited the most widespread participation. There were men's choruses, women's choruses, and children's choruses. There was a chorus specializing in Jewish liturgical music, another for Yiddish folk songs, still another for what was called "New Palestine" music, and yet another for folk songs of all nationalities.

This interest and involvement with vocal music led to the staging of operas, although "staging" may be something of a misnomer since most operas, especially at first, had to be performed concert style without scenery or costumes and with only a piano or sometimes an accordion for accompaniment. Yet they were eagerly asked for and well attended. As time went on, their producers and performers became adept at finding ways to add a bit of decor and at least some semblance of costumes. There were quite a few professional opera singers, both male and female, in the camp to sing the leading roles, assist the lesser trained, and to help generally with the productions.

These efforts reached a high point on November 28, 1942 with the performance of Smetana's "The Bartered Bride," the best known and, especially by Czechs, the most treasured of all Czech operas. Its opening chorus, "Why Shouldn't We Rejoice?" moved the audience tremendously in spite of, or perhaps because of, its irony, given the conditions under which it was being sung. As one teenager later wrote in her diary, "I have heard "The Bartered Bride" three times in Prague, but it was never so beautiful as here."

But music did not need national sentiment or narrative content or even a strong melodic line to captivate Theresienstadt audiences. Delicate and sophisticated chamber music could also hold them enthralled. Ruth Elias says she will never forget the first concert she attended in Theresienstadt. It was performed by a string trio at a time when SS interruptions were still feared.

> The room was relatively large but had only three chairs and these were for the musicians. The listeners had to stand and they did so as quietly as mice in order to hear the sounds. Sentinels were posted at the windows and on the stairs to give warning if an SS man appeared. This was, I believe, the most seriously listened to concert I have ever attended. There was such a reverential quiet among the audience that one could hear a pin drop, while on many a cheek tears rolled down.

Although Theresienstadt had an abundance of professional musicians, it did not have many professional actors and actresses. It had a few, however, as well as some producers, directors, and set designers. It also had Karel Schwenk.

Professionally, the 35-year-old Schwenk was as unversed in theatre as he was in music. Before the war, however, he had belonged to a rather freakish Prague group called "The Club of Unused Talents," and Theresienstadt gave him a chance to put his own unused, and unusual, talents to work. After having written, composed, and produced the first musical review, Schwenk went on to develop a more or less ongoing and clandestine cabaret. Soon other cabarets sprang up, all of them amateur affairs. Jana Sadova staged her successful cabaret production in the women's barracks without ever having visited a cabaret.

The arrival of the Germans and Austrians spurred on this trend. The Viennese proved especially adept at such entertainment and soon had three cabarets running. As the barriers between the sexes became less rigid, or less rigidly enforced, virtually all cabaret groups became mixed. All were mobile operations, performing in attics, courtyards, and such other space as might be available. Most also went out of their way to give presentations in homes for the aged, children's homes, and hospitals.

Gerty Spies describes one such performance. "As with other presentations, the older people sit on benches while the younger ones stand. The entertainment consists of comedians, a harmonica player, a dance troupe, and a young pair of singers with *he* singing soprano and *she* singing tenor. In the middle of the entertainment an elderly spectator has a fit and has to be led off, but the program continues." Private cabaret productions often were initiated by various groups with attendance by invitation only. The use of private invitations was dictated not so much by a desire for exclusiveness as simply by a lack of space. One such invitation informs Herr, Frau, or Fraulein (the individual's name is then inserted) that "The Cleaning Service HB introduces itself and takes pleasure in inviting you to a cabaret evening on January 12, 1943 at 8:00 P.M. in the potato peeling room of HB."

Cabaret presentations eventually led to more formal and elaborate theatrical offerings. Initially, writes Fryd, "Most of the stages were located in the garrets of larger buildings, and this in itself created a fantastic atmosphere. There were 2-story high roof supports made of gigantic 150-year-old beams. Feeble rays from the flickering spotlights gleamed spectrally through the dusty room, giving a grotesque appearance to the rags hanging on ropes which were serving as a curtain, and transforming the dirt into the cozy atmosphere of a stable. . . ." Such a setting, says Fryd, provided Kurt Gerron with a more authentic atmosphere for "The Beggars' Opera" than he had ever had in Berlin.

As congestion in the camp eased, a large hall in one barracks was cleared and transformed into something resembling a regular theatre with a modern stage, an orchestra pit, and even dressing rooms. It used for major dramatic and operatic productions. At the same time, smaller-scale theatrical programs continued to flourish in out-of-the-way spaces.

As previously noted, German theatre in Theresienstadt specialized in the classics. The Germans not only staged Lessing's pro-Jewish play, *Nathan the Wise*, but presented over two evenings Part I of Goethe's monumental *Faust*. Czech theatre was more enterprising and experimental for their thespians were not only younger but were also less subject to scrutiny from the SS, none of whose members, of course, could understand Czech. At the outset, the Czechs did keep innocent texts on hand, ready to insert them in place of risky passages should an SS man appear. But when they saw their Nazi superiors showing little interest in their activities, they grew bolder. Eventually, says Sadova, "Not a single Czech performance could have passed the Nazi censorship unpunished."

The Czech gendarmes posed no problems. Some even smuggled in scripts for their fellow Czechs and then, clad in civilian clothes with a Jewish star carefully pinned to their breast, smuggled themselves into the audience to watch the show.

The Czech Jews presented the only full-length play known to have been written in Theresienstadt. Entitled *The Last Cyclist*, it was, as might be expected, written, produced, and directed by Karel Schwenk.

Schwenk based his play on a parody of the persistent complaint of anti-Semites that Jews are responsible for all society's problems. It shows a dictator who, deciding that bicyclists are the cause of all his country's misfortunes, deports to Horror Island all cyclists who cannot prove their families were pedestrians for at least six generations. One of the cyclists, however, manages to escape to the mainland. He is caught and is about to be executed when the dictator is warned that no country can exist without cyclists since they have always been our best scapegoats. So the dictator places the cyclist in a zoo where the people can come to revile him for his misdeeds. In the end, the cyclist manages to turn the tables on the dictator and emerge triumphant.

The parody's parallel with Nazi Germany was so clear and cutting that an alarmed Jewish administration ordered Schwenk to at least change his ending. Schwenk said he would do so but did not, and when the SS took no action, the show understandably became the camp's most popular play.

One Czech group dramatized a series of Yiddish stories, which included Sholem Aleichem's *Tales of Tevya, the Milkman*. In this way, a precursor of the world-famous musical *Fiddler on the Roof* had its premiere in Theresienstadt.

Theresienstadt's artists enjoyed a somewhat more privileged position than its musicians and thespians, for a professional painter in Theresienstadt could work full time at his profession. The graphics office of the Technical Department employed 20 artists headed by Fritz Taussig, who, under the name of Bedrich Fritta, had been one of Prague's foremost illustrators. Fritta and his staff drew charts, graphs, and cartoons.(29)

Their cartoons were designed to drive home messages to the camp's population, such as the need to observe camp rules, take precautionary health measures, etc. One poster, for example, shows a mop, a broom, a cylinder of soap powder, and other cleaning articles all dashing someplace. It bears (in German) a rhymed couplet reading, "To work is a blessing; join the cleaning squad."

The Lautscher workshops, located above the library, also employed artists to design greeting cards, souvenirs, haberdashery and other products which the camp was producing for the Reich. In addition, the SS frequently ordered them to design frescoes and other decorations as well as to paint portraits of themselves and, from photographs, their families. Some SS men who wanted to pass themselves off as members of noble families called on the workshop to create for them imaginary coats of arms. A Theresienstadt artist could also do artwork for fellow inmates in exchange for food or other necessities. Troller, an architect, would sell sketches to bakery employees for half a loaf of bread each.

But if the position of a Theresienstadt artist was in many respects more privileged, it was often more precarious as well. For more than the camp's other creators of culture, the artists often led a double life. While they were ostensibly working for the SS and the Jewish administration, most were privately working for posterity. In secret they drew sketches and painted pictures showing Theresienstadt as they saw it. Those pictures which have survived provide a graphic record of what life in the privileged ghetto was like.

This secret artwork consists largely of sketches in india ink, pencil, or charcoal since paints were hard to obtain. Many were done on the blank sides of medical forms, on the back sides of old plans for the Fortress, or on other available scraps of paper. Once completed, they were hidden, sometimes sandwiched between official charts and graphs in the files or in the library, but more often in the walls of the drafting office. Some of Fritta's work was placed in a tin can and buried in the ground.

A Czech businessman with Nazi connections, who was also an avid collector, managed to smuggle some of this artwork out of the camp and to smuggle in food and cigarettes as compensation. The latter were certainly welcome but in taking such risks the artists were also motivated by the hope that their work would survive if they did not.

Their artwork may remind the casual viewer of Van Gogh's portraits of impoverished Belgian miners for it depicts, in Fryd's words, "a nightmarish world of gaunt faces, semi-clothed, emaciated bodies and disfigured humans." As one of the most talented younger painters, Alfred Kantor, says, "It was not so much that I wanted to draw my own story, but rather to capture this extraordinary place so that I could show the world something of it if and when I was ever free."

Literature provides the most accessible avenue for artistic expression since it requires little in the way of equipment and no specific skill beyond mere literacy. It should therefore come as no surprise that literary activity flourished in Theresienstadt. People of all ages and backgrounds scribbled away feverishly, using whatever writing materials-- usually pencil stubs and wrapping paper--they could find.

Most of this activity took the form of diary entries along with simple sketches and essays. Although artistic intentions and expressions usually played a secondary role in such outpourings, many do provide revealing and moving descriptions of Theresienstadt life. One of the more notable is the journal kept by Karel Fleischman, the Czech physician who initiated the psychological "Assault Squad."

For those with more specifically literary intentions, poetry soon became the most popular form of expression. Poems poured out by the thousands. Ilse Weber, a former Czech writer of children's books, wrote over one hundred poems, some in Czech, some in German, during her two years at the camp. Others may have penned still more since much of the poetry has been lost and much is unsigned.

Most Theresienstadt poetry reflects deep longings for the past, dismay at the dismal present, and bright hopes for the future. Such hopes are especially emphasized by Czech writers and are often bound up with expectations of a new and shining social order.

But if Theresienstadt's output of poetry was notable in quantity, it was far from notable in quality. Adler dismisses most of it as suffering from "rhyming sickness," while a more recent and more methodical German scholar, Ulrike Migdal, claims it lacks creativity as well as objectivity. She also offers a reason for this: the conditions existing in Theresienstadt made it impossible, she says, for its authors, whether professional or amateur, to achieve the "inner distance" and perspective necessary to write for "eternity."

If poetry became Theresienstadt's most common medium of artistic expression, lecturing became its most frequent cultural event. There could be as many as 70 to 80 lectures in a single week with subjects ranging from food chemistry to the philosophy of Nietzsche, from how to explore for oil to the history of the Catholic Church. One could hear a lecture in French on the writings of Andre Gide or a recitation of selections from *The Iliad* and *The Odyssey* in ancient Greek, with commentaries in German and Czech. Theresienstadt, in Baeck's words, came to resemble a small university.

Baeck himself became the most popular lecturer. A series of talks he initiated entitled "Philosophical Thinkers from Plato to Kant" regularly drew several hundred. Standing in a drafty attic with a biting late fall wind blowing through its many crevices, they would listen to his words in rapt attention.

The day following one of his talks, two men, a former Hamburg judge and a former Prague businessman, began discussing what he had said while pulling one of the camp's hearses. (These vehicles, it will be recalled, were used for carting goods and carrying away rubbish in the camp.) So involved did the men become in the subject that they failed to notice how two other hearse haulers had slyly hitched their own wagon to theirs, leaving them to pull both vehicles. Word of the incident spread quickly through the camp, producing much mirth and earning the discussants the title of "The Two Philosophical Horses."

Although the SS paid more attention to lectures than to other cultural happenings, they usually confined their scrutiny to merely scanning the titles. Aware of this, the Leisure-Time Activities Bureau, as previously mentioned, took pains to make the titles seem innocuous. But sometimes they failed to fully assess their captors' point of view. On one occasion, the SS ordered the title of a talk changed from "German Jews in German Literature" to "German-Speaking Jews in German Literature." The Nazis apparently could not accept anything which might suggest that a Jew could also be a German.

Speakers were free to talk on Jewish subjects and many did so. Predictably, rabbis emphasized religious themes and Zionist speakers stressed nationalistic ones. Robert Stricker, the camp's best known Zionist, did not generally lecture but held open discussions on Zionism in his room on Saturday afternoons. He did address a memorial service on Theodor Herzl's birthday.

The birthdays of other prominent Jews, along with a few highly regarded non-Jews such as Goethe and Schiller, were also observed. Franz Kafka's 60th birthday was commemorated with a talk by his sister Ottilie followed by remarks by some of his cousins and two of his former schoolmates. Unfortunately for his later biographers, no transcript exists of what was said, but the memorial meeting was probably well attended for many of Kafka's writings, especially his masterpiece, *The Trial*, must have seemed particularly relevant in Theresienstadt.

Since lectures, like cabarets, could be delivered most anywhere, speakers, including some of the most prominent and popular, spoke frequently at old age homes, children's homes, and hospitals. Outstanding in this regard was the German writer Else Dornitzer, who delivered 275 talks covering 22 themes during her stay in Theresienstadt. She was a welcome visitor everywhere.

But since lecturing, like writing, requires no specific skill or equipment, many who indulged in it had relatively little to offer. Some merely described what they had done or what they had been in their past lives. A few sought to pose as authorities on things they knew little about. Among the latter was a man who, claiming to be a former professor of Egyptology at the Sorbonne, offered to give a series of talks on his "specialty." It turned out that he had been an advertising man for a travel book publisher and, in that capacity, had once written the ads for a travel guide through Egypt.

Children participated in almost all areas and aspects of Theresienstadt's cultural boom. They attended many of the concerts and plays designed for adults as well as other events planned exclusively for them. As noted earlier, many of the leading figures frequently called at the children's houses to speak or perform.

The youngsters were also encouraged to make their own contributions to the camp's cultural life. Virtually all had some access to paper and pencil to write and draw, while those showing musical talent would usually receive special attention. Bernhard Kaff, the camp's premier pianist, established a miniature conservatory whose students "paid" for their lessons by coming once a week to clean his small room. When one of his students fell ill with scarlet fever, Kaff called at his bedside to present him with a precious book of music. Alisha Sommer-Hertz, a prominent prewar pianist who worked at splitting feldspar during the day and practiced or performed in the evening, taught a few talented youngsters during her lunch hour. Budding violinists could usually find plenty of good teachers and could sometimes borrow Zucker's instrument for practice and performances.

The youngsters also became involved in theatre, especially light opera. The German-speaking children put on a musical adaptation of the German children's novel, *Emil and the Detective*, while the Czech children staged a musical written especially for them. Entitled *Brundibar*, it became the camp's most popular theatrical attraction.

Brundibar was actually written in Prague after the Nazi takeover and was premiered at the Jewish orphans' home in the winter of 1943. Its composer, Hans Krasa, was not present for the occasion, having already been sent to Theresienstadt. However, his work had greatly impressed those who attended its debut and when the children themselves arrived in Theresienstadt a few months later, efforts immediately got underway to revive it.

Both Krasa and his librettist, a lawyer named Adolf Hofmeister, were decidedly left wing, and their opera in its original form reflects this orientation. It portrays the efforts of an impoverished brother and sister to raise money to buy milk for their seriously ill mother by singing on the streets. An evil organ grinder named Brundibar, however, fears their competition and together with various street vendors, his fellow capitalists as it were, prevents them from doing so.

In Theresienstadt the story was changed from an anti-capitalist to a subtle anti-fascist point of view. Brundibar became more of a dictator than a monopolist while the other capitalists, i.e., the street vendors, were eliminated. Its last lines were changed from "He who deeply loves his mother and father and his native land can play with us" to "He who loves justice and will befriend it and is not afraid is our friend and can play with us."

The show premiered in Theresienstadt on September 23, 1943 and became a smash hit overnight. Even German-speaking residents wanted to see it and tickets were so scarce that their acquisition became a status symbol. Eppstein himself, though he knew no Czech, was so impressed that he gave Honza Teichlinger, the teenager who played *Brundibar*, a job in the meat department so that the youth could keep up his strength. In the year following its premiere it was performed 55 times, setting a record for any Theresienstadt production.

Theresienstadt's children also produced numerous poems and drawings. Many of their drawings compare favorably with those done by adults while one children's poem, written by a 9-year-old named Pavel Friedmann, has become the best-known piece of writing to emerge from the camp. Entitled "To A Butterfly," it runs, in more or less literal translation, as follows:

It was the last, the very last,
It was so rich, so bright, so dazzlingly yellow,
It was like a tear from the sun
Singing against a white stone.

Such a flash of yellow
Soared freely way up high,
Going away I'm sure because
It wished to kiss our world goodby.

For seven weeks I've lived here,
Penned up inside this ghetto.
I have seen the dandelions reaching out to me,
And the white chestnut candles in the courtyard.
But I have never seen another butterfly.

That butterfly was the last one, for

Butterflies do not live here in the ghetto.(30)

Providing sustenance and support for much of the camp's cultural life was the library. It opened in the fall of 1942 at about the same time as the bank, coffeehouse, and stores. Unlike these other operations, however, it soon became a vital and popular component of camp life.

Situated in a former store, it started out with less than 5,000 volumes. Within a year, however, the number had increased to nearly 50,000 as the SS began bringing the contents of several Jewish libraries and private collections to their Model Ghetto. The library opened a reading room which became a haven for the elderly and it organized a mobile operation, sending out boxes of books to house blocks and barracks. It had also set up branches in hospitals, old age homes, and children's homes as well as specialized subunits such as a medical library, a technical library, and a Hebrew library for young people. Each adult borrower had to pay a deposit of 50 ghetto crowns and present proof of literacy, neither requirement being at all difficult to meet.

Like other ghetto institutions, the library confronted an array of distinctive problems. Its book collection started out and remained heavily unbalanced. Nearly a third of its volumes were prayer books and only about ten percent were fiction, the most sought-after reading material in the camp. In another sense, however, it was the best balanced library in the German Reich since it was the only one offering works by Jewish authors. It had, for example, 587 copies of Heine's poems.

About half of all the books it loaned out were never returned, for books in Theresienstadt were such precious commodities that people tended to hold onto them or trade them. Deportations were especially devastating, for the deportees would take their borrowed books with them and would even trade things they could not take for an additional book or two. Interestingly, this did not greatly upset the library's director, Emile Utitz, a former professor of psychology and philosophy who had taught at both German and Czech universities. Utitz believed that every book was fulfilling its mission as long as it lay in appreciative hands.

In normal life libraries are often regarded as semi-sanctuaries which afford their staff some escape from the rigors of everyday existence. Such was hardly the case in Theresienstadt for its library staff put itself perpetually at risk. They concealed certain forbidden works, secretly supplied books for the children's homes for teaching, and provided the artists with large squares of stiff paper, which normally served to separate maps and prints. The artists used this paper to paint and draw sketches of Theresienstadt life. They would then return the squares to the library staff who would put them back in their original places with the forbidden artwork on them.

Library work also entailed another kind of danger. The circulation of books encouraged the spread of disease as the volumes passed from one set of dirty hands to another. One result was that half of the library staff were always out ill and many never returned from their sickbeds.

Despite such hazards and difficulties, which the frequent deportation of staff members only compounded, the library consistently managed to function at a high level. It even staged exhibitions, such as one featuring Jewish artists. But perhaps its chief claim to distinction lay not in its productivity but in its probity.

Because of the value attached to books in Theresienstadt--many would trade a piece of bread for a short-term loan of a desired volume-- the library offered numerous opportunities for corruption and favoritism. Yet no reports of such misdoings ever surfaced. The books were distributed as fairly and as equitably as possible.

One reason for this rectitude, says Starke, was the great respect for books which the staff members shared. As she puts it, "We came from different countries but all from the same milieu." But another, more important reason, she says, was the behavior of its director. Utitz never took a book for himself and never showed partiality to anyone, whether staff member or borrower. As a result, the library demonstrated that even under concentration camp conditions, institutions of integrity were still possible.

In assessing all three of the ghetto's areas of achievement, certain aspects stand out. Those responsible not only benefitted as much, if not more so, as those for whom they labored, but they benefitted in often unforeseen and unusual ways.

Teachers could teach without having to obey numerous rules and regulations and, since teaching was not officially sanctioned, without processing the numerous forms which encumber most school systems. They could and indeed had to improvise quite freely. In living with their charges they could also get to know them and could thus more effectively help them learn. Theresienstadt offered dedicated teachers, and most of them fell into that category, a chance to make a real difference in the lives of their pupils.

Doctors in Theresienstadt often got a chance to pursue specialties they could not have developed before. As we have seen, Victor Frankl started on a path that would make him one of the world's foremost psychiatrists. Others benefitted by working alongside some of the most respected practitioners in their fields. Still others benefitted by the opportunity to work at all since patients and practices were not that numerous in prewar Central Europe.

Even the more esteemed and established physicians could reap rewards from Theresienstadt's unique conditions. Julius Spanier had been Munich's foremost pediatrician and as such was offered Prominenten status when he arrived in the camp. The 62-year-old physician, however, rejected it and plunged into work. "I have always wanted to be strictly a doctor and not have to worry about payment," he said. "Here I can do so." When asked later how he liked Theresienstadt, Spanier replied, "Here there is no telephone, no cashier's office, no bills or insurance forms to fill out. Why shouldn't I like it?"

As with the physicians, so with the musicians, painters, thespians, and other artists. While laboring under numerous limitations, they also enjoyed an exciting, indeed, often exhilarating freedom. For one thing, they could test and hone their capabilities for it was often possible to perform a program 20 or 30 times. They could experiment and even branch out into entirely new areas. An attorney who had always wanted to be a puppeteer got his chance in Theresienstadt while a tailor from Prague discovered he had a beautiful voice and began singing operatic arias. (His name, appropriately enough, was Alexander Singer.) A Berlin attorney who had lost his dominant right hand, along with his right foot, in the trenches of World War I found he could paint and draw with his left hand.

Gifted young people could study under revered masters, while amateur actors, singers, and musicians could perform with seasoned professionals. Only in Theresienstadt could one find an amateur violinist playing in a string quartet alongside a former concertmaster. Only in Theresienstadt could one find a prominent pianist cheerfully accompanying a far less well-known and less accomplished soloist.

Like the physicians, even the more established performers found the freedom from financial worries and administrative problems gratifying. As the Prague violinist, Karel Froehlich, later recalled, "For an artist it was a tremendous opportunity to work during the war in his own field, with excellent colleagues and actually, in a certain sense, in an ideal milieu, for there were no problems with renting the hall, advertising, pianists; all that cost a lot of money."

It should be noted, however, that the camp's near intoxication with cultural and semi-cultural pursuits has generated a certain amount of controversy. Adler claims such involvements became a way of distorting and denying reality and therefore proved detrimental. Utitz does not go that far but points out how such events often became an escape into the past. He notes the aching nostalgia with which the Czechs heard *The Bartered Bride*, the Austrians heard the songs of Vienna, and the Germans heard the words of Goethe and Schiller.

Most, however, take an entirely different point of view. To Lederer, the cultural activities provided consolation to the old and inspiration to the young, giving the inmates the "only sense of freedom they had." Karney finds in the theatre "the prisoners' weapon of defense against human decimation. It became the battlefield where the struggle to maintain the camp spirit was waged." Fryd views the inmates' cultural involvement as "a measure of their unbroken will to live."

Given the plight of the Jews and the paucity of their options, these more positive assessments, while perhaps overstated, seem essentially correct. Without the music and the theatre, the paintings and the poetry, there would have been much greater despondency and despair and, as a result, much more illness and death. While cultural outlets often served as an escape from reality, they also enabled many to endure reality.

Brundibar, the camp's most popular cultural offering, vividly illustrates and exemplifies this. According to Ella Weissberger, one of the few surviving members of its cast, the show meant more to its young performers than food for it helped them overcome feelings of helplessness while giving them a sense of membership in the human race. This was especially true, she says, for the orphan Teichinger, who had begged for the title role and performed it superbly. Their director was working during the day on a dangerous construction project outside the camp, and when he was late for rehearsals the children would tremble with fear that something might have happened to him. But, weary and dusty, he invariably showed up.

The audiences, both young and old, seemed to derive the same benefits. Their enthusiastic, often wild applause would prompt the cast to sing the finale again and again. Musically superior to Schwenk's early anthem, the opera's finale became the inmates' victory march and was whistled or hummed throughout the camp.

But accepting the more positive view of the camp's cultural activities should not blind us to the many ironies it engendered. Even those involved were aware of them.

Spies describes the sight of a long line of raggedy, half-starved people who, while waiting for their scanty bowl of soup, and while watching the stretcher bearers carry off the sick, the dying, and the dead, hear from an open window the voice of a concert singer practicing for a performance. Gerta Haas recalls being taken on a bright spring day to the top of the church tower by the young Czech who regularly adjusted its clock. As she felt the sun shining on her face and heard the joyful strains of *The Bartered Bride* rising from the concert hall below, she could observe a group of beaten-down, almost lifeless men being escorted into the Little Fortress. As Redlich notes in his diary, "Oh, my God, what a life! . . . Colorful, horrible, full of contradictions. . . A cabaret on one side and on the other, old people dying. . . A richly colored mosaic of life and death."

But beyond these contradictions and contrasts, there were paradoxes which characterized all three of the camp's areas of achievement. These paradoxes make one survivor, Dita Loewy, label Theresienstadt as a Theatre of the Absurd. Most of those patients whom the physicians exerted all their expertise and energies to save from death would eventually succumb to still another illness or get shipped off to the Auschwitz gas chambers. Most of the musicians and artists who worked so hard to develop their skills and perfect their presentations would suffer similar fates. And as for the children on whose welfare the camp placed such emphasis, 11 out of 12 would never have the chance to build the Jewish future for which they were being so carefully prepared.

---

26. Kaltenbrunner, an Austrian who had replaced the assassinated Heydrich as number-two man in the SS, wrote to his boss Himmler in early February seeking permission to deport an additional 5,000 of Theresienstadt's elderly, saying they were the most likely to catch and spread the disease. He also claimed that maintaining them was draining too much of the ghetto's manpower. But Himmler was apparently having second thoughts about his and Germany's future in the wake of the German defeat at Stalingrad a few weeks earlier. Though he had approved the deportation of the elderly the previous fall, he now replied through his adjutant that Theresienstadt was designed for the elderly and they should therefore be allowed to remain there.

27. In deference to the medical service, it might be noted that conditions generally in such institutions in prewar Europe, to say nothing of America, were hardly much better. Moreover, the camp's few psychiatrists had all they could do to treat the less mentally ill who could articulate their complaints and demand treatment.

28. It should be noted that Frankl, along with Fleischmann, Jonas, and others, took the view that Theresienstadt did not represent time out from normal life, a provisional layover as it were, but a confirmation test for life

itself. It therefore represented something of an epiphany in a resident's existence.

29. Some of the other more prominent professional artists in Theresienstadt were Leo Haas, Otto Ungar, Ferdinand Bloch, Maria Klanova, Hilda Zadikow, and Alfred Bergel. All but Bergel, who was from Vienna, were Czech. Friedl Dicker Brandeis, a prominent prewar painter originally from vienna, would have been a welcome addition to the studio but she chose instead to work as a drawing teacher in the children's homes.

30. Some sources give Pael Friedmann's age as 21 when he wrote the poem. Most anthologies, however, describe him as a 9-year-old.

PART III

JULY 1943 to AUGUST 1945

CHAPTER 8
EXODUS I: THE END OF EDELSTEIN

The first half of 1943 ended on a rather triumphant note with the completion of the railroad spur to Bauschwitz. Both the SS and the Jews treated its opening as a festive occasion, each side apparently regarding the ambitious project as demonstrating what *it* could accomplish. This buoyant mood continued into July as efforts went forward to make Theresienstadt more livable. Construction crews partitioned attics, widening their air vents into small windows and installing electricity and stoves. The camp workshops turned out increasing amounts of furniture, much of it for the inmates themselves. More and more families, or at least married couples, were finding ways of living together.

The camp was also busily turning out goods for the Reich. The assembly of tank engine kits, begun in May, was now employing 1,000 workers under three tents in the town square. Nearly 200 women were still splitting feldspar, while other women along with some men were making uniforms for the German army. Goods for the SS itself as well as for the German civilian population were also being produced.

The medical service continued to have its hands full for 24 percent of the population were still reporting sick on an average day. But there were now 635 active physicians in the camp, or one for every 73 residents. Furthermore, the nonprofessional nurses were becoming more proficient, while equipment as well as furniture was becoming more plentiful. The medical service was giving more inoculations-- 24,000 for scarlet fever in 1943 as compared to less than 15,000 in 1942-- while its radiology division was now taking 100 x-rays a day, ten times as many as a year earlier. Toward the end of July the camp doctors took over the coffeehouse for two weeks to hold a series of medical seminars.

The camp's cultural life was also moving forward. Rehearsals began for *Brundibar*, while Raphael Schaecter's success with *The Bartered Bride* had encouraged him to produce another Czech opera, *The Kiss*. It premiered on July 20 in the attic of the Dresden barracks and would be performed at least 15 more times. Following the premiere, Schaecter began assembling a chorus of about 150 singers and four soloists for a rendition of Verdi's *Requiem*. It was the most ambitious cultural project yet undertaken in the ghetto.

It should be noted that not all the cultural enterprises were uniformly well received. Many, for instance, felt Schecter should have chosen a Jewish work, or at least one with Jewish content such as some of

Handel's Oratorios, rather than an expressly Christian work such as the Verdi *Requiem*. A still greater controversy arose over Wolfgang Lederer's production of *Die Fledermaus* which many felt was too light-hearted for a concentration camp. On the other hand, some were delighted with the colorful scenery and costumes which the producers had managed to procure. They were also impressed with the way Renee Gaertner-Geringer singlehandedly provided the music by alternatively playing the piano and a reed organ, using the latter to imitate reed instruments.

Sports also continued to thrive. In mid-summer the better nourished meat department workers defeated the warehouse workers 4 to 3 to win the soccer cup.

Another encouraging sign was a renewed effort by the Jewish administration to curb corruption. It reorganized and put tighter controls on food distribution with the aim of making it more equitable. It also eliminated the peeling of potatoes which not only improved the camp's nourishment but eradicated one major area of theft.

But contributing most to the camp's more confident mood was the news of Allied advances. For the first time, the Russians were pushing back the Germans without the Russian winter to help them, while the western Allies were now inching their way up the Italian peninsula. Many felt it would only be a matter of weeks before their ordeal would be over.

The SS in some ways seemed to confirm these hopes. In early July it instructed the Jewish administration to cease using the terms "Camp Commandant" or "Camp Inspector," but simply to refer to the officer's military grade. A week later it changed the designation of the town's streets. Before, they had been denoted by simple numbers; now they were given names, such as Lake Street, Tower Lane, etc. Most encouraging of all was a mid-summer visit from Eichmann who used the occasion to state, in the presence of both the SS and Jewish administration officials, that Theresienstadt would experience no more comings and goings. The deportations had ended. Or so it seemed.

But other SS developments were proving more troublesome and more ominous. On July 22 Seidl was suddenly replaced. The reasons for his removal remain unclear. Murmelstein believes that Seidl's closeness to Edelstein was making it difficult for Eppstein to function. Others speculate that it reflected tensions between the Prague SS and the Berlin SS headquarters. Still another report says Seidl had been slapped by an underling during a drinking bout in the headquarters lounge and the incident had weakened his authority. In any case, while

Theresienstadt's inmates had always detested Seidl, they soon began to miss him, for his successor turned out to be Anton Burger.

A former elementary school teacher from Vienna, Burger violently hated Jews, especially Czech Jews. He did not wait long to make his feelings apparent.

Seidl had always been lax in enforcing the ban on births, but Burger immediately began to crack down, and in response to his orders 350 pregnant women reported to the health service for abortions on July 14. He subsequently decreed that henceforth all parents of children conceived in the camp, along with the children themselves, would be deported. (The order was apparently issued before Eichmann's visit.) Although Burger later modified these actions and even allowed a few births, his manner and methods made those of Seidl seem almost benign.

Burger also forbade any SS member from speaking privately to a Jew and rigorously observed this order himself by never conferring with Eppstein or any member of the Jewish administration without having another SS man present. He did not, however, show the same commitment to another of his commands, for although he strictly forbade any of his garrison from using Jewish doctors or dentists, he had himself treated for an eye disorder by a noted camp specialist from Vienna. Since he could never bring himself to say "thank you" directly to a Jew, he would end each visit with the impersonal, *Mann dankt*, or "One thanks."

Soon after Burger's takeover, Bergel, the camp's inspector or second-in-command, suffered an illness that would eventually put him in a wheelchair. He remained in the camp but his position was taken over by a former electrician from Vienna named Rudolph Haindl. As was the case with Seidl, the replacement proved worse than the replacee.

Haindl quickly became known and feared for his viciousness and violence. He would strike people when they did not salute him quickly enough or when their Jewish star was not properly attached. Once he spotted a woman in the Schleuse who had arrived with a folding stool slung over her shoulder. He yanked the stool off her shoulder so violently that the woman, who was neither young nor strong, collapsed and died on the spot. When her sister bent over her, Haindl gave her a kick which sent her sprawling.

In his relentless search for misdoings and misdoers, he would turn up at the most unexpected places at the most unexpected times. He would even leap through a barracks window to catch inmates unawares. Or he would suddenly appear at the SS farm and, peering through his field

glasses, try to detect farm workers secreting food. Smoking especially enraged him. Once he came across an older mason with a pipe in his mouth and asked him what he was smoking. Though the man was actually smoking straw,
he replied, out of terror and perhaps because he did not know the German word for straw, "tobacco." "Come along," said Haindl. The mason was never seen again. Like Burger, Haindl particularly hated Czech Jews. On the other hand, he did show some tolerance for Viennese Jews, or at least for those few who would become his informers.

Some other SS developments were to prove more fateful to the privileged ghetto. On July 28 the residents of one of the largest barracks, along with those in some adjacent buildings, received notice to vacate their quarters within 24 hours. Suitcases, boards from dismantled bunks and shelves, and other materials came flying out of windows as the 5,700 affected inmates hurriedly sought to comply. Since the housing office had little extra space to offer, the men desperately combed through other buildings looking for new places to sleep. The whole episode created enormous confusion and consternation. It was, said Adler, as if a tornado had swept through the camp.

The vacated buildings lay empty for three weeks. Then a group of 220 Gestapo members and employees arrived, bringing with them truckloads of files. The Gestapo had become fearful of losing its records in the stepped-up Allied air raids on Berlin and so were moving them to Theresienstadt knowing that the camp would not be bombed even by mistake. The buildings taken over were surrounded with barbed wire and connected by a footbridge to the main SS headquarters. The whole northern end of the town was now cordoned off; a German ghetto had been created within a Jewish one.

Another SS move that caught the camp off guard was the dissolution of the Ghetto Watch in August. The constabulary force was soon reconstituted, but on a much different basis. The new Ghetto Watch was much smaller, having only 150 members compared to 420 on the former one. It was also much older, for 45, which was the maximum age for the former Ghetto Watch, was now the minimum age for the new one.

What prompted this move? While various explanations exist, the real inspiration probably came from the Warsaw ghetto uprising of the previous spring. The Nazis could hardly look with equanimity on a disciplined force of 420 young men, most with some military training, after seeing the trouble which a handful of half-starved Polish Jews could cause. The revolt in Treblinka that month, in addition to the approach of the Red army, may have further increased their fears.

Then, on August 24 a large and mysterious transport arrived. It pulled up to the camp on the new railroad spur but no one other than SS guards emerged. Finally, at around midnight, the train doors opened and some 1,260 ragged, emaciated and terrified children straggled out. Barelegged and often barefoot, clutching knapsacks and small bundles and, in some cases, prayer books and phylacteries, they were marched through the dark, silent streets to the delousing station.

The children, all boys ranging from 6 to 14 years of age--some may have been a year or two older but because of malnourishment looked younger--were very nearly the sole survivors of the Bialystok ghetto in Russia which had been liquidated the week before. When they saw the delousing station, they panicked and started to run away. They had seen some of their parents enter a building marked 'Baths' never to emerge.

Quickly rounded up and herded into the building, they clung together and refused to go under the showers. But a few Yiddish-speaking camp residents had been recruited to help care for them, and when one caretaker persuaded an older boy that the showers were really showers, the youth went under them and the rest soon followed.

The boys were lodged in an outlying building that had apparently been set aside for this purpose. Circled with barbed wire and guarded by Czech gendarmes, it was sealed off from the rest of the camp. Not even Eppstein or Edelstein could enter. The two physicians and 52 nurses and youth workers assigned to the youngsters not only had to speak Yiddish but had to have no family members in Theresienstadt. Among these caretakers were Ottilie Kafka and Aron Menczer.

At first, only silence emanated from the building but soon sounds of laughter and singing became audible for the children were being given food and other kinds of special care. Moreover, the other children in the camp made or collected toys and other things for them. Aron Menczer became the leader of the caretakers and saw to it that the youngsters received moral as well as physical care. When two boys were found to have stolen suitcases from others, he held a public "trial" to teach all of them the value of honesty and justice. Those children who fell ill were taken out secretly at night by the SS to the Little Fortress and killed. (Presumably the SS had told the other children and caretakers that they were being taken to the hospital.)

Although some of the children had confided to their caretakers their reasons for fearing gas, no real awareness of the horrors of the Nazi extermination policy spread through the camp. Earlier reports of such activities had also reached some members of the camp, but those reports had also failed to gain much credence. During the month of August, however, a prominent camp resident learned for a certainty what was going on.

Leo Baeck was awakened one night by a Czech engineer who had shortly before received a visit from a good friend, a half-Jew who had worked for a while in Auschwitz. The latter had escaped into Czechoslovakia and by bribing a gendarme had made his way to the engineer's quarters, where he told what he had seen in Auschwitz. After his visitor left, the engineer went to Baeck's room to tell him what he had heard. Baeck wrestled with the idea of telling others. He finally decided not to do so since it would demoralize the entire camp. Moreover, not all Theresienstadt's deportees may have been sent to Auschwitz and even some who were would probably have survived since there was a work selection at the camp. So he decided to keep mum. As a result, most residents continued to believe that deportation, though unwelcome, was by no means synonymous with death.(31)

If the residents of Theresienstadt did not realize the dangers which the deportations entailed, they soon began to suspect that they had not ended. During the final days of August rumors started circulating about a new transport. As one resident wrote in her diary on August 27, "The transport specter is here once again! Everyone is anxious, horribly anxious. It does not appear to be a work transport but a usual Polish one." The official announcement came a few days later.

Selection for this transport took a different tack than previous ones, however, for Burger, unlike Seidl, was not leaving the list simply to the Council of Elders to make up. Instead, he became actively involved in its composition. He seemed especially eager to include Czechs not employed in manual work. As a result, school teachers began dressing in old, dirty clothes and rubbing their hands on the barks of trees to make them look calloused. Members of the first two work details, who had previously been exempt from deportation, were summoned, and those who appeared well dressed were put on the list, while those in working clothes were not. Large numbers of the former Ghetto Watch were also selected, along with two of the more prominent figures in the camp: Leo Janowitz, head of the central registry, and youth leader Fredy Hirsch.

The SS had earlier searched Janowitz's room but had found nothing incriminating. Burger had nonetheless ordered his removal, probably to undermine Edelstein by depriving the Czech leader of one of his closest aides. As for Fredy Hirsch, he had made an unauthorized visit to the Bialystok children to see how they were getting along. (Hirsch had developed a fairly good relationship with Bergel and perhaps thought this would protect him from recrimination. But as we have seen, Bergel was no longer a force in the camp.)

On September 4 the list was posted. It numbered 5,007, about one-ninth of the camp's population. Of these, 933 were over 60, while 256 were under 15, the youngest being 2 months old. Some 4,800 or 96 percent of the deportees were Czechs.

Despite the inclusion of elderly residents and children, the transport was billed as a work detail for constructing a new camp. Supposedly Janowitz would head the new facility while Hirsch would direct its youth program. Former Ghetto Watch members were assured of being assigned similar posts at the new facility. The transport left on two trains on September 6, the largest contingent ever to leave on a single day. Some 20 passengers would be dead by the time the trains arrived at their destination.

Undoubtedly, fear of revolt was one reason for the deportation. The fact that it included so many of the former Ghetto Watch and the early work details, groups which consisted of young, able-bodied Czech males who had developed a sense of solidarity, reflects this. Also, there was Burger's hatred of Czech Jews and his wish to weaken their leader, Edelstein. But another and quite possibly more important factor was that the arrival and installation of the Gestapo records and record keepers had once again made the camp fearfully overcrowded. Density in the Jewish section had nearly reached the levels of the previous September.

The resurgence of intense congestion bothered the Nazis for with their prospects of victory shrinking, their interest in developing showplaces to deceive the outside world, and even their own people, about their treatment of the Jews was growing. Though few in Theresienstadt knew about it, the SS had already stepped up their efforts to use Theresienstadt for this purpose, and the previous spring had invited representatives of the German press and the German Red Cross to visit the camp. (These visits will be discussed in detail later.) But after the arrival of the Gestapo record office the following month, they could not help knowing that Theresienstadt had now become too congested to be shown to anyone, including fellow Germans. The September deportations eased this situation considerably by carting away almost as many people as the Gestapo record office had dispossessed.

The September transports had a shattering effect, however, on the camp's morale. The residents had been lulled into a sense of security by the softening of their situation and the long hiatus since the last such transports the previous February. When the list was posted, people crowded the transport office, some claiming that a mistake had been made, others simply begging for reconsideration. When it came time to load the trains, the SS turned out in force, forming narrow lines from the *Schleuse* to the railroad cars.

Nevertheless, once the transports had departed, the residents, as was their wont, began to resume their regular lives. They were encouraged by continuing postcards and a few letters from the deported, saying they were in Birkenau which, though Theresienstadters did not know it, was merely a branch of Auschwitz. (In any case, they did not really know what Auschwitz represented.) They were also encouraged by the news that Italy had imprisoned Mussolini and surrendered to the Allies. Since the residents were unaware of how insignificant Italy's contribution to the Axis war effort had been, they assumed its defection meant the war was now nearly over.

So Baeck went forward with his lecture series on great thinkers, *Brundibar* went into its final rehearsals, and Schaecter, whose chorus for the Verdi *Requiem* had been decimated by the deportation, began assembling a new group. (Fortunately, none of his four soloists had been sent off.) Another factor helping to rebuild the camp's shattered spirits was the arrival of considerable quantities of sardine packages from Portugal, arranged and paid for by the Joint Distribution Committee, an American-Jewish relief organization.

Although the transports had taken a disproportionate number of able-bodied workers, the camp still managed to function. The Jewish administration, in what Starke calls "one of its finest hours," saw to it that food was cooked and distributed, the sick attended to, and that the other services continued to operate. On September 29, Rosh Hashanah Eve, the Council of Elders posted a bulletin wishing all their fellow inmates a good new year and thanking them for their efforts in maintaining the "community."

The following month brought a further deportation, but this one actually raised the camp's spirits. On October 6 the Bialystok children and the 53 adults looking after them left Theresienstadt. The children, now well nourished, had been outfitted with new clothes on which no Jewish star had been placed. Their caretakers had been required to sign declarations vowing not to spread any "horror stories" about Theresienstadt. It was widely believed that their transport was going to Switzerland.

There were some bases for such a belief. Eichmann, acting on orders from Himmler, had been negotiating with the British to exchange 5,000 Jewish children for a number of Aryan civilians in Allied hands. He was planning to bring all these children to Theresienstadt literally as well as figuratively to fatten them up and otherwise prepare them for their transfer. The Bialystok boys represented the first contingent of such transferees. To house those who would come later, work crews had begun constructing a complex of small buildings in the Bauschowitz Basin, the low, grassy plain which lay just outside the town gates. The British, however, wanted the children to go to Palestine, while Eichmann and presumably Himmler wanted them to go to England. Sending them to Palestine would only antagonize the Arabs, whose support the Nazis had been successfully cultivating; sending them to Britain would, in their view, intensify anti-Semitism in that country.

When the British refused to take the children into Britain, the project was aborted. So despite their joyous departure, the Bialystok children and their attendants, including Aron Menczer and Ottilie Kafka, were taken to Auschwitz and gassed.(32)

The day before the Bialystok children departed, a transport arrived that would have considerable consequences for the camp. This transport brought the first of three groups of Danish Jews to Theresienstadt.

The Nazis had originally planned to send nearly all of Denmark's 8,000 Jews to Auschwitz but the Danish underground, acting on a tip from the German Marine attache in Copenhagen, had whisked most of them to Sweden in a daring overnight operation. The action had of necessity been carried out so quickly, however, that nearly 500 were left behind. Confronted with such opposition to their plans from the Danes, the Nazis decided to send the country's few remaining Jews to their "model ghetto." They apparently felt that such a small number would not add significantly to the congestion and would not stir up any unwanted resistance in Denmark.(33)

On their arrival the 456 Danes were given a reception unlike any accorded those who had come before them. Ushered into a courtyard, they were served a lavish meal alfresco on covered tables. Burger smiled cordially at them while Haindl actually walked from table to table, asking how they liked the food. Neither SS officer seemed to mind their cigarette smoking or their lack of yellow stars. (Christian, the Danish king, had prevented the Nazis from imposing the yellow star on his country's Jewish citizens by threatening to wear one himself.)

Once the meal ended, the Danes were given cards to send back to friends at home. They were then hustled inside and promptly searched, robbed of anything valuable, and outfitted with yellow stars. Yet they continued to enjoy privileges exceeding even those afforded the Prominenten. They could send letters fairly frequently, were lodged in comparatively comfortable quarters, and were exempted from deportation. They received four packages a month from the Danish Red Cross, all identifying the King of Denmark as the sender. They received parcels from the Swedish Red Cross as well. Although nearly one-third were actually immigrants from other countries who had fled to Denmark, all benefitted equally.

The two most notable Danish deportees were Peter Deutsch, former conductor of the Copenhagen Royal Orchestra, and Dr. Max Friediger, chief rabbi of Copenhagen. Friediger, who with his bearded and bespectacled countenance and his Ph.D. seemed more like a professor than a rabbi, became their leader and spokesman.

The Danes added a new and still higher rung to the camp's ethnic pecking order. But if a few used their privileges to procure sexual favors and other preferments, most conducted themselves superbly. Their cheerful good humor and their willingness to work, often at undesirable jobs, soon endeared them to the other inmates. They got along especially well with the Czechs even though they could communicate more easily with the Germans and Austrians whose language most of them could speak.

The real impact of the Danes, however, lay elsewhere--in Copenhagen, Geneva, and Berlin. Pressures were set in motion which would grow and culminate during the coming year.

On November 30 a letter from Theresienstadt arrived at the headquarters of the International Red Cross in Geneva. After acknowledging receipt of a shipment of medicines two months earlier, the letter went on to say, "We are so well supplied with medications that we ask you to refrain from further shipments. The health situation of the Jews consigned to our care must be characterized as completely favorable." The totally misleading letter, which had obviously been written under Nazi supervision, was signed by Eppstein and Murmelstein. Edelstein's name did not appear.

Things had been going downhill for Edelstein ever since Seidl's departure. As leader of the Czech Jews, he naturally bore the brunt of

Burger's hatred of them. The new commandant had not only deported many of his countrymen and his chief aide, Janowitz, but had also moved Germans and Austrians into key positions formerly held by Czechs. Burger had apparently also stirred up his own superiors against him for during the fall some bakery workers, looking out the window, saw and heard Eichmann sharply dressing down Edelstein and even threatening to have him shot.

The incident alarmed Edelstein's many loyal followers and the next day the leaders of Hechalutz, the largest Zionist organization in the camp, met with him to urge him to flee. They said they could help him escape with his wife and son through the sewers and could even provide them with funds to find a hiding place outside the town. But though he suspected a Nazi scheme to get rid of him, Edelstein refused to run away.

As it turned out, the Nazis needed to fabricate no plot to end Edelstein's career. They discovered a discrepancy in the ghetto records stemming from the deportations of the previous fall when he was camp Elder. The discovery showed that 55 persons were currently being carried falsely on the registers or were in some way unaccounted for.

There is still some confusion as to what exactly occurred, but it seems that dead people had been put on the transport list while others slated for deportation, had remained in the camp. Still others who had escaped from the camp were also being carried on the registers. It seems likely also that the ration cards of the escapees were being used by some of those who had eluded deportation. As Ze'ev Shek put it in an interview many years after the war, "I know of cases under Edelstein where he had simply not sent away people and they then "by error" remained and no one found out about it. I know many such cases. A false count was made at the railroad station. . . They had not reported children whose parents had died, falsified the situation, and sent away 960 instead of the 1,000 ordered."

How the SS learned of the "crime" remains unclear. According to one account, the disparity was discovered when an escapee arrested in Prague was found to be still listed on the camp's registers. Another account claims a new employee at the central registry came across the discrepancy and reported it lest he be blamed. Some even accuse Eppstein, saying that he had heard of it and thought it wiser to tell the Nazis himself than to let them find out about it on their own.

The discovery resulted in the immediate arrest of Edelstein and three registry employees. It also resulted in the most terrifying day and night in the camp's history.

Edelstein and his three compatriots were imprisoned on November 9, the fifth anniversary of *Kristalnacht*. The next day the SS announced that a census would be taken. All camp residents were to fill out a detailed form. The following day they were to assemble outside their buildings at 5:30 A.M. to march to the Bauschowitz Basin for an actual head count. Only the hospitalized and those necessary to maintain the camp were exempt.

On November 11 the residents assembled at the stipulated time and in rows of 5 marched through the gates. Many, especially the elderly, feared they would never return and some even tried to bring their entire belongings with them. But others were elated at being allowed to go outside the walls of their prison community. As they passed through the town gates and reassembled on the grassland, they could see farms and farmers, along with cows, trucks, and cyclists crossing the highway. These were sights that most had not seen since their incarceration. Such scenes also reassured them that the SS would not use such a public spot to undertake any horrible enterprise. Still, the presence of the Czech gendarmes who surrounded the field with guns in hand did lend a disturbing note.

By 11:30 the last groups had reached the field and by early afternoon the SS appeared. The residents were ordered to march in rows while SS men on motorcycles darted between the lines, keeping order. Everyone not marching was counting, including Eppstein.

Whatever festive mood had manifested itself at the outset soon evaporated. The SS census takers could never agree amongst themselves on the count and so became increasingly testy, cuffing freely anyone who incurred their displeasure. A 7-year-old girl screamed in horror as an SS man smashed the butt of his rifle into her mother's back.

The inmates became increasingly weary as well as worried and the older and weaker among them began collapsing from exhaustion. Those having to relieve themselves had to do so in public, although fellow inmates sought to shield them by forming rings. One woman delivered a baby on the field. The small rations they had received made them hungrier than usual. The cloudy, chilly weather only added to their misery.

At around 5:00 P.M. the SS men abandoned the effort and departed, leaving the residents still standing in the field. As night fell and fog accompanied by a light drizzle settled over them and as no order to return was heard, their tension turned into terror. Many feared death awaited them, saying, "Don't you see, we are perfect targets! They will shoot us all." Parents, themselves gripped by fear, desperately tried to comfort their sobbing children. Some of the younger Czechs began to think of bolting and wondered whether their fellow Czechs, the gendarmes who still girded the field, would fire at them. Exhaustion was also taking an increasing toll, prompting some to crawl into the half-finished buildings which had been designed for the Jewish children to be sent to England. In these primitive and open structures, they quickly fell asleep, many never to awaken. Others who collapsed on the spot were picked up by stretcher bearers.

Finally, at about 8:30 the order came to return to camp. The crowd began moving back as rapidly as it could. In the process some people were trampled on and only decisive action by the Ghetto Watch prevented outright catastrophe as they jammed the re-entry gate. By 11:00 P.M. only about half had returned. Many elderly and ill were still lying on the ground and the stretcher bearers worked through the night to bring them in. But it was almost dawn before even all those who could walk had managed to stumble back to their quarters.

Although 40 had died on the field during the night, many more succumbed during the next few days, largely from cold and lung inflammations. The total death toll from the aborted undertaking has been estimated at between 200 and 300. As for the census itself, it was done easily and satisfactorily a week or so later by simply having the residents appear alphabetically in groups in a designated courtyard to be counted. The hospitalized were counted in their beds. The census determined that Theresienstadt now contained 40,145 inmates.

Among those who had not taken part in the census count was the imprisoned Edelstein. But when he heard the sounds of marching feet from his basement cell in SS headquarters, he feared the worst for his people and in desperation put on his phylacteries and prayed. His SS guard, seeing him wrapping the phylacteries around his head and believing he was trying to commit suicide, burst into his cell. When Edelstein explained what he was doing, the guard actually became sympathetic. As Redlich later wrote in his diary, "Pity stirred in the heart of the guard and a wonderful thing happened. . . An enemy of the Jews learned to love the Jews. A miracle came to pass through the donning of phylacteries."

On November 24 the Jewish administration posted a bulletin marking the second anniversary of the camp's creation. The statement reminded the residents of how hard they had worked and how much they had accomplished. The recent arrest of Edelstein and the deportation of over 56,000 of their fellow inmates during the past two years were not mentioned.

The number of deportees would soon sweep past the 60,000 mark for on December 13 a new transport was announced. It left two days later carrying 2,504 Jews to an unknown fate. Then, on December 17 a further transport of 2,504 Jews was announced. It departed the next day.

The composition of the two December transports was similar to those of September. While not billed as "work detail transports," their destination was given as the "Reich Area." No appeals from either transport were allowed.

The December deportees did not, in fact, go to the "Reich Area," but to Auschwitz. There all but one of their members joined the September group in a unique settlement established exclusively for them in Birkenau. Since the "Auschwitz Family Camp," as it was usually called, has been described in numerous Holocaust works as well as in two lengthy interviews in the film "Shoah," its functions and fate will only be briefly summarized here.

The "Family Camp" was established for the September deportees and in some respects afforded living conditions unknown to Auschwitz or any other ghetto or concentration camp, including Theresienstadt itself. While food rations for the former Theresienstadters remained inadequate, they could receive food packages and nearly 2,500 such parcels reached them from or through the International Red Cross. Each resident was actually required to send one postcard and could send up to four more, either to friends or relatives in Theresienstadt or in the Protectorate. The September and December groups even organized separate soccer teams to play matches against each other.

Hirsch, who apparently impressed the SS with his perfect German, his athletic good looks, and his authoritative and somewhat militaristic demeanor and dress--he still wore his polished boots--got permission to set up two children's homes, one for small children, the other for 8- to 16-year-olds, plus a school and a library. Later the youngsters presented an opera based on the Snow White story with a lone harmonica player providing the music.

Though the Family Camp was strictly segregated from the rest of the Auschwitz complex, SS personnel from Eichmann on down regularly visited it. Eichmann showed a special interest in its children's program and told Hirsch to prepare a report for the International Red Cross. Several SS guards frequently dropped in to play with the children and to attend their programs. SS physicians also paid calls and conferred congenially with the Jewish doctors whom they addressed as *Herr Kollege*.

Nevertheless, many conditions at the Family Camp were far from idyllic. Space was at a minimum and despite the word "Family" in its title, men and women were housed separately. With almost no plumbing, the residents washed in cold, often half-frozen water and used outhouses, 300 of which had been hastily built for the 10,000 displaced Theresienstadters. Although they were not required to wear standard Auschwitz garb, their clothing was inadequate for the harsh Polish winter. By March over 20 percent of the September group and an almost equal percentage of the December group had died.

Still, the camp did maintain a superficial semblance of decent living and in March some representatives of the German Red Cross were brought in to inspect it. Then, almost immediately afterward, the SS began preparing to exterminate those from the September transport. A few days later, on March 7, they were separated from the December group and were told they were going to a new labor camp.

The September transport had included quite a few communists, many of them teachers. They and some non-communists had already formed a clandestine organization in the Family Camp which had forged links with the Auschwitz underground which was also largely, though not exclusively, communist. The Auschwitz underground learned of the extermination order and one of its leaders urged the communists from the September transport to stage a revolt, saying other Auschwitz prisoners would join them. Such a step, however, required the participation of Fredy Hirsch who, though only 28, had emerged as the camp's most influential leader.

Hirsch at first refused to believe the extermination report. When finally convinced, he expressed fears over what would happen to the children if the adults rebelled. When told that the children were doomed in any case but that a revolt might save many children in the future, he asked for an hour to consider. He was later found lying on his bunk, dying from an overdose of sleeping pills.

That night, March 8, the September group was taken to the gas chamber. Only 11 pairs of twins, whom Dr. Mengele wanted for his research, and 13 doctors and nurses who had been assigned work elsewhere in Auschwitz, were spared. Although no organized revolt occurred, some resisted their captors and many sang the Czech national anthem and the Zionist song, *HaTikvah*. Hirsch, who might have been of some comfort to the children in this agonizing moment, was still alive but comatose.(34)

For the time being, the December deportees remained where they were, but four of the group were nevertheless selected for special treatment. They were Jacob and Miriam Edelstein, their 12-year-old son Ariah, and Mrs. Edelstein's mother, Mrs. Olliner. Miriam, Ariah, and Mrs. Olliner had ridden with the other deportees in the first December transport and on arrival were sent with them to the Family Camp. Freddy Hirsch promptly made Miriam an assistant housemother, a position which afforded somewhat better living conditions.

Jacob had also been aboard the transport but had ridden in the last, or prisoners', car. On arrival he had been hustled off to an isolation cell and was soon being intensely interrogated regarding escapes and other events in Theresienstadt. He does not appear to have been tortured, although he was later taken to the camp hospital for ambulatory treatment. While he was there, an earlier Theresienstadt deportee who had been selected out for work managed to speak with him. He asked the former Elder whether he had known of the gas chambers. Edelstein vigorously shook his head.

Though Edelstein betrayed no one during his interrogation, he did agree to write letters back to Theresienstadt. Miriam also wrote three postcards, one of them to Fritz Ullmann in Geneva, saying she, her son, and mother were healthy and "that is what is really important." She said she had received no word from or about Jacob.

Eichmann called on her in February and asked if she had any requests. He also deceptively asked if she had had any news of her husband. She said no and asked to send him a letter. Eichmann agreed to accept the letter and to consider carefully her request to see him.

On June 20 a car pulled up at punishment block 11 where Edelstein was now lodged. The SS officer in charge told the former Elder he had been sentenced to death. Edelstein then began saying goodby to his fellow inmates, all of whom had come to love and admire him. (One later described him as "like a saint.") When the impatient SS officer snapped, "*Schnell, schnell*" (quick, quick), Edelstein calmly replied, "I am the master of my last moments." He then completed his leavetaking and departed.

The car deposited him at crematorium III and then went to fetch his family. Miriam was suffering from the measles and her doctor refused to let her be taken away. The SS men drove off but soon returned, saying they had orders to take all the family regardless of their condition. Miriam was removed on a stretcher.

When the four of them were assembled, the SS guards made derisive remarks while allowing Edelstein to watch as they shot his wife, his son, and mother-in-law. They then turned their guns on him. According to two eye witnesses, one a prisoner whose job it was to hold other prisoners being executed, all four members of the family met death in a calm and composed manner. Their bodies were burned a few hours later.

---

31. After the war Paul Tillich, a then widely admired Protestant theologian, criticized Baeck for his decision to remain silent. But others feel that his silence prevented a wave of suicide and other calamities. The Theresienstadt survivors when Bondy interviewed said, "Had we known the deportations really meant, we would not have been able to endure."

32. Kurt Weigel, who is today one of Israel's leading orthopedic surgeons, but who as a youngster knew and admired Aron Menczer in Theresienstadt, says Menczer seemed to know they were not going to Switzerland but at the same time did not believe they were going to another concentration camp.

33. The name of the marine attache who tipped off the Danes was Georg Duckwitz. He did not contact the underground directly but informed the country's former prime minister and the president of the Jewish community. Duckwitz was never, in my view, been properly honored for his brave and noble action.

34. A certain amount of controversy has arisen regarding some of the details of the Family Camp. Miroslav Karny questions whether the Auschwitz underground really promised to join the September transport revolt. (See his two articles on the subject of the Family Camp in the bibliography.) Also at Beit Terezin, the Theresienstadt museum at Kibbutz Givat Chaim in Israel, I was told about one survivor who believes that Hirsch's death was not a suicide.

CHAPTER 9
ON DISPLAY

Theresienstadt began 1944 with less than 35,000 inhabitants, its lowest number since it had been an all-Czech camp. Czechs, however, now comprised less than half its population since the December transports, like the one in September, had taken away mostly Czechs, many of them young able-bodied men. The camp's labor department, a particular haven for Edelstein loyalists, had been especially depleted.

Nevertheless, some 40 percent of the population were considered fully work-capable, while another 30 percent were deemed partly work-capable. Zucker had replaced Edelstein as deputy Elder and the camp continued to function. So did its lively cultural life. Schaecter, whose chorus for the Verdi *Requiem* had once again been decimated by deportations, began assembling a new one. The camp's Catholic Jews prepared and performed a Schubert Mass for New Year's Eve.

Although no sizable transports had come to the camp since the arrival of the Bialystok children in August, small numbers of Jews, sometimes only single individuals, were continually trickling in. Some were Jews in mixed marriages that had been dissolved through death or divorce; others were Jews in such marriages who had been caught violating one of the Reich's anti-Jewish regulations. Since these were numerous and complex, this was quite easy for a Jew to do. Simply being caught out on the street after 8:00 P.M. could end one's exemption from deportation.

Czech Jews in such marriages were especially vulnerable since their marriage partners and in-laws were usually less able to effectively complain or protest or defend them in other ways. At the start of 1944 a large number of Czech Jews in mixed marriages lost their exemption, and in mid-January some 140 arrived in Theresienstadt.

A few days later, on January 18, a trainload of 876 Jews arrived from Holland. They were the largest number yet to come from that country. They were also the first group of Dutch Jews, for previous transports from Holland had consisted of Jews who had immigrated there from other countries, chiefly Germany.

The 876, like the nearly 4,000 other Dutch Jews who would follow them during the next ten months, were considered privileged in having international reputations or having worked under the Nazis in operating Jewish institutions, or in having some other claims to special status. (Some 100,000 other Dutch Jews were being dispatched to far worse places than Theresienstadt.) Yet, unlike the German and Austrian o had also been considered privileged, this initial group of Jews received a red carpet treatment almost as special as that given the Danes. Eppstein made a welcoming speech to which their leader, David Cohen, responded. A smiling Burger helped the aged out of the train while an equally genial Haindl played with the children.

Once they entered the Schleuse, however, they were treated much like the German and Austrian Jews. If anything, they fared somewhat worse. Why, then, were they given such a warm welcome on the railroad platform? The answer lies in the fact that cameramen were filming their arrival. The Nazis were planning to put their model ghetto on public view.

Since their massive setback at Stalingrad, the Germans had begun giving more thought to using Theresienstadt as a showplace ghetto. The subsequent spread of reports about the extermination camps further encouraged such efforts. As mentioned earlier, the Nazis had invited some German press representatives to the camp the previous May. The journalists visited the rooms of a few Prominenten, saw the bank in operation, attended a theatre performance, and witnessed the trial of an accused thief in the ghetto court. The trial, although screened and selected in advance, did not proceed as planned, for the defense attorney pleaded hunger as the excuse for his client's crime, and hunger supposedly did not exist in Theresienstadt. Still, the Nazis did not seem unduly alarmed.

No accounts of the visit appeared in the German press. Instead, the Nazis were probably counting on the journalists to give glowing reports of what they saw to their fellow journalists from neutral countries who were stationed in Berlin. Such first-hand, personally delivered oral reports would undoubtedly impress these neutral correspondents, and through them eventually journalists in hostile countries as well, far more than would laudatory accounts of Theresienstadt published in the controlled Nazi press.

The Nazis apparently felt the visit went well despite the defense attorney's unexpected plea at the trial, and the following month they went a step further and invited two German Red Cross officials to inspect the camp. The two were Walter Hartmann, head of the German Red Cross's foreign department, and his deputy, Dieter Neuhaus. The pair arrived on June 28 and Eichmann, along with one of his top aides, personally escorted them around. Presumably, the SS expected Hartmann and Neuhaus to subsequently tell their Red Cross colleagues from Switzerland and Sweden how well off the Jews of Theresienstadt were.

If this was the Nazis' intention, they had miscalculated for the German Red Cross had become a sanctuary for anti-Nazi Germans, and Hartmann and Neuhaus apparently fell into that category. The two were horrified at what they saw in Theresienstadt. Eichmann, for example, took them to a Prominenten house to meet Baroness Bleichroeder, apparently thinking they would be favorably impressed. But the two Germans were shocked at finding the granddaughter of Bismarck's financier living with her family in one room.

On returning to Berlin, the two Red Cross officials kept their real impressions to themselves as far as the SS was concerned but conveyed them secretly to a Swiss Red Cross representative named dePilar, who was stationed in the German capitol. They told him of finding congestion, malnourishment, and generally wretched conditions, as well as an elaborate infrastructure created by the Jewish administration. They had not been able to determine whether any residents had been deported from Theresienstadt to the East.

DePilar relayed their findings to Geneva. Whatever direct impact his report may have had on the International Red Cross remains unknown, but a copy of it reached Reigner of the World Jewish Congress, possibly sent by dePilar himself. It caused Reigner and the representatives of other Jewish organizations in Geneva, as well as Kopecky of the Czech government-in-exile, to step up their pressure on the International Red Cross to arrange a visit to the camp.

Pressure for such a visit emerged from another source with the arrival of the Danes in the fall. They had hardly reached the camp before King Christian and the Danish Red Cross began seeking to send a delegation to see how their Jewish countrymen were faring. The Nazis, on their part, were growing more amenable to such a visit as word of the gas chambers continued to spread abroad and as the war continued to go against them. They hoped to show off Theresienstadt as an example of their humane policies toward the Jews, as, in short, a model "Jewish settlement area."

On November 4 Eichmann responded to the Danes' repeated requests with a conditional 'yes.' He would allow a visit but refused to set a date, saying only that it could not take place before spring. The Danes pressed for an earlier date but he refused to budge. Then, in January the Swedish government received a report that Theresienstadt was going to be liquidated and that its 10,000 residents (sic) stood in imminent danger of death. When the Swedish foreign minister asked the German foreign office about it, he was told that no such plan existed and that only ten (sic!) Theresienstadt residents had been sent to the East. Still, the report and the publicity it had received startled the Nazis and subsequently the German ambassador to Sweden dropped hints that if the Swedish government formally asked to visit Theresienstadt, such a visit could be arranged. Again, no date was mentioned, for before Theresienstadt could be shown to foreign visitors, much work needed to be done.(35)

The work of making Theresienstadt look more like what it was supposed to be had already begun. Shortly before the end of 1943, the Nazis launched a *Stadtverschoenerung* or city beautification. The task of carrying it out naturally fell to Murmelstein as head of the camp's Technical Department. He tried at first to dodge the assignment, fearing that with the limited time and resources available he would never succeed in fulfilling the Nazis' orders and would therefore suffer the consequences. But when he sought to pass the project on to Zucker, the latter demanded a broad range of authority that Eppstein could not accept.

Although unversed in the technical work that would be required to carry out the beautification, Murmelstein did possess substantial administrative skills. Realizing that his own future hinged on the success of the project, he suppressed his natural authoritarian tendencies and adopted a democratic device which Edelstein had first utilized. This was the cabinet coordinating conference in which department heads involved in a particular project would meet regularly to discuss problems and coordinate efforts.(36)

On February 8 an event occurred which would facilitate Murmelstein's task as well as foster his own advancement. Burger had shown little aptitude or ardor for the beautification, so Guenther, who still headed the SS in Prague, used this as an excuse to send him back to Berlin. In his place Guenther put his own deputy, Karl Rahm.

Like his two predecessors, the short, stocky Rahm was an Austrian. Unlike them he had only an elementary school education. A former Social Democrat and skilled toolmaker from the Vienna working class suburb of Klosterneuburg, Rahm had become a 1st Lieutenant through a certain amount of native intelligence combined with a zest for work more typical of a German than an Austrian.

The new commandant took the beautification project personally in hand. He continually toured the various areas of activity, issuing commands even on minor details. His interest in and knowledge of manual work led him to make changes, most of them improvements, in many technical matters such as the operation of the carpentry shop. He also developed a new type of bunk that was far superior to the ones being used.

But wherever he went he generated fear for he had brought with him from Prague a reputation for brutality. His reputation was not unfounded since he soon showed himself to be extremely hot-tempered. Once he got caught in a rain shower while riding through the SS farm. Drenched, he galloped up to a shed only to find a group of Jewish farm workers taking shelter under its roof. Enraged, he grabbed one of them, Baron Rudolf von Hirsch from Bavaria, and beat him so severely that von Hirsch could no longer do farm work but had to take a position in the camp library instead. (Farm work, because of its access to food, was by far a more desirable position even for a baron.)

Rahm's temper showed little respect for position. Some time after his appointment, Eppstein returned with a black eye from a morning conference. (Eppstein's wife, however, claimed he had bumped into a clothes chest in the middle of the night.) On another occasion, when inspecting a cleaning operation with Murmelstein, he noticed a flashlight dangling from the rabbi's belt. He immediately ripped it off with a snarl, evidently feeling that no Jew should wear such a sign of authority.

Yet Murmelstein would later refer to Rahm as not completely heartless, and while some, such as Adler, find this outrageous, others agree. Eppstein claimed that Rahm's bark was worse than his bite, while Lederer notes that Rahm's bursts of temper, though frightening, were short-lived and often followed by signs of regret.

Unlike Seidl and Burger, Rahm allowed ordinary residents to address him. During a subsequent deportation, a young woman approached him on the railroad platform and said, "Herr Kommandant, I am a Viennese and you are from Klosterneuburg. Help me. Please let me stay." The deportation proceedings immediately ground to a halt as the SS men, the gendarmes, and the deportees waited to see Rahm's reaction to such an audacious act. But Rahm, though somewhat taken off guard, barked, "What do you do here?" and when she replied "Nurse," he told her to put down her knapsack. Then, after shouting "Carry on" to the others present, he turned to a gendarme and said, "*Raus mit ihr*" (Out with her).

Rahm's appointment proved advantageous for Murmelstein in two ways. The first stems from an incident in Vienna when Murmelstein was deputy director of the Jewish Gemeinde and Rahm, then a young sergeant, was an aide to Eichmann. Eichmann customarily let Jewish functionaries stand during conferences with him no matter how long such meetings lasted. But during one exceptionally long conclave with Murmelstein, he had turned to Rahm and said, "Fetch the rabbi a chair." This left the impressionable Rahm with a certain respect for the portly rabbi.

The second and more important factor facilitating their new relationship was language. As anyone who has spent time in Vienna knows, the city's dialect exercises a deep hold over its people. Even highly respected professors at the University of Vienna often lapse into it during their lectures. With comparatively little formal education--he continually referred to the camp's medical laboratory as the *Kueche* or kitchen--Rahm lapsed into the dialect constantly, often making it difficult for others to understand him. But Murmelstein had spent nearly 20 years in Vienna and was a gifted linguist in any case. He could converse easily with the new Kommandant. So, despite occasional run-ins and relatively minor eruptions, the two got along well as they worked industriously to make the beautification a success.

The beautification project brought many changes. Some were largely superficial and symbolic. Thus the Order of the Day became "the Daily Bulletin of the Jewish Self-administration" and the Ghetto Court became the Community Court. The sign saying *Transport* over the transport office was taken down and the transport numbers of the Theresienstadt inmates became their identification numbers instead. The saluting requirement was also abolished.

Other changes were more substantive. Food parcels from abroad as well as from the Reich were expedited and their contents were less carefully searched. Such delicacies as marmalade, condensed milk, and chocolate began reaching some residents. Some were also allotted small plots between the embankments to grow food.

The library was transferred to a more spacious building and this allowed thousands of books hitherto lying in a garage to be put on the shelves. German physicians visited the camp on March 18 to inspect its medical service and subsequently more medical supplies became available. Additional musical instruments, along with operatic costumes, wigs, and other theatrical gear, also arrived. They allowed Schaecter to stage a costumed production of *Brundibar* with a nearly complete orchestra instead of a single piano providing the musical accompaniment. On April 30 a new concert/recreation hall/ community center was inaugurated with music, poetry recitations, and a speech by Murmelstein. The rabbi turned administrator had obviously emerged from the shadows and was rapidly gaining stature and influence.

But the beautification was running into the problem that had been plaguing the camp for almost two years: overcrowding. The December deportations had alleviated the situation, but the arrival of transports from Holland, along with the ongoing influx of individuals and small groups from other countries, had partly offset their effect. Fortunately, construction crews finished the complex of buildings in the Bauschowitz Basin that had been designed for the children to be sent to England, and most of the camp's workshops were transferred to them, thereby freeing up more space in the camp itself for living quarters. But there was still no way that Theresienstadt, especially with its whole northern end occupied by the SS, could harbor 35,000 Jews without showing signs of severe congestion.

The situation was driven home to the SS in early spring when a group of German army officers came to the camp, apparently to check on its work for the war effort. One of them wandered into a barracks by mistake and was startled to see rows of 3-tiered double bunks with hardly any space between them. He and/or his fellow officers conveyed their reaction to the SS. The latter responded by ordering another deportation.

The SS may have been planning a deportation in any case since they realized that not only did Theresienstadt contain too many people but that it also contained too many of the wrong people. It had too many ill or infirm inhabitants for a community whose population was supposed to be enjoying excellent health conditions. It also had too many children whose parents had died or been deported. Their presence could lead to embarrassing questions concerning the where-abouts of their elders.

On May 12 Rahm announced a deportation of 7,500 in three transports, the first of which was to leave in three days. Although some effort was later made to speak of it as a "work detail transport," it was to include many sick adults, including 1,200 TB patients, as well as orphaned children. These were groups that had hitherto remained largely exempt. Rahm apparently even wanted to get rid of unattractive people. Seeing a dwarf on the street, he shouted at him, "You there. You are spoiling the beautification. Report to the Council of Elders for deportation." On the other hand, he did not single out the Czechs since he did not share Burger's particular aversion to them and, in any case, he realized that he needed the younger Czechs to complete the beautification and maintain the camp in satisfactory shape.

Following Rahm's guidelines, the Jewish administration prepared a transport of 2,500 for departure on May 15 and another transport of an equal number for departure the following day. But when it came to completing the third transport, the task began to bog down. With less than 30,000 remaining in the camp, it was becoming impossible to assemble 2,500 without including people who were either officially exempt or who were truly needed for the camp's operation or who had influential contacts with higher functionaries. The list had to be constantly revised as friends, relatives, bosses, patrons, as well as the deportees themselves, pleaded their cases.

When a group of 2,500 plus a reserve was finally assembled, Rahm bicycled over in late afternoon to the Hamburg barracks, which was serving as the evacuation center, to inspect them. Flanked by members of the Council of Elders, he ordered those selected to march past him. He stopped some to ask about their work and selected some of *them*, especially robust young men and handsome, healthy women, to stay. He repeated this procedure two more times.

As darkness fell, searchlights came on. They swept over the area, illuminating in turn the anxious faces of the scheduled deportees, as well as those of worried friends, family, and reserve members watching from the balconies. One who was present describes the macabre scene as a combination of the November census and an Auschwitz selection.

By 11:00 P.M. Rahm had removed 600, or nearly a quarter of those chosen. Zucker then reminded him that the transport, even with the reserve, would not be complete. Rahm immediately exploded in anger. Cursing the Council of Elders, he lunged first at Zucker, who stood his ground, and then at Eppstein, who stepped back. He then calmed down and by 12:30 had put 450 back on the list. But his exemption of several others the next day, plus the hiding out of some already selected, forced the administration to draw heavily from the reserve. The transport left on May 18.

German Jews comprised 40 percent of the three transports. Among them were approximately one-third of the disabled war veterans who had up to now been automatically exempt. Austrians constituted another 20 percent, while Czechs made up only a third. The remaining 559 came from the recently arrived Dutch. Though these transports were announced as going "to the area of Dresden," they followed the others to Birkenau. There all 7,500 joined those of the December deportations in the "Family Camp."

On May 11, the day before the transports were announced, Himmler flashed the final go ahead for the foreign inspection. It would take place on June 23.

With a date set and a deadline to meet, work on the beautification accelerated. Artistically decorated signposts pointing "To the Cafe," "To the Baths," etc. started to appear. So did benches, grass, and 1200 beds of roses. The shop windows began bulging with desirable goods and even with advertising posters to incite "customers'" interest. Those who had received allotment gardens now received time off from work to tend them. The prayer room, the offices of the Jewish functionaries, the bank, and various other sites, including the soccer field, received extensive refurbishing.

The dead also received consideration. Hebrew lettering was inscribed on the ritual chamber of the crematorium, while a monument was erected and a grove of trees was planted outside the urn depository. A new, richly decorated hearse replaced the old ones which temporarily disappeared.

The children came in for special attention. The SS authorized the construction of an extensive playground complete with sandboxes, splash pools, swings, rocking horses, and other delights. In lavishness and expense it outdid any being built for German children in the Reich. The youngsters were carefully rehearsed in how to behave before the foreign visitors. They were, for example, to call Rahm "Uncle Rahm," and on receiving tins of sardines they were too exclaim, "Not sardines again, Uncle Rahm," as if they had already received too many sardines. The Jewish administration used different children for each rehearsal so that a greater number would receive the extra food.

The Jewish Rescue Committee in Budapest had scraped together $10,000 for Theresienstadt, and as part of the new policy to promote public awareness of the camp, Eichmann allowed the Committee to send it along with a letter. Although the SS, of course, pocketed the money, it ordered the Jewish administration to send back a letter containing not only warm thanks but a glowing description of life in Theresienstadt. For example, the writers described the camp's health conditions as "thoroughly favorable" and attributed this to its "modern health service" equipped with "fully adequate supplies of medication and food." Eppstein, Zucker, and four others signed the letter, Murmelstein not being one of them. It was sent one week after the last May transport to Birkenau.

In early June, however, SS hopes for deceiving world opinion suffered a setback. Word had leaked out to the Vatican and to the Polish underground regarding the fate of the September transports, and on June 9 the Polish emigre press in London reported the gassing in Auschwitz of 7,000 Jews from Theresienstadt the previous March. The Czech government-in-exile in London immediately began pressing for more information, while its alarmed representative in Geneva, Kopecky, met with a still more alarmed Ullman and Reigner on June 13. Kopecky had received a further report that the September transport was gassed following a six-month quarantine period, and that the December transport--his information did not yet include the May transports--would meet the same fate when its six-month quarantine period ended on June 20. This was only one week away.

As a result of their meeting, Kopecky sent a telegram back to his government in London conveying his information and "appealing most urgently that this news may be broadcast immediately through BBC and American radio in order to prevent at the last moment this new massacre." The BBC's Czech transmission broadcast the news the next day followed by a warning from the Czech government that after the war it would punish severely all those responsible.

The broadcasts were, of course, picked up immediately by the Gestapo monitoring service and relayed to those higher up. The latter responded by canceling whatever plans they may have had for liquidating the camp on that date and by ordering the residents to send postcards back to Theresienstadt dated June 21 to show that no gassing had occurred. The SS also became more concerned than ever with the upcoming visit to Theresienstadt. Representatives from the SS office in Prague and even from the Berlin headquarters began calling almost daily at Theresienstadt to check and spur on the beautification.

Virtually no effort was now spared to make the visit a success. Buildings were painted or whitewashed, fences were torn down or repaired, and every nook and cranny was inspected. As the day of the delegation's arrival neared, the streets through which they would pass were thoroughly cleaned and the sidewalks washed with soap and water. Jewish women had to use their hairbrushes for this task. The streets were then roped off so that no one would walk on them.

Cripples and poorly dressed people were told to keep out of sight, while nicer clothing was distributed to those who would be on view. Thus, Lauscherova, a children's matron who was assigned to lead her charges along a walk where the Commission would repeatedly see them, received black high-heeled shoes, a light dress, and a white coat. These, she later said, "were my props."

The day before the scheduled visit the gendarmes suddenly and temporarily disappeared. The Danes were transferred to better quarters, but about 70 were ordered to report the next morning to an out-of-the-way location and to bring food with them. One Danish woman and her two children were temporarily transferred out of the camp entirely. Her husband, an engraver, had been sent earlier to Bergen-Belsen to work on a highly secret counterfeiting project. (The Germans were planning to destroy the British economy by flooding the country with counterfeit pounds.) The SS was obviously taking no chances.

The reasons for placing most of the other Danes under lock and key, however, were fears about how they would behave. As one young Danish woman later told Gerda Haas, "At rehearsal when we were told what to say to the Commission and what to answer to questions, I'd let it be known that I'd tell the truth, and on inspection day a Jewish orderly picked me up and kept me in a room with dozens of other people who had also refused to go along with this comedy. Oh, the *Judenrat* (Council of Elders) apologized, but they explained that Commandant Rahm had threatened mass punishment to the ghetto should anything go wrong, so they wanted us out of the way of the visitors."

As darkness fell, a feeling of tense expectation spread through the camp. The lights in Eppstein's office burned into the wee hours as the Jewish Elder carefully dictated a list of possible questions that the visitors might ask and the answers he should give them. Then, with his secretary coaching him, he committed the answers to memory. The Jews themselves, or at least their leaders, were also taking no chances.

At 11:00 o'clock on a bright, early summer morning, two limousines pulled into Theresienstadt. The foreign delegation had arrived.

It was not much of a delegation, consisting as it did of only three people, two Danes and one Swiss. The Danes were Frants Hvass, who headed the political section of the Danish Foreign Office, and Dr. E. Juel-Henningsen, an administrator from the Ministry of Health. The Swiss was Maurice Rossel, deputy head of the International Red Cross Berlin Office. Rossel had come in place of his boss, who said he had to make another trip. The Swedish embassy, though invited, had not sent anyone, claiming the visit conflicted with a Swedish holiday. After all the concerns voiced over Theresienstadt, no neutral country or organization seems to have been that eager to inspect it.

The group first called at the refurbished offices of the Chancery, where a smiling Eppstein, looking like a German mayor in a frock coat and cylinder hat, greeted them. The SS had decided to let Eppstein do most of the talking, and from their point of view the decision proved a wise one.

The Jewish Elder gave the visitors a carefully crafted and deceptively distorted description of his community. To cover up the deportations, he added over 7,000 to the ghetto's existing population and to enhance the ghetto's image as a haven for the elderly, he placed the fictional people in the over-60 category. He expanded the Council of Elders to 66 to make the Jewish administration look more democratic, independent, and vigorous. He spoke of the SS farm as if it were designed to produce food for the residents and not for their captors. He mentioned an experiment then underway of raising silkworms as if the project were producing the ghetto's only export to the Reich. (In reality, the silkworm experiment was a failure and would soon be aborted.) His talk, which included many more falsified figures and fictitious or semi-fictitious facts, ended with the words, "What you are going to see here is a normal, provincial German city."

The visiting party then set out to inspect Eppstein's "normal, provincial German city."

The two limousines now became three, since Eppstein had been given a car and chauffeur for the occasion. The visitors numbered at least 14 in all, for six SS officials and a member of the German Foreign Office and a member of the German Red Cross had accompanied the foreign delegates to the camp, while Rahm had joined them in Eppstein's office. Germans thus outnumbered non-Germans by almost 3 to 1. Only Rahm, however, was in uniform.

The caravan criss-crossed the camp in a carefully predetermined route. They visited the bank, the newly erected band pavilion, the laundry, the living quarters of some Prominenten, the ground floor of a barracks, one or more hospital wards, the allotment gardens, the post office, the cafe, the pharmacy, and other sites. They saw a group of healthy, tanned young women with rakes over their shoulders singing and laughing as they marched off to work in the fields; bakers wearing white gloves while handling white bread; elderly people listening to band music; chess players studiously plotting their next moves; and soccer fans erupting in cheers as a goal was kicked. They saw Schechter rehearsing the Verdi *Requiem* and they saw and heard the children's cast of *Brundibar* singing the opera's finale.

Their tour ended with a visit to the children's pavilion where they observed healthy-looking youngsters happily at play. They also heard them ask, "When are you going to play with us again, Uncle Rahm?" and heard Rahm reply, "I can't right now, children. I have no time."

The visitors did not know that the "mayor" who greeted them had barely escaped receiving a beating just the previous month and that his chauffeur, who so deferentially opened the door for him, was considered one of the cruelest SS men in the camp.

They did not know that the bank manager who was puffing away on a cigar when they called, and who offered them cigarettes, had just completed a three-month jail term for, of all things, smoking!

They did not know that the SS had held up the distribution of parcels for several days so that they would see scores of them being passed out when they called at the post office.

They did not know that most of the men peering so assiduously over their chess boards had never played the game in their lives or that the people so contentedly lying between clean white sheets in their hospital beds were actually healthy individuals, the real sick having been moved out of sight for the day.

They did not know that the schoolhouse they passed, which displayed a sign "Closed for summer vacation," had never been used as a school since the Czech townspeople left, that the dolls in the hands of little girls playing so joyfully with them had been given them only an hour or so before, and would be taken from them an hour later, and that the kindly "Uncle Rahm," whom the children had beseeched to play with them, had during the previous nine months deported nearly 1,500 of their playmates to their death.

And they certainly did not know that advance men had preceded them every step of the way, giving signals so that the young women with rakes over their shoulders would march past, the soccer goal would be kicked, and the finale of *Brundibar* would be sung at just the right time. As Rudolf Franek, the conductor of *Brundibar*, later recalled, "I got the first signal when the car entered the street; the second signal meant they were mounting the stairs; and at the third signal I dropped my arm and the music started. . . ."

At 7:00 P.M. the visitors departed for Prague where the SS treated them to a lavish dinner. They had spent eight hours in Theresienstadt, only 5 hours, 40 minutes of which were actually devoted to inspecting the town. But if it was a short inspection tour, it was the most

176 --George E Berkley

elaborate, drawn-out farce ever staged since the time Catherine the Great took her foreign visitors on a trip down the Volga to see the mock villages put up by her prime minister Potemkin.

Did the visitors suspect that the "normal, provincial German city" they were inspecting was in reality a Potemkin village? Did they seek at all to probe beneath Theresienstadt's smiling surface?

The two Danes mostly concerned themselves with their fellow Danes. They inspected their quarters and talked with quite a few, including Rabbi Friediger, to whom they brought personal messages of goodwill from King Christian and from the Protestant bishop of Copenhagen. But these meetings lasted only a few minutes and there was always one or more SS men present. Still, they managed to open up some holes in the curtain of deception. On entering the especially pleasant room of one Dane, they asked him how long he had lived there and then heard him reply, "Since yesterday."

The Danish officials also asked some questions which Eppstein and the SS found hard to answer. An inquiry about the camp's mortality figures produced only a vague reply. Also, when the physician of the pair expressed an interest in seeing the maternity ward that Eppstein had mentioned, he was told that it would not be possible at this time. (Theresienstadt, of course, had no maternity ward.)

Rossel, in a brief, private moment with Eppstein, asked him what he thought would happen to the ghetto population. Eppstein said he knew no answer to the question and that he personally "saw no way out." When they stopped at the pharmacy, Rossel asked about a shipment of medical supplies from the International Red Cross. His question produced a certain amount of confusion for those at the pharmacy knew nothing about it. (It had apparently been confiscated by the SS.)

Most inmates they encountered, however, did little to encourage their skepticism. Murmelstein later claimed he tried to convey the real truth about the camp through his inflections, and the doctor who showed them the hospital ward added, in pointing out how wonderful everything was, the Hebrew word *Lo*, which means no or not. But hardly any Jews, let alone Gentiles, knew the meaning of this word, while whatever shadings of speech Murmelstein may have used could hardly convey the real nature of Theresienstadt. The Danish visitors did notice a certain "psychological pressure" in the inmates they briefly spoke with.

On their return to Copenhagen the Danish officials reported on what they had seen. While obviously impressed, they indicated they had not been completely taken in. Doctor Henningsen expressed "complete astonishment over the Jewish accomplishments" thanks to which "the situation has improved, especially in the past year." While the high population density posed some peril in terms of sanitation, "there can be no doubt that the Jewish administration is confronting the sanitation danger as effectively as possible under the circumstances."

His colleague Hvass also expressed total amazement at what the Jewish administration had achieved. But, he added, "whether or not their positive attitude persists depends on whether the population regards their stay in Theresienstadt as permanent."

Their findings were sufficiently positive to permit the Nazi-controlled Danish Press Service to report on July 13 that "two Danish representatives, a physician and an administrator from the Foreign Ministry, have returned from a trip to Theresienstadt where deported Danish Jews have been sent. Conditions there are described as relatively favorable and rumors that a number of Jews will be sent to forced labor have been denied." The report was promptly picked up and published by the Swedish press and a few other foreign journals.

A few days later the two Danes went or possibly were sent to Stockholm to report on Theresienstadt in person. They were even allowed to meet with a small group of Swedish Jewish leaders at the Danish legation. They told of the positive sights they had seen and the encouraging assurances they had received. But Hvaas intimated that they had opted for a prudent approach in making their reports so as to permit continued deliveries of food and medical supplies to their incarcerated Jewish countrymen. Hvaas also let it be known that all their conversations in Theresienstadt had been "discreetly observed."

That the Danes were hardly free agents was certainly well known, and consequently anything they said would be judged accordingly. Much more importance would be attached to Rossel's reaction since he was a Swiss citizen representing an international organization that carried considerable clout, at least when it came to influencing world opinion. By early July Rossel had finished a 15-page report. It proved to be a glowing testimonial to the model ghetto, its Jewish administrator and, most significantly, its Nazi overseers.

"This Jewish city is truly astonishing," said Rossel. "Out of Jews from various countries a communist-type society has been fashioned which is under a 'Stalin' [Eppstein] of much greater worth." He found living conditions a bit congested but still comfortable, with more than enough furniture. As for food, "One found in the ghetto foods that were almost impossible to find in Prague." As for clothing, "The smarter women were all wearing silk stockings, hats, scarves, and carried modern handbags," while some of the young men seemed "flashily dressed." As for the population's health, "Certainly there had seldom been a people who had better medical care than those at Theresienstadt." Moreover, the residents could count on their good fortune continuing for Theresienstadt was, he said, a final destination camp from which no one is normally deported.

"We will say," wrote Rossel in summing up, "that our amazement was extraordinary to find in the ghetto a city that was leading an almost normal existence. We told the SS officers accompanying us that the most surprising thing about our visit was the difficulty we had experienced in getting to make it."

The Swiss representative's use of "we" and "our" would seem to indicate that he was purporting to speak for the two Danes as well, though neither of them had seen his report or consulted with him since they all had left Prague. His concluding paragraph is especially informative. "Our report will not change anyone's judgment; each remains free to condemn the position the Reich has taken to resolve its Jewish problem. If, however, this report dissipates a little the mystery surrounding the ghetto of Theresienstadt, it will be enough."

The reference to the Reich's "Jewish problem" indicates that this supposedly neutral and impartial observer was far from being such. The Jews of Germany had numbered less than one percent of their country's pre-Hitler population but had won 25 percent of their country's Nobel prizes. They had also helped develop its economy, contributed greatly to its cultural life and, when permitted, fought valiantly in its wars. Only anti-Semites believed that the Reich had ever had a "Jewish problem." This Swish Red Cross official was apparently one of them.

Although Rossel's report was supposed to be confidential, intended only for the International Red Cross in Geneva, a copy almost immediately came into the hands of the SS. Whether Rossel himself gave it to them remains unknown. What is known is that he sent pictures he had taken of Theresienstadt to the German Foreign Office, which thanked him warmly and said they would make use of them to counter the "horror propaganda of the Allies."

They wasted no time in doing so. They sent copies of the pictures to the Swedish embassy and on July 19 held a press conference for foreign journalists at which they used Rossel's materials to deny what the International Red Cross, among others, knew to be a fact: Jews were being gassed en masse in Poland.

The (justifiably) guarded tone of the reports of the two Danes and the (unjustifiably) enthusiastic tone of Rossel's report had immediate consequences in Auschwitz. Early in the year Himmler had told the IRC that he would permit them to inspect not only Theresienstadt but a "Jewish work camp," evidently meaning the family camp at Birkenau. After the success of the Theresienstadt visit, however, he apparently felt the family camp was no longer needed and on July 7 gave orders for its elimination. After a work selection as well as a selection of twins for Dr. Mengele, over 11,000 more Theresienstadt Jews were sent to the gas chambers.

Reaction to the Red Cross visit in Theresienstadt itself was mixed. For Leo Baeck, it was a catastrophe. "The commission never bothered to climb a single flight of stairs," he remarked after the war. "Perhaps they knew the real conditions--but it looked as if they did not want to know the truth. The effect on our morale was devastating. We felt forgotten and forsaken."

Eppstein, however, did not share these sentiments. He invited a few long-time associates--they had accompanied him from Berlin--to his quarters and assured them that the visitors were seasoned observers "who would not be fooled by what they saw and heard." According to one who attended, the Jewish Elder did not feel any need to justify his own role in the charade.

Eppstein's attitude seems to have been more representative of the camp's reaction than Baeck's. For the beautification had taken hold of the residents and, in a manner reminiscent of that of the Colonel in *The Bridge on the River Kwai*, many seemed to have become genuinely excited over its execution. The oppressed had unwittingly become almost eager partners of their oppressors. In their defense, it should be noted that the beautification had brought them benefits, that it also brought some foreign attention to the camp, and that, like Eppstein, they did tend to believe that it could not really deceive anyone. Their mood was further buoyed up by Allied landings in France two weeks previously, as well as the Russian penetration into Poland.

A day or two after the visit, the Jewish administration held a get together in the largest dining hall for all those who had worked on the project. Eppstein, Zucker, and Murmelstein all spoke in turn. Murmelstein wisely limited himself to thanking the workers in both German and Czech, and then adding, with reference to the tensions generated in having to do so much in such a short time, "I'm grateful to you for not beating me up." Schwenk staged a satirical sketch showing the same furniture being dragged from place to place to deceive the visitors. When an alarmed Eppstein stood up to stop the program,

Murmelstein shrewdly took the side of the performers, offering to assume full responsibility for any adverse consequences. It was, in all, a festive occasion.

In a way, the visit had deceived the visited as much as the visitors. This too would have consequences for the camp. Two months earlier a former Theresienstadt firefighter named Vitezslav Lederer had escaped from Auschwitz. After making his way to Prague and establishing contact with the Czech resistance, he got himself smuggled back into the ghetto. (The Czech barber who came to shave the SS arranged it.) Once back, he told a small group which included the head of the fire department, some members of the Ghetto Watch, and the head of the economics department, Schliesser, about the Auschwitz gas chambers, including the liquidation of the September transport. They believed him, although many of those to whom they repeated his story did not since post-dated postcards from the September transport had started arriving in the camp.

The Red Cross visit undid most of his efforts for it convinced even his former fire brigade comrades that they had nothing to fear. "The Nazis are losing the war; they will need us for an alibi," they now responded. "Why even think of revolt when the IRC is taking an interest in us?" When Lederer sensed that his friends were growing cold to his exhortations and to him personally, he departed to join the Czech underground. He left behind a Ghetto population more confident than ever of its future.

The SS rewarded the residents for their good behavior during the visit by granting the Ghetto a work-free one-and-a-half-day holiday. The Nazis also retained many of the beneficial changes which the beautification had produced. Those with allotment gardens could continue tending them, with the result that vegetables other than turnips became available. Those given more comfortable beds in place of the bunks could, in many instances, continue using them. The band pavilion and the concert/theatre/community hall erected for the Red Cross visit remained, as did most of the musical instruments, stage lighting, costumes, and other theatrical equipment and gear. However, many of the toys distributed to the children, including the dolls handed out to the little girls, were snatched away as soon as the delegation departed.

The nightly curfew was extended to 9:00 P.M. for the summer and the population was allowed greater access to the embankments and other hitherto restricted areas. One could now wander fairly freely in the evening, only taking care not to stumble over others lying on the ground. At the same time, with congestion at its lowest point in over two years, more and more married couples were finding opportunities to live together, although most still had to share their rooms with other couples.

A German doctor with SS connections came to the camp to try out a new treatment he had devised for abscesses. His experiments, while apparently unsuccessful, enabled Theresienstadt's own doctors to acquire additional medications and equipment.

These and other improvements, added to the ongoing reports of Allied advances, kept up the camp's morale. When the SS changed the name of the camp's money from Ghetto crowns to Theresienstadt crowns on July 9, the residents saw this as still another sign that the Nazis knew the war was lost and were counting on the camp to cover up their misdeeds. The summer of 1944 was easily the best summer, indeed the best period, in the camp's troubled history.

On July 16 the Zionists observed the 40th anniversary of Herzl's death with a day-long celebration featuring several sports events followed by a dance. The sports events included not only a soccer game and a relay race through the town but also a bicycle race with the SS providing bicycles for the occasion. This last gesture seemed to represent still another sign of a softening in the Nazis' attitude toward them.

The Zionists were not the only ones who were becoming more active. The camp's rabbis began to hold impressive Friday night services with the camp's two best cantors alternately singing. Attendance at the services was consistently, and surprisingly, high.

Attendance at Catholic and Protestant services on Sunday mornings had also increased, for most of the mixed marriage partners who had trickled into the camp during the past year were converts to Christianity. Christians now made up nearly one-sixth of the Jewish Ghetto's population.

The camp's cultural life continued to flourish, helped by the new concert hall, the new theatrical equipment and musical instruments, and the newer arrivals. On June 28 Bernard Kaff thrilled an overflow audience with his rendition of Moussorgsky's *Pictures at an Exhibition*. Although the piece can hardly be called political, Karas speculates that the approach of the Russian army may have figured into its selection and reception. Its last resounding section entitled "The Great Gates of Kiev" may have had a particularly strong effect in reminding the residents of what they believed to be their approaching freedom.

Rehearsals began for a new opera called *Der Kaiser von Atlantis*, or *Der Tod Dankt Ab* (The Emperor from Atlantis, or Death Abdicates). It portrays a cruel emperor who orders Death to lead his army into an unnecessary war. Death, however, refuses and goes on strike. Chaos ensues and order returns only when Death resumes his work and makes the emperor his first victim.

The libretto, written by a young painter and poet named Peter Kien, contains obvious political connotations. Less obviously, so does the score. The composer, Viktor Ullmann, smuggled into the music a minor key variation of the German anthem, *Deutschland, Deutschland Ueber Alles*, and ended the opera with an adaptation of Martin Luther's triumphant hymn, *A Mighty Fortress Is Our Lord*. The new opera was scheduled for presentation in the fall but would never be performed in Theresienstadt.

A much shorter piece of music composed in the camp would fare better. This was Pavel Haas's *Study for String Orchestra*. Unlike Kien and Ullman's opera, Haas's work would not only be premiered but also preserved.

The high point of the summer's cultural activities was Schaecter's production of the Verdi *Requiem*. It represented a year's work by its conductor, soloists and those of its chorus who had managed to avoid deportation. (Replacements for those who had been sent off had been found among newer arrivals.)

Despite the controversy which its Christian content had created, it thrilled all those who heard it. As one of them later wrote, "Conductor Rafael Schaechter had no baton, the singers had no score, but the *Libera Me* [Liberate Me] has never before or since been so well understood."

During the latter half of the summer, two unique cultural or culture-related events occurred. One was a poetry contest; the other was a film production.

The poetry contest was held on August 3. Although all entries had to be in German and approved by the SS, 3,000 poems were submitted. Not unexpectedly, Leo Strauss, the Viennese cabaret writer and son of Oscar Strauss, was one of the winners. (His entry did not, of course, include the lines quoted in the frontispiece.)

Then, on August 16 a camera crew arrived from Prague and production began on a film. Its title: *The Fuehrer Presents a City to the Jews*.

It was not the Nazis' first attempt to make a Theresienstadt film. In the fall of 1942 they had assigned a Czech director named Irina Dodalova to produce a film that would encourage Jews and their Gentile relatives and friends to cooperate in carrying out deportations to the town. It showed a Jewish family in Prague getting their deportation notices, calling at the Gemeinde, packing their luggage, appearing at the train station, arriving at Theresienstadt, going through the intake process, and then beginning their new lives.

The project ran into difficulties, however, for the paradise ghetto did not appear to be much of a paradise. The film's footage showed quarrels, confusion and, above all, congestion. In addition, it was clumsily shot and crudely put together, since the director had been given only eight days to finish the script. When it arrived in Berlin, a last-ditch effort was made to whip it into shape before it was scrapped altogether.

Interest in filming Theresienstadt revived in 1944 as horror stories of the extermination camps spread abroad and as the course of the war convinced more Nazis that they might soon have to account for their actions. As noted earlier, cameras had recorded the arrival of the first large transport of Dutch Jews in January. Although these scenes were presumably designed only for newsreel clips, during the beautification one Theresienstadter heard Haindl say to another SS officer, "We should film Theresienstadt so that the Jews will not say later we mistreated them."

Some delicate dealings which the Nazis were conducting during the summer of 1944 may also have influenced their decision to try once again to make a Theresienstadt film. Eichmann was negotiating with a Swiss Jewish leader named Saly Mayer to release a substantial number of Jews in return for a substantial amount of money. The Nazis were demanding five million dollars. Mayer, however, had only about $2.7 million at his disposal. Moreover, he lacked authorization from the Swiss government--he was, after all, a Swiss citizen--as well as the blessing of America's War Refugee Board for various aspects of the deal he was trying to make. (The War Refugee Board consisted of humanitarian non-Jews who wanted to save Jewish lives but, understandably, did not want to see the Germans acquire resources that could prolong the war.) So Mayer and other Jewish leaders involved had begun dragging out the negotiations, hoping that the course of the war or other developments might eventually make an agreement possible. If not, the delay could at least forestall the fate of those Jews in Nazi hands who were still alive.

As part of his stalling tactics, Mayer had expressed doubts that the Reich still had any large number of living Jews in its custody. The Nazis may have believed that a film on Theresienstadt would show that they had.

Although the SS brought in a two-man camera crew from Prague to shoot the film, they assigned Kurt Gerron to produce and direct it. The former stage and screen star plunged into the task with gusto. Working from a script which he co-wrote with a fellow inmate, a former lace manufacturer, Gerron shot 1200 scenes within four weeks.

His footage actually presents a more falsified picture of Theresienstadt than that which the Red Cross visitors saw. Among the scenes it shows are the following: a group of distinguished-looking elderly Jews sitting under sunshades on a terrace sipping drinks through straws (the deception here needs no explanation); a well-dressed couple with their children, opening a food package in a comfortable living room (the room was in Murmelstein's apartment, the package was from Denmark, so that one could be assured of its generous contents, and the "parents" were not married and not related to the children); a group of young Jews swimming joyfully in the river (such swimming had never been and never again would be allowed); Karel Ancerl, wearing a tuxedo while leading an orchestra (flowerpots had to be placed on the stage to conceal Ancerl's wooden clogs).

The production did not proceed without hitches. When it came to filming children eating apples and rolls, the hungry youngsters gulped down these goodies so greedily that the scene had to be shot several times until they had eaten enough to quell their hunger pains. Another difficulty less easily overcome was the lack of residents who clearly looked like Jews were supposed to look. In filming crowd scenes, the SS, or Gerron himself, would occasionally send a blonde Jew to the rear and call a more Semitic-looking Jew to the foreground. The fact that many residents were far from enthusiastic about participating in the project also did not help. On one occasion, Gerron tried all kinds of stratagems including flattery, promises of extra food, and jokes in an effort to get a group of teenage Czech boys to laugh. When none of these devices worked, he began laughing himself, keeping it up until the boys finally broke down and laughed with him.

Rahm and even Guenther occasionally showed up and, whenever they did, would often interfere with the filming. Two lower-ranking SS men who had been assigned to keep watch on the proceedings had to be continually asked to keep out of camera range. Their constant presence, however, did not prevent one of the Czech cameramen from thrusting cigarettes into the hands of Gerron's assistant, Hans Hofer, and from whispering words of encouragement in his ear.

Despite the many obstacles he encountered, Gerron forged ahead. In fact, he got carried away with his task and, though he would never see one foot of the 50,000 feet he shot, he felt confident he was making a superb documentary. He even boasted that it would win international acclaim. He also believed he was ensuring his own future, for he told one fellow resident that the Nazis had promised him good food and better living quarters for his efforts.

He would soon find out differently.(37)

---

35. In further reaction to the rumors of Theresienstadt's possible destruction, the Nazis suddenly allowed Baeck and certain other prominent Jews to write additional letters to Jewish organizations and friends abroad. Baeck and the others gladly did so without knowing the reasons behind this sudden relaxation of SS restrictions on mail.

36. Murmelstein later claimed that he and all the others involved in the project knew it was only designed for propaganda purposes but they did not think it would fool anyone. At the same time, they believed it offered them a chance to improve conditions in the camp.

37. If the film, as we shall see, did not do Gerron and those who helped him much good, neither did it do the Nazis much good. At the Prague studio where it was to be assembled, Czech editors did all they could to sabotage or at least hold up its completion. One scene showing Eppstein addressing the Council of Elders had to be designated, for by the time the film was finally finished, most of the people in the scene were no longer alive. In the interim, the Nazis reportedly did not incorporate some scenes from the film into newsreel interspersed with shots of German troops fighting at the front. The commentary pointed out that "while the Jews in Theresienstadt lounge in their clubs and coffeehouses, our soldiers must bear the burden of the war and defend the Fatherland."

CHAPTER 10
EXODUS II: THE END OF EPPSTEIN

If Theresienstadt were having its best summer, so, in a vastly difference sense, was Auschwitz. Its ovens and gas chambers were operating at a faster rate than ever. What accounts for such a divergence? How does one explain a softening of conditions in one concentration camp and a step-up of horror at another?

The anomaly reflects a developing disarray in German policy and practices regarding the Jews. It first began or at least first revealed itself following Stalingrad, a defeat which many historians regard as the turning point of the war. As we saw earlier, a few days after the German disaster, Himmler rejected Kaltenbruner's request to deport more of Theresienstadt's elderly to Auschwitz. Although the SS chief subsequently dispatched 17,500 Theresienstadters, including many elderly, to the extermination camp, he nevertheless showed himself willing to bargain with the British for the possible release of some Jewish children. Signs of hesitation were slowly surfacing in the Nazis' hitherto unremitting and ruthless war against the Jews.

By the summer of 1944 some Nazis wanted to slow down or even stop the executions. They hoped to use the Jews as bargaining chips with the Allies (most Nazis greatly overestimated the power of the Jews and their influence on Allied decision making); or they wanted to utilize more Jewish labor for their country's hard-pressed war industries (they hoped Germany could still put up enough of a fight to force the Allies to negotiate a peace); or they simply felt that the fewer Jews killed, the easier time they would have when the final collapse came (the Russians were already closing in on one extermination camp, Majdanek).

But the course of the war made others more eager to speed up the extermination program. They wanted to get rid of witnesses to their misdeeds and eliminate possible uprisings such as had occurred in the Warsaw and Vilna ghettos and at the Sobibor concentration camp. More important, they saw in the continuance and intensification of the Jewish Holocaust a way of snatching a measure of victory from defeat. For if their war against the Allies was largely lost, their war against the Jews could still largely be won. Ridding Europe of most of its Jews would mean that all their efforts had not been in vain.

The Germans, especially the north Germans, involved in the extermination program tended to opt for the more moderate approach; the Austrians, including Eichmann, Kaltenbruner and, most of all, Hitler himself, favored the harsher one. But the divisions were by no means clear-cut. Indeed, the same individual might waver between the two approaches, now favoring one, now the other, and even on occasion favoring aspects of both simultaneously.

These confusions, contradictions, and cross currents had already produced inconsistent policies and decisions regarding Theresienstadt. They would do so even more as the war moved closer to its inevitable end.

Although the summer of 1944 was turning out to be an excellent one by Theresienstadt standards, it did not elapse without signs of trouble. On July 17 Rahm suddenly summoned to his office four of the camp's leading artists, Fritta, Unger, Bloch, and Leo Haas. As they were leaving to go, they ran into Zucker who suggested they take warm underclothes and a coat with them. This certainly seemed strange advice for a midsummer meeting but Zucker, who apparently knew more than he could disclose, explained that they might have to wait for quite a while in the cellar before they met with the commandant.

As it happened, the four had no such wait. They were ushered almost immediately into Rahm's office where they found not only Rahm but Eichmann, his adjutant Moehs, and Guenther. The three high-level SS officers showed them pictures and drawings which the artists had made depicting the sordidness and squalor of Theresienstadt life. The SS, it seems, had arrested the Czech businessman who had been buying and smuggling out some of their secret art work.(38)

The Nazis began questioning the four in an unusually polite and even rueful tone. "Do you really think there is hunger in the ghetto when the Red Cross could find no signs of it?" they were asked. When the interrogators did not elicit the desired responses, their manner became more threatening. At the end of the session, the Nazis ordered the four artists transferred after dark to the Little Fortress along with their wives and *Fritta*'s 4-year-old son Tomas. Bloch was beaten to death soon after their arrival at the prison for not holding his pitchfork straight, while the other three artists, but not the four women and the boy, were subsequently sent to Auschwitz.(39)

The art smuggling did little to quell the Nazis' suspicions and fears of their Jewish underlings. They now prohibited all cultural presentations in any language but German and disbanded the common billets of the transport section, evidently fearing that such a cohesive group of young Czechs might become the corps of a resistance movement. The following month, their fears further fed by a break-out in Sobibor, they compiled a list of all Czech Jews who had had military service. They also required all former military officers of whatever army to register. They even transferred to another part of the town a children's home that was too close to their own quarters. House searches increased and efforts to check smuggling intensified.

None of these measures greatly affected Theresienstadt's daily life which, as noted, had improved. Even the ban on non-German presentations did not create too much unhappiness since the three deportations of the past year had left fewer Czechs in the camp and most of those who remained spoke German. *Brundibar* could no longer be performed but most camp residents had already seen it more than once.

Still, these measures caused some to become distrustful of Nazi intentions. When *Hechalutz* leaders held their second annual conference in August, a bitter dispute arose over whether to allow members to accompany their parents should the latter be deported, or to require them to remain in Theresienstadt to continue working for the community's benefit. (The former view finally prevailed.) A few young Czechs even feared that with the war apparently ending, the Nazis would liquidate the camp and its residents. They began making plans with some Czech gendarmes to attack the SS headquarters should such a move appear likely.

On September 6 another transport of Dutch Jews reached the camp. It brought 933 women, 782 men, and 372 children, or some 2,087 in all. Unlike those who had come earlier in third-class and even second-class railroad cars, this group had traveled for 58 hours in sealed boxcars with no food, no water, and only one bucket per car for human waste. They were assigned to a section of the Hamburg barracks where Eppstein later called to welcome them. Mindful of the problems the earlier Dutch arrivals were having in adjusting to Theresienstadt, he urged them to accept the camp and its difficulties. "Learn to live in a community even though it is a compulsory community," he said. This large, and as it would turn out, last transport from Holland showed that the Nazis were still able and willing to deport Jews. It was not a good sign.

As it so happened, deportation rumors resulting from an indiscreet remark of an SS man had already started to circulate. A transport of 5,000 to 7,000 was being mentioned. On September 27, Moehs arrived at the camp to inspect all its production facilities involved in the war effort. This included primarily the feldspar-splitting plant which had resumed operations only three weeks earlier after having suspended production at the beginning of the year.   (The tank kit assembly operation had long since been closed down.)

Moehs's inspection alerted the entire camp to his presence, and since he had always appeared at deportations, by the following morning the camp was gripped by tension. By late afternoon, however, the anxiety began to ease as no announcements appeared. Then, at 5:30 P.M. Eppstein, Zucker, and Murmelstein were suddenly summoned to Rahm's office. There they were told that since Theresienstadt lacked the space and facilities for increased defense work, a new camp would be built within the Reich itself. Zucker would head it up.

A bulletin conveying this decision was posted almost immediately. It read, "It is imperative that Theresienstadt provide more manpower than hitherto for the war effort. After careful consideration, it has been concluded that the ghetto lacks the space needed for additional war industries. Consequently, it has been decided that 2,500 able-bodied men will leave Theresienstadt for this purpose on Tuesday morning, September 26, to be followed by the same number of able-bodied men on Wednesday, the 27th." The men, it was said, would set up a new work camp while their wives and children staying behind would receive good treatment. As to location, the announcement merely said, "The destination of the transports is in the direction of Dresden."

The announcement came in the middle of Holy week with the first transport scheduled for Yom Kippur. When the railroad cars failed to appear on schedule and Kol Nidre services went as planned, many felt the deportations had been canceled. But the next day the trains arrived and the first transport of 2,500 left on September 28, followed by a second transport of 1,500 the next day, and still another of 1,500 two days later on October 1.

Though scarcely welcome news, the announcement of the deportations did not cause as much consternation and concern as most previous ones had done. The reason is quite simple. Most inmates fully believed what the Nazis had told them.

There was certainly some reason to think that the deportees would not be going to Auschwitz to die but to Germany to work. The previous March some 235 young men from the camp had been sent to Zossen, a wooded area southwest of Berlin. There they were building a new headquarters for the Gestapo. They were joined three months later by 25 young women sent to do their washing, cleaning, and cooking. All were allowed to write back frequently to family and friends in Theresienstadt so that no doubts ever arose as to where they were or what they were doing. While their worsening living conditions were forcing them to supplement their meager rations by eating acacia plants in the woods, their heavily censored mail only relayed the reassuring news that they remained alive and well. The Nazis sought to capitalize on this by describing the deportation as "a work assignment similar to that of Zossen."

The guidelines governing the deportation only reinforced the credibility of its announced purpose. It would include only able-bodied men from 16 to 50. (The upper age limit was later raised to 55.) Indeed, not only were women, children, the elderly and the sick, including the mentally ill and the retarded, excluded but, most surprising of all, so were "asocial elements" who were usually the first to go. Such stipulations made inclusion in the transport seem almost like a privilege and this feeling was further fostered by a provision allowing Mischlings and other hitherto protected groups to volunteer.

That Zucker would head it up also allayed the deportees' anxieties. Many considered him the most able member of the administration and thus it seemed impossible that the Nazis would send him off unless they desperately needed his capabilities elsewhere. Zucker himself apparently believed this as well for he tried to take as many engineers as possible with him, claiming he needed them for his "new work camp." The news that Schliesser, the head of the economics department, would go with him added further credence to the deportation's putative purpose.

The Jewish administration worked with the SS in bolstering such beliefs. Ansbacher, who was on the first transport, recalls how Rahm and a member of the Council of Elders came to the Schleuse to bid them goodby. The Elder read a speech on Rahm's behalf saying, "Now you are going to a labor camp. You will be better off there than here. You will be getting good food and there is no reason to worry. We are very proud of you because you will be able to represent those you are leaving. You will be able to build there what you were unable to complete here."

So the deportees departed, some almost cheerfully. "Our best youth went off, many in high spirits," recalls one older deportee, "for they believed the Nazis now desperately needed them for their futile last-ditch war efforts. Already they sensed the dawn of a new day." Several of the camp's leading musicians even volunteered to go. Zucker had always favored and protected them and they believed he would do the same at the new camp. Egon Ledec managed to drop a postcard from the train addressed to his sister. It expressed more concern for her future than for his own. "Be well. Let the dear God protect you. Love and kisses. Egon."

Zucker, however, would not be able to protect anyone, including himself. For though he and Schliesser traveled in a passenger car while the others rode in boxcars, and although Guenther and Moehs came to their compartment before the train left to talk to them about the importance of their new mission, the transport went straight to Auschwitz. Zucker and Schliesser were removed from the train first and were last seen standing handcuffed together on the platform, not a single muscle moving on their stony faces. They were then hustled off to the gas chamber where, after a work selection which spared less than half, the rest soon joined them.

As was customarily the case, those left behind in Theresienstadt knew nothing of the deportees' fate. So when the Nazis announced they would "allow" 500 wives and relatives to go on the third transport to join their menfolk, Zucker's wife Fritzi quickly volunteered and urged other wives to do the same. Although the full women's allotment of 500 places was not reached and had to be completed through conscription, several hundred signed up. In one room of 34 women, all but two registered to go.

When Mrs. Zucker showed up on the railroad platform with eight trunks, the SS dutifully had the trunks put aboard the train while Rahm introduced her to the train commander, saying, "This is Frau Zucker. You must promise me that Frau Zucker will tonight lie in the arms of her husband." In one sense the promise would be kept, for she, along with most of the other women, would share her husband's fate.

Another prominent camp figure had already shared Otto Zucker's fate. This was Paul Eppstein. Only he had not had to travel so far.

As the first transport was being readied on September 27, Rahm told Eppstein that the SS needed 30 knapsacks and that he should take them from the men who were going off. Eppstein, however, did not want to upset the deportees and felt he could meet the demand with knapsacks stored in the camp's warehouse. The warehouse lay in a normally out-of-bounds area on the other side of the perimeter street, but Eppstein, as camp Elder, had the authority to issue passes to residents to go there. So he hopped on his bicycle and, accompanied by a member of the Ghetto Watch, pedaled to the site.

A gendarme at the building, however, demanded to see his pass and when Eppstein said he did not need one, a bitter argument broke out. It ended with Eppstein's arrest.

Murmelstein was at his apartment while this was happening. He was suddenly summoned to headquarters where Rahm called him into his office. Almost immediately after his entrance, however, Rahm got a telephone call and so Murmelstein started to leave. But Rahm told him to stay and to continue talking. When, confused and confounded by the order, Murmelstein lapsed into silence, Rahm shouted, "Talk further," while the commandant continued his phone conversation which he obviously did not want Murmelstein to overhear. "As far as I remember," says Murmelstein, "I talked about the wonderfully positive attitude of the Danes toward hard work."

Suddenly, and simultaneously, Moehs entered through one door while Eppstein, escorted by Haindl, came through another. Rahm demanded to know why Eppstein had argued with the gendarme. The desperate Eppstein tried to remind him that "I have the right to go there; you have given it to me." Moehs then interceded, saying, "This could be interpreted as an escape attempt. I'll have you locked up until the transport leaves." Eppstein was ordered to turn over his portfolio to Murmelstein and was then led away.

Rahm and Moehs also left, leaving the anxious Murmelstein sitting alone in the commandant's office. A half hour later Rahm returned and ordered him to inform the Council of Elders that Eppstein had been arrested for attempted escape.

At about the time Rahm was telling this to Murmelstein, a car containing Eppstein and two SS men arrived at the Little Fortress. (Since the prison was only a few minutes' walk from the camp, the SS probably chose to use a car to prevent the residents from learning what was going on.) Eppstein reported to the deputy commandant in prescribed Little Fortress fashion, saying, "I am the *Stinkjude* Eppstein." These are the last words he is known to have spoken for he was promptly taken to a potato field north of the prison and shot. His body was put in a coffin for cremation, but since the delivery of a single coffin to the camp crematorium might have aroused suspicion that it was his, three other coffins were filled with wood and sent along with it. The prison's commander ordered complete secrecy over the matter.

If the events surrounding Eppstein's arrest and execution are reasonably certain and clear, the reasons behind them are not. Obviously, the fuss over his entering an off-limits area he could authorize others to enter served only as a grotesque pretext. Deeper and more deliberate forces were at work.

Lederer attributes Eppstein's removal largely to a speech Eppstein gave before 1,200 listeners as part of a Rosh Hashanah greeting on September 19. Concerned over the buoyant mood spreading over the camp, and wanting to keep it from getting out of hand, he told the group, "We are like people on a ship that lies outside the harbor and which finds its way to port impeded by a heavy minefield. Only those in charge of the ship know the narrow way which leads safely to land." He urged them to continue obeying the rules and to work hard. He had previously shown the speech to Baeck, who warned him of its imprudence. But he supposedly had then shown it to Rahm, who had raised no objection.

Murmelstein offers other possible explanations. With a decline in the ghetto's population and an increase in available food thanks to the allotment gardens and a stepped-up influx of food packages, there was now more than enough food to meet the stipulated rations. As a result, so Rahm later told him, Eppstein, at Schliessers urging, had been allotting some individuals extra food. Rahm had learned of the situation but did not want to acknowledge it officially since he feared the wrath of his superiors and colleagues who would think he had been allowing the Jews too much food, a heinous offense by SS standards. Getting rid of the officials involved supplied a solution.

Murmelstein does not specifically give this as the reason for Eppstein's arrest, and certainly such a situation does not in itself seem to have warranted such drastic action. More significantly, it does not explain why Moehs seemed more eager than Rahm for Eppstein's elimination.

In another section of his manuscript memoirs, Murmelstein provides what could be the most critical cause for Eppstein's removal. Citing testimony of some SS men at a trial in Leitmeritz in 1947, Murmelstein says the Nazis had come up with a truly macabre idea. They would have one of their own planes bomb and destroy the town and then blame it on the British. Eppstein, who apparently would have been evacuated earlier, would deliver a radio broadcast in English from a city in mid-Germany protesting the destruction of a "Jewish settlement area" by British "terror pilots."

The Allied advance into northern Italy had put Czechoslovakia within bombing range and in late summer one Allied bomber had destroyed a chemical plant not far from the ghetto. The bombing had caused a lot of soot and heavy dust to fall on Theresienstadt, creating a good deal of elation among its residents who saw it as still another sign of their approaching liberation. But it may have suggested to their captors a scheme to get rid of them.

When confronted with the idea, Eppstein, according to Murmelstein, who was scarcely one of his fans, refused to go along with it. The generally compliant Jewish Elder had once said, "I know the time must come when I can no longer say yes." Such a time had apparently arrived.

But while this may be the main reason for Eppstein's demise, it is probably not the only one. The previously mentioned factors must be taken into account. Furthermore, there was the Nazis' desire to eliminate those who knew too much, which may explain the deportation of Zucker.(40) Finally, we cannot exclude the continued frustration which the Viennese toolmaker must have experienced in working with a former professor who spoke only high German and who in some respects seemed more Aryan than Rahm himself. Certainly, Murmelstein was much more Rahm's man.

And Rahm's man he now became. Told only that Eppstein had been "reassigned" and that he should "temporarily take over his duties," the scholarly rabbi became in fact, if not in title, Theresienstadt's third Elder. Eppstein's signature stamp was used for a short time afterward, but the residents soon learned that Murmelstein had replaced him. Most did not consider it a welcome development.

As previously noted, Murmelstein had come to the camp with a reputation for having done too much to accommodate the Nazis in Vienna and for having done too little to accommodate his fellow Jews. In Theresienstadt he had made some efforts to overcome these sentiments. He began learning Czech and always made some remarks in that language when addressing a mixed gathering. He also helped put Czech books in the central library and books, it will be recalled, were important items in Theresienstadt. He cultivated Czech leaders, such as Franz Kahn and the young Zionist activist Ze'ev Shek. He even appointed Shek to the Hebrew library, although Shek's knowledge of Hebrew was, by his own admission, inadequate for the library's scholarly task. However, Murmelstein was seeking to curry favor with the Zionists, for he told Shek that whenever he needed time for his clandestine *Hechalutz* activities, he should let him know and Murmelstein would tell the others that he was using him for some special work of his own. (Murmelstein was apparently well aware of and somewhat sensitive to his own reputation for the first time he met Shek he asked him if he had heard much bad talk about him.)

These efforts, however, had not made his fellow Jews in Theresienstadt like him any better than did his fellow Jews in Vienna. He was widely referred to as "Murmelschwein" and during the beautification some wall graffiti appeared, saying, *Aussen rein. Innen Schwein. So ist unser Murmelstein.* (Clean outside. A pig inside. So is our Murmelstein.) When news of his elevation spread through the camp, Karel Fleischmann, who in addition to being a physician and writer was also an artist, drew a satirical sketch showing a fat, jowly Murmelstein wearing a crown and holding a scepter.

The reasons for the continued hostility toward him are not hard to fathom. Despite his conciliatory gestures, he often treated harshly those whose favor he did not need. Once he showed a visiting Nazi professor around the Hebrew library, and the academic, deeply impressed, congratulated him on his good work. After the visitor left, a rabbi on the staff half jokingly remarked, "You, Mr. Vice Chairman of the Council of Elders, get all the *Koved* (honor) while we get all the work." Murmelstein, infuriated, dismissed him from his post.

On another occasion, Murmelstein came across a young woman walking on the street during working hours. She had recently recovered from an illness and, in accordance with general ghetto practice, had been assigned to the commissary so that she could build up her strength. Although she was executing an errand for her boss, Murmelstein accused her of promenading around and transferred her to feldspar-splitting, one of the hardest jobs in the camp. Only later was he persuaded to restore her to her former position.

It was perhaps not so much what he did as the way he did it that stirred up so much sentiment against him. He would not only reject most pleas for help but would do so in an arrogant and abrasive, if not abusive, manner. Eppstein and even Edelstein might well have done the same, but they would at least have offered some consoling words. Edelstein also made himself accessible at almost all hours, while even the more aloof Eppstein had reserved an hour a day for people without appointments to see him. Murmelstein had never been easily available and during his first days as Eppstein's replacement hardly anyone could even find him.

Murmelstein's close aide, Robert Prochnik, did little to boost his boss's popularity. He was a clever but crude and uneducated young man whose black boots and overbearing manner gave him the appearance and demeanor of an SS man. If he was more accessible than Murmelstein, he was not much more approachable. (It was Prochnik, however, who persuaded Murmelstein to restore the convalescent commissary worker to her job.) Edward Seinfeld vividly recalls the vigor with which Prochnik, in his breeches and boots, slammed shut the door of the boxcar that was taking Seinfeld and those with him to Auschwitz.

Murmelstein had come across Prochnik in Vienna. It was there that Murmelstein had also acquired his reputation for several repellent

196 --George E Berkley

characteristics. In Theresienstadt, however, he earned the reputation for still another unsavory trait: lechery. The rabbinical scholar has been repeatedly accused of having had several sexual liaisons in Theresienstadt and of even threatening women whose spurned his advances.

These are certainly serious charges against any camp administrator and especially against one who is a rabbi. What evidence exists to validate them?

Alisa Shek says that a 28-year-old friend of hers in the camp admitted to having an affair with Murmelstein. According to Seinfeld, a children's nurse was well known to have been sexually involved with him. Jiri Lauscher reports that a man once coming to visit him told of having come across Murmelstein "with a woman" on the stairs. Lustig says the camp's teenage girls all feared Murmelstein. But most significant of all is the response of Murmelstein's former secretary, Sidoni Koralek, who was asked in 1985 whether her boss had deported women who refused to go to bed with him. Mrs. Koralek lowered her eyes and sadly nodded her head.

That the 39-year-old rabbi was sexually active in Theresienstadt there can be no doubt. In an interview many years later he admitted to having had one affair with a woman in her twenties. She may well have been Mrs. Shek's friend who incidentally claimed to be in love with Murmelstein, described him as a wonderful lover and insisted that the rest of the camp had grossly misunderstood and misjudged him. The charge of forcing his attentions on women under threat of deportation, however, seems exaggerated for his position alone, even when he was only number three in the camp hierarchy, assured him of ample female favors. Furthermore, his authority to specifically designate someone for deportation had been and would remain rather limited. What seems more likely is that he protected from the transports those whom he made love to. (The question to Mrs. Korelek on this point, which was phrased in English by a third party, may have been understood in that sense.)

So we are left with the certainty that he had one sexual relationship, the probability that he had others as well, but the unlikelihood that he had quite as many as some believe or that he deliberately used his position to force his attentions on anyone.

To better understand though not necessarily justify his behavior, one should note several circumstances. He had been a fat, generally unappealing young man who had not been able to find a wife for himself. Therefore, his family had arranged a marriage with a slightly older cousin from Budapest.

In Theresienstadt he found himself suddenly in a position of increasing authority which automatically made him desirable to many of the camp's destitute and desperate women. He also found himself in a place where sexual indulgence was fairly flagrant. One might also note in assessing him that as his power grew, so did his uncertainty over his own fate. Had the beautification been a failure, for example, his life would certainly have been on the line. In his new position as acting Elder, he had to live with the scarcely reassuring knowledge of what had happened to his two predecessors. (He did not know the specifics of what had happened to them but he could have little confidence that either still lived.) One of his first steps as acting Elder was to have a ghetto doctor give him a poison which could be taken easily and quickly without water. He would keep it with him at all times.

As for his rudeness and roughness in dealing with fellow inmates, he later insisted that such demeanor was necessary to keep favor-seekers away from him. It certainly helped, although such deportment also undoubtedly fitted his personality. (Even as a young religious teacher in the Viennese public schools he had become known for his arrogance and dictatorial manner.) But if he faithfully followed SS orders, then most others, including his two forerunners, did pretty much the same.(41)

Murmelstein does have his defenders. While Edelstein never ceased distrusting him, even warning his fellow Zionists from his jail cell before his deportation to beware of him, and while Adler calls him "clever, arrogant, cynical and sly," Artur Goldschmidt, leader of the camp's Protestants, sees him in a different light. According to Goldschmidt, the "learned rabbi" was an "unusually clever, organizationally gifted and energetic man with no sentimentality who naturally fell into the role of 'Leader.' He was viewed with hostility by many and only his unpleasant sides were placed in the foreground."

More exculpatory yet are the words of Lederer who after the war claimed that Murmelstein took "great moral risks by looking for loopholes whereby he could foil the Nazis' efforts to exterminate the Jews. It appears," he writes, "that he saw himself as another Flavius Josephus [Jewish historian] who, undeterred by the vociferous contempt of his people, worked for their salvation."

In the pages which follow we may obtain a clearer picture as to how much truth these various assessments contain of the man who would become, and who still remains, Theresienstadt's most controversial Jewish administrator.

Murmelstein plunged into his new duties with a vigor for which he had become known and, by many, despised. To help him, he called on Rudolf Bergmann, a former member of the Council of Elders, and Herbert Langer, a member of the secretariat, as well as his faithful Prochnick. Together, the four arranged the three deportations and kept the camp running.

On October 2, the day after the third transport left, Rahm assured his new Jewish administrator that the deportations had ended. The barracks used as the Schleuse could now be restored into living quarters. Murmelstein posted a bulletin thanking the residents for their cooperation in handling the transports and urging them to continue working hard. He then went to his apartment to rest.

Two hours later he received a summons to headquarters. There he found Moehs along with Rahm. There he also learned that more transports would be dispatched. Many more.

During the next 26 days a succession of transports carried away a majority of the camp's remaining inmates. So sweeping was the outflow that it can best be described in terms of who was selected to stay rather than who was selected to go. The SS in fact used this approach. They exempted certain groups, most notably the elderly, and shipped off almost everyone else. As Adler puts it, "No one under 65 was permitted to stay who did not belong to a special category or who did not receive a personal dispensation by the SS."

Besides the elderly, the special groups included those so sick they could not survive the move from the hospital to the train itself; most though not all the women working in the feldspar-splitting plant; the families of those sent the previous April to build the new Gestapo headquarters in Germany; and a corps group of workers and functionaries needed to keep the camp in operation.

They also included all the Danes and three subgroups of the Dutch. The latter consisted of 600 prominent scientists, artists, business people, and scholars for whom the Dutch government had obtained special protection; some one hundred Protestants who had converted to Christianity before the German occupation and whose bishop had wrangled a promise from the Nazis not to send them out of Theresienstadt; and, finally, David Cohen, former head of the Amsterdam Jewish Council, along with his wife and mistress. (Cohen's daughter, who still lives in Holland, had gone into hiding and had not accompanied her parents to Theresienstadt.)

Those with "Aryan blood" or Aryan family connections were no longer automatically excluded. Rather, their cases were considered individually. Liselotte Neuhause, the illegitimate daughter of a Jewish mother and non-Jewish father, was called to SS headquarters and asked if she had had any contact with her natural father who was still serving in the German army. When the young teenager innocently answered "No," she was shipped out. Spies, who had left a son and daughter in Germany, both half Aryan, was asked by Moehs whether her son-- Moehs showed no interest in the daughter--was working for the war effort. In reality, her son was in a mental hospital but Moehs satisfied himself that the son was helping the Fatherland and granted her an exemption. That she was working in the feldspar plant was also in her favor.

As these incidents indicate, the SS had not just set the guidelines but were actually composing the list. Toward the end they simply summoned whole groups alphabetically or by blocks, selected some to stay and sent off the others.

While most of those who escaped the transports fell into the previously mentioned exempt categories, a few did not. Veterans had long lost their exempt status but Moehs went over the list and, ignoring war decorations, allowed some seriously disabled veterans to stay. Rahm continually paraded inmates, each time removing a few whom he wished to keep. He also appeared on the platform at each deportation and, when approached by someone wishing to stay, occasionally said yes. In general, he seems to have favored women over men, probably because of the fear of a revolt which was almost certainly one of the reasons for the entire proceedings.

But aside from such individual instances, Rahm, Moehs, and the rest of the SS carried out the deportations rigorously and ruthlessly. Those so sick they could not walk but were yet able to be moved were taken by stretcher to a boxcar. There two teenage girls, one Dutch and one Czech, at first tried to lift them to the floor as gently as possible. Suddenly Haindl appeared and, waving his riding crop in a threatening manner, ordered the girls to tip the stretchers on their side, dumping the patients on the floor. With tears streaming down their faces, but with Haindl standing over them, they complied. One of the girls, Netty Vanderpol, still shudders when recalling the look of terror on the patients' faces as the girls carried out the order.

Rahm did not engage in such brutality himself but he rejected Murmelstein's attempt to slow down the human shipments, and when the rabbi sought the help of another SS officer, Rahm summoned him to the train platform where he was overseeing a transport and threatened him with a beating. Rahm also rejected far more petitions to remain than he granted. When a youth asked him whether TB could exempt him from going, Rahm waved him away; when a children's nurse asked if a healthy youth could stay behind with his seriously ill twin brother, Rahm replied, "Not unless they are Siamese twins."

The October transports met with much less acceptance than those in September. As Josef Polak describes it, "People no longer go to bed because nobody can fall asleep anyway. Everything disintegrates, nobody is interested in anything, only transports loom in everybody's mind. Night changes into day, nerves are tense to the breaking point. . . ."

Polak, however, left on the eighth and last transport (it was actually the eleventh if one counts the three "work transports" in September), and those sent out earlier in the month were less anxious and more hopeful. The SS still maintained that a new camp was being erected and the fact that the elderly were spared supported such a claim. As for the sick, the new camp, it was said, had ample facilities to care for them. Postcards arriving from those in the September transport provided still further assurances. The postcards carried a Dresden postmark for the train did stop in the German city, where the cards were distributed. But once the cards had been written and collected, the trains swerved eastward on the way to their destination.

One member of the September transport had left a note on his seat saying simply, "Birkenau." The cleaning squad found it when the train returned to Theresienstadt, but the message it conveyed did not reach many residents. Moreover, those who did learn of it, such as the transport commission and Murmelstein himself, could not fully comprehend its meaning. While they knew that Birkenau was in Poland and not in the Reich, they had only a vague idea of what it really represented.(42)

Thus, most left, if not willingly, at least initially without despair. A few even seemed eager. One middle-aged man entered his transport clasping an overcoat which had belonged to his son who had gone in September. The young man had mistakenly left the coat behind and his father was looking forward to surprising him with it. Some women who had not volunteered for the third September transport now wanted to go to rejoin their men or, in some cases, merely their friends. "I will never forget a conversation I had in the middle of the night with a woman who had voluntarily elected to leave in order to join her friends who had gone on earlier," writes Murmelstein. Since she was not listed for the transport currently being assembled, which might also have been the last, Murmelstein says he tried to talk her out of it. But she would not be persuaded. "The next day she boarded the train beaming with joy at having overcome all obstacles."

A young orthodox woman, married for one year and pregnant, was consigned to one of the first October transports since she had refused to have an abortion. Her husband desperately tried to talk her into having the abortion in order to escape the transport but she still refused. When a transportation commission member at the loading platform tried, at the husband's request, some last-minute persuasion to get her to change her mind, the young woman replied, "Tell my husband that I still love him but I simply cannot do it." (The abortion probably would not have helped since her husband was sent off on a later transport and she would no doubt have been sent with him.)

Inflated reports of Allied successes in the war eased and were used to ease the fears of many. When one early deportee expressed concern for his future, Robert Stricker sought to cheer him up, saying, "The Allies are already at the German borders. In four weeks it will all be over." Actually, it would be almost another six months before the Allies would cross the Rhine. In one sense, however, Stricker's words proved all too true for he and his wife Paula were shipped out soon thereafter.

Many other prominent residents were also sent off. One of them was Mrs. Paul Eppstein.

Hedwig Eppstein had never learned of her husband's true fate: only that he had been arrested. She had asked for and received permission to bring a plate of food for him to headquarters every day, and every day she faithfully did so. She never, however, received a plate back and soon was having trouble finding new ones. Now she was told she could join her husband in the new camp. In deference to her former position and perhaps to indicate to others that her husband still lived, she and her family were allowed to sit by themselves in a waiting room at the evacuation center while other deportees milled around in the corridor. Whenever the door opened she could be seen sitting neatly dressed and patiently awaiting the train which she believed would take her to her mate.

The majority of the Council of Elders, some 16 in all, were sent off along with numerous high-level department heads and other functionaries. They included Drs. Munk and Fleischmann who had been told they would head the medical services at the new camp. Even one of the two dentists who had been secretly treating the SS had to leave.

As the deportations continued, they eventually took away Murmelstein's two newly appointed aides, Bergmann and Langer, leaving him only with Prochnik. The Hebrew library he had overseen was complete-

completely shut down and all of its staff deported. (The Jewish museum and archive project in Prague was similarly closed and its staff sent to Auschwitz as well.)

Although those over 65 were usually spared, some were not. Among the latter were Phillip Manes, who had headed the cultural activities bureau, and Otto Friedlander, a former vice marshal of the Austrian army who had become one of the bureau's most popular lecturers. Both men had been keeping journals and had made no efforts to conceal them since they regarded them as nonpolitical. But the SS wanted to get rid of anyone who might become a serious witness against them. Hence their deportation.

On the night of his own deportation, scheduled for 11:30 P.M., Friedlander delivered his last lecture. With all the freshness and charm of the young cavalry officer he had once been, he described some of the battles of World War I in which he had served with such distinction. He closed his talk with a prayer he had composed which was later duplicated and circulated. In bidding goodby to Spies, he said, "How often on the battlefield have I confronted death. In my talks and writings I have also fought for what I believe. I would be shameful to myself if I now blinked an eye." Then, embracing the tearful Spies, he added, "Work. Give back to humanity what has been given to you."

There were no restrictions at the other end of the age ladder: children and even infants in diapers were among those deported. All strays and orphans not deported the previous spring were now dispatched and, in a few instances, children who had parents were sent off by themselves. Some of the older youngsters left in a good mood, imbued with a pioneer spirit at the prospect of building a new camp and proud that the Nazis needed them for this purpose. As members of the boys' chorus from *Carmen* gathered on the platform, they sang the chorus once again, little realizing it would be the last song most of them would ever sing.

Many musicians who had not left earlier with Zucker also ended up on the transport list, along with nearly all other artists and artistes who were neither Danish nor in one of the protected Dutch groups. As a result, the Ghetto Swingers, the string orchestra, and most other musical and theatrical ensembles were completely dismantled. Kurt Gerron learned the value of Nazi promises when he received his summons to go. On the station platform Rahm gave him a cheerful "Auf Wiedersehen" (Until we meet again).

Gerron was not the only one whose faithful service the Nazis chose to reward in such fashion. For the eighth and last transport they rounded up and sent off all or nearly all of their informers in the camp. Indeed, this transport may have been designed primarily for this purpose for Murmelstein says the transport seems not to have been part of the original plan but the result of a last-minute decision by Moehs. Informers, too, would make serious witnesses against them.

Since over 900 others would have to go to complete the transport, Rahm held another parade. Among those marching past him were the last seven Czech musicians and singers of any distinction remaining in the camp. When Murmelstein asked whether the seven, all of them women, should be sent off, Rahm smiled and in Viennese dialect replied, "Let's let them stay. They should do some more singing and dancing." The seven were removed from the marchers and assigned to the feldspar plant.

Once completed, the train started off but stopped suddenly in Bauschowitz where 20 young men were removed. They were secretly taken back to Theresienstadt by night to dig up and destroy the remains of those hung during the two executions in the winter of 1942. After they finished the task, the 20 were taken to the Little Fortress and killed. The rest of the transport continued on its way to Auschwitz. The fall exodus had finally ended.

Like so many episodes in Theresienstadt's history, the fall exodus was with replete with ironies, most of them tragic. For example, Ilse Weber, a prominent Czech writer of children's books, could have remained in the camp along with her small son. But she elected to go in order to accompany her deported husband. She and the child perished; her husband lived for another 30 years.

Her husband owed his survival to work selection. Yet here too tragic ironies abound. So little did most Theresienstadters know about Auschwitz that some pleaded an incapacity for work, thinking it would lead to better treatment. One giant of a man claimed to have a dozen illnesses, and when the Nazis directed him to the left, which he felt was the wrong side, he went off, cut his hands, and went through the line again. This time he ended up on the side he wanted.

Others acted more wisely. Musician Karel Berman heard Dr. Mengele ask another Theresienstadt musician about his occupation, and when the latter replied, "Singer," he saw Mengele point to his right. So when Mengele asked Berman the same question, he replied, "Manual worker." Mengele pointed to his left.

Berman survived the war. So did another musician, Karel Ancerl, who had worked as a cook and therefore appeared strong and robust.

Ancerl attempted to use his heavy build to shield the shrunken Bernard Kaff through the selection process. But Kaff poked his head out from behind to see what was going on. When Mengele spotted the diminutive, bespectacled pianist, he immediately pointed to his right.

As might be expected, fewer members of the October transport passed work selection than did those of the "work transports" in September. In all, about 10 percent of the eleven transports were selected out. Some of these later died from deprivation, exhaustion, or individual execution. They include Kurt Gerron and George Kafka, the latter a highly regarded writer in his own right as well as a second cousin to the more famous Franz. In all, 1,574 or about 8.5 percent are known to have survived the war.

The last Theresienstadt transport was also the next to the last transport of Jews to arrive in Auschwitz. Two days later a transport of Slovakian Jews came and were promptly gassed. Then, on November 2, Himmler gave orders to cease operations. Jews, including Theresienstadt Jews, would still die, but the gas chambers of Auschwitz would claim no more victims.

CHAPTER 11
FROM POTEMKIN VILLAGE
TO GHOST TOWN

Before the first fall transport, Theresienstadt had contained 29,481 people. After the last transport, it contained 11,077 people. In exactly one month, from September 28 to October 28, the ghetto had lost nearly two-thirds of its population.

The camp's remaining population was not just smaller but different in other ways. It was, for one thing, much older. More than 4,000 were over 65, while less than 6,200 were 16 to 65. The number of children had shrunk from nearly 2,600 to a mere 819. The camp's average age now stood at 51.

The gender gap had also widened. As might be expected, women outnumbered men by more than 2 to 1 among the elderly. As might not be expected, they outnumbered them by nearly 3 to 1 among the 16- to 65-year-olds, for this group now included 4,543 women but only 1,642 men. Moreover, since these figures include the mostly male work detail building the new Gestapo headquarters at Zossen in Germany, the real gender gap in the camp's working-age group was greater still. Only among those 15 and younger did males have a slight edge.

The camp's ethnic mix had also shifted. Since Germans had made up a high proportion of the exempt elderly, they now held a 4,000 to 3,500 edge over the Czechs. The Austrians, with 1,500, had fallen into fourth place behind the Dutch, with 1,700. This represents no special favoritism to the Dutch, for although some 700 of them fell into protected groups, few of the rest held positions that made them indispensable to the camp's operations. Consequently, they had lost about 3,000 to the fall exodus, or roughly the same proportion lost by the camp as a whole. Only the 460-plus Danes truly escaped the effects of the exodus, having had only one member deported.

Theresienstadt's future was now unknown, but one thing was certain: it would be a different camp than what it had been.

The Dutch who now constituted Theresienstadt's third largest ethnic group, had up to now been its most discontented ethnic group. And, it must be said, they had much to be discontented about.

To begin with, they had come too late to obtain good positions and, until September, had been too few in number to wield any influence or make their collective weight felt. This made them feel excluded from the mainstream of camp life. Although Gerron recruited some of them for his production of *Carmen*, a former concertmaster named Tromp was turned down when he offered to play in the camp orchestra during the Red Cross visit. Other reasons may have prompted the rejection-- the orchestra was already formed and deep in rehearsals when he arrived--but he and many of his countrymen attributed it to the desire of the Czechs and Germans to protect their own.

Another factor which contributed to the alienation of the Dutch was their living conditions. These were wretched even by Theresienstadt's low standards. Since the ghetto's more desirable housing was already taken when they arrived, they were initially assigned to a section of the Hamburg barracks. There they slept crowded together on filthy straw pallets in a manner reminiscent of the camp's worst days. They received no parcels from home since no arrangements could be made at this stage of the war to collect and ship them. Much of the luggage of the September group, which made up nearly half of all the Dutch in the camp, had been lost in transit and the 50 Ghetto crowns each received as compensation hardly made up for such a deprivation.

The fact that they were lodged together also curtailed their contacts with the other residents, thereby further heightening their sense of estrangement. But several additional factors compounded this problem.

While the Dutch knew no Czech, most of them could speak and understand a decent German since the two languages are closely related and German is taught from the earliest grade in the Dutch schools. Yet most of the Dutch intensely disliked the German Jews. Their animosity sprang from their experience with those German Jews who had emigrated to Holland before the war. These immigrants, like so many German Jews generally, had tended to be passionate German national- ists who enjoyed pointing out how things had always been done differently, and better, in Germany. In Holland many had continued to conduct themselves like Germans. For example, in school their children sat strictly erect at their desks instead of slouching the way Dutch children, both Jewish and non-Jewish, liked to do.

During the 1930's, the Dutch government had set up a camp at Westerbork to house Jewish refugees from Germany. When the Nazi occupied Holland, they used the camp as a collection center for deporting Jews. In so doing, they let the German Jews who had been running the camp for the Dutch government keep their positions. These German Jews, like so many German Jews in Theresienstadt, sought to impress their new Nazi bosses by showing exemplary German efficiency and thus slavishly followed the Nazis' orders. Among other things, they refused to go along with efforts to arrange escapes from the camp.

The Dutch also felt antagonistic to their own leaders, or at least to those who had been designated as such. As noted earlier, their ostensible leader was the former Amsterdam professor David Cohen, whom the Nazis had appointed co-chairman of Holland's Jewish community. Most Dutch Jews not only disliked but despised Cohen, however, for he had become such a fervent Nazi tool that he actually tried to block efforts to place Jewish children secretly with Dutch non-Jewish families. When one Jewish mother begged for his help in getting her son released from deportation to the East, he blithely told her that the deportation would make a man of him. When one well-to-do Jewish couple were deported to Auschwitz, Cohen together with his wife and mistress ransacked the couple's abandoned apartment, picking out choice items.

That Cohen brazenly kept a mistress also understandably upset them. The mistress accompanied him and his wife to Theresienstadt where all three lived together in one room. (Cohen, on Nazi orders, was given Prominenten status and made an official "guest" of the Council of Elders.) Each morning the three could be seen standing outside their building picking fleas from their blankets and clothing. For the Dutch Jews it was a scene, and source, of daily disgust.

Another Dutch Jew, who had emerged as something of a leader, or at least as someone of influence, was the 43-year-old artist Jo Spier. But he too owed his status strictly to his Nazi ties. Though considered even by his detractors as one of the most talented painters in Theresienstadt, Spier had become a darling of the SS. They not only assigned him to paint frescos in their lounge headquarters but had also entrusted him with preparing an 18-page picture book on Theresienstadt, copies of which were given to members of the Red Cross commission. Spier's pictures, of course, provide a totally falsified representation of Theresienstadt life. His depiction of the coffeehouse showing joyous, well-dressed people, for example, presents a startling contrast with a drawing by Fritta showing gloomy, skeletal figures jammed elbow to elbow at their tables while mournfully listening to music played by a specterlike trio.

Spier came to the camp early and the Nazis used him to welcome later Dutch arrivals. Well-dressed and healthy looking, he addressed the newcomers in a jaunty manner using inflections and phrases that made him sound almost like a Nazi himself. As far as is known, he at no time used his Nazi connections to help any of his countrymen.

The Dutch did have one or two natural leaders. Foremost among them was Walter Suskind, a low-keyed businessman who had quietly smuggled nearly 1,000 Jewish children to the Dutch resistance which placed them with non-Jewish families. On some occasions Suskind had personally wrapped up a Jewish infant to look like a bundle of laundry and then, after giving the child a few drops of brandy to keep it quiet, had boldly carried it out of the Jewish day center literally under the noses of the Nazis. The loose-knit network he headed also worked with the Dutch resistance in placing 2,000 Jewish adults in hiding. His activities put him at loggerheads with Cohen who had once threatened to tell the Gestapo if he didn't cease such operations.

Although the Nazis never suspected Suskind, they gave him no special status when he arrived in September and shipped him and his family out on one of the October transports. He had been in the camp only six weeks.(43)

The Dutch found a further cause for aggravation and alienation in the camp's moral standards. They were aggrieved at the rampant corruption which not only offended their sense of justice but, since they lacked both connections and tradeable goods, left them far worse off. They were offended at Theresienstadt's sexual morality as well. Though most of what they knew about the camp's sexual activities was based on rumors or wildly exaggerated reports, occasionally one of them would encounter a disturbing incident. Thus, a teenage Dutch girl who went to work for the internal mail service once entered the Danes' quarters to deliver a message, only to come across three young men engaged in a joint homosexual encounter. Horrified, she fled the building and found another job.(44)

The effect of all these conditions on the Dutch varied greatly from one individual to another. Frank Goperts, a young Dutch artist who lost both an arm and a leg as a soldier in Holland's four-day war with Germany, insisted on weari..g his Dutch uniform in Theresienstadt even though SS men frequently cuffed and kicked him for doing so. Businessman Adolph Schwarz, seeking to make the best of things, organized weekly seminars where former Dutch professors could discuss philosophical questions. Schwarz's wife, however, nearly broke down under the strain and for a long time spent most of each day sobbing.

Perhaps the most distinctive Dutch response to the ghetto came from a Mrs. Pop, a widow in her early 60s. She became a latrine warden and showed up for work every day in a trim hat, a delicate veil, and white gloves. She even traded some of her scanty food rations for lipstick and other cosmetics. Properly attired and made up, she would do virtually no work but sit primly in her chair in the latrine while urine sometimes sloshed around her feet. Jokingly referred to as "Malka" (Hebrew for queen), she managed to preserve not just her dignity but her sanity in the Theatre of the Absurd known as Theresienstadt.

The fall exodus had solved Theresienstadt's most persistent and pervasive problem: congestion. To be sure, the town still contained nearly twice as many people as it had before the Jews arrived, but its housing stock had been greatly expanded and its facilities extended. With the loss of so many people in so short a time, the once swollen ghetto now resembled a ghost town.

And not a pleasant ghost town at that. "Theresienstadt became empty," writes Spies. "A stillness engulfed the houses, the streets. The steps of walkers rang with a hollow sound." In some instances, entire buildings stood vacant. Where once electricity was scarce and had to be conserved, lights now burned night and day. Where once water was in short supply, some taps now ran constantly, flooding the rooms and corridors. Where once personal belongings had been carefully protected and preserved, now heaps of goods, some of them costly items, lay strewn about on the floors.

Some basic services had nearly come to a standstill. In the infirmaries patients who fell out of bed remained on the floor the entire night for lack of nursing personnel. Adolph Schwarz, hospitalized for an illness, was put in a bunk under the bunks of two men with diarrhea. Each day when Schwarz's family came to visit him, they found him soaked in urine.

One factor temporarily hampering customary camp functions was the need to carry out a noncustomary one. The last transport had hardly left when the SS ordered the removal of the funeral urns. This proved a painful project in more ways than one. Writes Willy Groag, who first witnessed the operation on his way to work, "What was this black mass of people standing on both sides of the open gate and what about the truck they were loading with boxes? As I approached I saw something terrible. In the middle of the gate stood the chief Jewish Elder, Murmelstein, giving orders, his face contorted with grief." Groag remembers hearing a little boy whispering words of comfort to his mother. "Don't cry, Mama. If I come across grandmother, I'll steal her."

Many a member of the work crew did indeed come across the ashes of a departed loved one, and every so often an anguished cry would go up from a woman handling the remains of her husband or parent or child. Some of the older youths only made matters worse by adopting a coarse gallows humor, making such remarks as "Watch out, here comes my uncle. Don't drop him."

Some 200 people worked on the project, mostly women and children. Forming human chains, they passed the boxes, many of them really paper bags, from hand to hand. The Nazis said they were taking the urns to a Jewish cemetery in Prague for interment. Few believed them and in reality the SS dumped them in the river. Each member of the work crew received a can of sardines for his or her efforts.

If Murmelstein was visibly upset at the removal of the urns, he had an added reason for being so. As he notes in one of his manuscripts, Eichmann had once said that as long as the urn depository and its urns remained, the ghetto would have nothing to fear. The removal of the urns could thus be signaling the coming liquidation of the ghetto itself.

Eichmann seems to have made his statement before a small group of high-level functionaries since Murmelstein says he was now the only person alive who had heard him make it. Murmelstein decided to keep it to himself lest he spread panic among the residents. He also decided to move forcefully to put the ghetto back in shape, apparently hoping that if he could make it into something the Nazis could once again exhibit, they might keep it and its residents in existence.

His biggest problem was lack of manpower. Even many of the 6,200 people of normal working age left in the ghetto could not be used to restore it, for their number included the ill and the infirm, such as most of the 175 remaining war veterans; those employed in the war effort, such as the women splitting feldspar or making uniforms; and the men building the new Gestapo headquarters in Germany. But realizing that preserving the ghetto meant saving himself and his family as well, Murmelstein decided to take desperate and drastic measures.

On November 9 the Jewish administration, which now consisted essentially of Murmelstein, issued a bulletin saying, "The Jews of Theresienstadt have in the past week demonstrated anew their commitment to order, discipline, and communal responsibility. Especially praiseworthy are the accomplishments of those who have untiringly fulfilled a multitude of their tasks and duties. A reformation of the Council of Elders and a restructuring of the Jewish self-administration is now under way. In the meantime, all the needs of the Jewish settlement area must be fully met and the communal work must go forward without interruption."

Murmelstein followed up his congratulatory peptalk a few hours later by issuing a second bulletin spelling out just how the community was to meet the challenges it now confronted. Henceforth, all residents capable of working, starting at age 10, would work 70 hours a week. (Some children as young as 8 joined the work force as well, for with most of their teachers and caretakers gone there was little else for them to do.)

The ghetto's precarious situation provided the rabbi with an incentive and an opportunity to tackle its inflated infrastructure. He abolished some organizational units, merged others, and streamlined still others. Positions once held by political favorites, most of whom had been deported, were either eliminated or taken over by others whom Murmelstein considered as technically competent. In this respect, his very unpopularity may have helped both him and the ghetto for he had few favorites of his own. At the same time, he knew all too well that only the most qualified people could carry out the program he had in mind.

His drastic administrative reforms brought a welcome reduction in the camp's corruption. Meal portions became larger and more uniform and neglected or slighted groups, such as the elderly, the infirm, and the Dutch, all benefitted.

Murmelstein also sought to crack down on corruption in more direct ways. He made supervisors responsible for any misdeeds within their area of responsibility. Thus, when a break-in occurred at one kitchen, he warned its manager that if any further such incidents occurred, he would place the manager himself under arrest until the culprit or culprits were caught. The camp's lawyers and jurists were outraged at such a step, but Murmelstein ignored them and, so he claims, no further break-ins occurred.

Murmelstein also invalidated all mail proxies which had allowed some clever wheeler-dealers to collect as many as 60 food packages a month. Henceforth, all packages addressed to dead or deported people- -nearly 120,000 one-time residents now fell into this category!--became the property of the Jewish administration, which in turn distributed them on the basis of need. Each elderly, sick, or disabled person would now receive a package each month. Each child under 16 would receive a package each week.

Several factors facilitated the rabbi's bold moves. The recent deportations had disrupted and largely destroyed the ghetto's elaborate hierarchy. Even the Prominenten had lost their special status. Furthermore, many of the remaining residents owed or thought they owed their omission from the transports to him. He did apparently intervene, sometimes successfully, to keep people whom he claimed the camp needed. Others realized that only forceful measures could keep the camp operating, and that only Murmelstein could carry them out.

A relative abundance of food also helped. Food packages were now arriving from Sweden while those from Switzerland and Portugal had increased. The ghetto also had reasonably adequate stocks of its own on hand since the deportations had left it with far fewer mouths to feed. This along with a relative abundance of living space and personal goods left behind by the deported further reduced the pressure for favoritism and partiality. The fact that women were now playing a greater role in camp life may also have encouraged more honest, humane conduct. Finally, as noted earlier, Murmelstein's own unpopularity may have helped; he had no entourage of courtiers and cronies to succor.

Although running a one-man show obviously suited his personality, he was shrewd enough to solicit support from and maintain communication with those he governed. Discarding the Council of Elders, of which only a remnant remained in any case, he established a new body of his own. It consisted of a single leading figure from each of the camp's major ethnic groups. It included Baeck, the former Czech cabinet minister Alfred Meissner, a former Viennese judge named Heinrich Klang, and Rabbi Friediger. For the Dutch, Murmelstein wisely passed over the detested David Cohen and appointed another and more popular former professor, Edward Meijers, instead.

At the outset, this new body was not officially a Council of Elders for Murmelstein himself had not been appointed Chief Elder. Moreover, he had no intention of letting it make many decisions. Rather, it functioned as an advisory committee and as a communications link to the various groups its members represented.

Being dictatorial in nature, Murmelstein frequently squabbled with most of its members. He later claimed that the legalistic Klang wanted a written law for every action, that Meissner, a staunch social democrat, wanted him to go easier on the work force, that Meijers felt he should do more for the Dutch, and that Friediger wanted to run a separate welfare system for the Danes. Only Baeck, who was easily the most respected figure in the camp, seems to have exercised any real influence over him, and it was probably at Baeck's behest, and certainly with his backing, that Murmelstein took forceful steps to ease the plight of the elderly.

Murmelstein's efforts soon proved effective; the camp almost miraculously began to revive. Women, children, and the elderly took over jobs previously held by able-bodied men and performed them usually as well as and sometimes better than they had been performed before. When a shipment of potatoes arrived on November 19, oldsters up to the age of 83 helped shovel them into the bins. Each received a shovelful for himself as a reward.

The health service struggled back onto its feet. Its new director was Dr. Richard Stein, a noted Czech ophthalmologist. Although such a highly specialized physician seems an odd choice for the post, Rahm, like his predecessor Burger, suffered from an eye problem and Stein had begun treating him for it in Prague. Rahm had brought Stein to Theresienstadt with him and kept him in the camp during the deportations. It was almost certainly at the commandant's dictation that he became its new medical director.

Stein had only 75 other working physicians and dentists, many over 65, to assist him. But together with such nurses as remained, and such others as could be recruited, they managed to restore most of the ghetto's medical programs. Despite a greater proportion of the elderly, the death rate actually dropped; occasionally a day elapsed without a single reported death.

The deportations had decimated the Ghetto Watch and virtually destroyed the fire department, sparing only its chief. But both units at least partially rebuilt themselves with older, younger or, in some cases, even semi-crippled recruits. Despite the shortage of men, both departments remained all-male bastions.

Appreciating the value of cultural activities in maintaining camp morale, and believing such activities to be still possible despite ten-hour work days and seven-day work weeks, Murmelstein moved quickly to make them once again a part of camp life. Czech singer Hedvika Grabova, one of the seven artistes whom Rahm had spared from the last transport, received word three days after the deportations ended to prepare a new concert program. She and some other women, most of them feldspar splitters like herself, began rehearsing after work in the unheated recreation hall. Pianist Alisha Herz-Sommer, another feldspar splitter, started preparing for an all-Chopin recital with which she would thrill the camp in the coming winter.

Since most of the camp's remaining Czech, German, and Austrian musicians were women singers and pianists, the distinguished instrumentalists in the protected Dutch group now had more opportunities to utilize their talents. When the coffeehouse reopened in December, the Dutch constituted the core of a band which most residents considered superior to the largely deported Ghetto Swingers. The Danish musicians also became more active, especially former Philharmonic conductor Peter Deutsch, who organized and conducted a band for light music.

Murmelstein also sought to strengthen the ghetto's religious life by instituting its first official rabbinate. Although only four rabbis were left besides himself, and though only two of them were under 65, regular Sabbath services were held and Jewish rites were performed for the now greatly diminished, and never very religious, Jewish population.

The new Chief Elder had always maintained good contacts with the camp's Christians and he continued to do so in his new position. When Rahm rejected their request for a Christmas tree, Murmelstein ordered a ghetto workshop to make an artificial one complete with simulated branches and electric lights. He also organized a Christmas party for their children at which the youngsters sang carols and acted out a fairy tale before being entertained by a (non-Christian) camp magician. The Czech gendarmes, becoming a bit bolder perhaps, placed a lighted Christmas tree outside their barracks for all the ghetto residents to enjoy.

Christians now made up close to a quarter of the ghetto's population. They owed their relatively greater numbers not to any particular immunity to deportation, for except for the protection granted the 100 pre-occupation Dutch Protestants, the Nazis showed them not the slightest favor. Rather, a larger proportion were either over 65 or had close Aryan connections.

The fall deportations, however, had shattered the Catholic congregation by taking away their religious head, Brother Kuhnert, and several of their leading laymen. With less than 1,000 members, they were now outnumbered by the 1,200 Protestants. Moreover, the Protestants now had an ordained minister, The Reverend Max Enker, who had come with the last Dutch transport in September. Good relations continued between the two congregations, as Enker performed funeral rites for the Catholics and otherwise assisted them. A young German Catholic named Ruskowitz, who was actually dying of tuberculosis, also tried to fill in the leadership gap left by the deportations. He impressed and inspired not only his fellow congregants but the Protestants as well with his deep devotion.

If some of the camp's organized groups had managed to survive, its most influential groups had virtually died out. The deportations had taken away nearly all the Zionist activists, including Redlich and his wife, who were gassed, and Zev Shek, who was selected for work. Most of Theresienstadt's remaining Jews, like most other Jews exposed to the Holocaust, had more or less come to believe in a Jewish homeland, but the camp's Zionist movement as such had perished along with most of its leaders. Also gone as an organized group were the communists.

Rahm had, however, retained its Council of Elders member, Jiri Vogel, presumably because of the latter's engineering skills and indispensable knowledge of the ghetto's now extensive water system. (Rahm almost certainly knew nothing of Vogel's politics.)

On a day-by-day basis the presence of the SS had also diminished. They were showing less interest than ever in enforcing many of their own rules. While the customary 8:00 P.M. winter curfew was officially reinstated, it was largely ignored. So was the rule requiring non-Prominenten families to live apart in barracks. Murmelstein even turned over a now-empty Prominenten house to some of the ghetto's skilled workers to use for family quarters.

All these changes soon began bearing fruit. As Adler admits, "Amazingly, conditions in some respects became better than before." On December 5, hardly more than five weeks after the last transport left, an SS official from Berlin visited the camp. After inspecting it, he remarked, "*So kann es bleiben*." (Literally, "So it can remain," but carrying the connotation that thanks to the shape it is now in, it can be kept in existence.)

A week later the SS officially announced Benjamin Israel Murmelstein's appointment as Chief Elder and his five hitherto unofficial ethnic representatives as elders. The 71-year-old Baeck, who now headed a unified welfare department, was designated deputy elder. The bulletin also outlined the ghetto's new streamlined administrative apparatus and ended with an announcement of cultural events, including a daily 6:00 P.M. program at the coffeehouse and a Mozart evening on the 19th. Theresienstadt was a ghost town no longer.

All through 1944 Jews continued to come to Theresienstadt. In addition to the Dutch, over 2,000 Germans and Austrians and more than 900 Czechs reached the camp in dribs and drabs. Nearly all were previously protected Jews who, for one reason or another, had lost their special status. But toward the end of the year, two quite different transports arrived.

The first reached the ghetto in late November bringing 70 Dutch children and two nurses, virtually all near death from starvation. They had been traveling for weeks with a stopover in another concentration camp, Bergen-Belsen, which did little to alleviate their plight. The children had been placed by their parents with Dutch Christians but had been discovered by the Nazis. A few of the camp's Dutch residents found children of their own among them. Because of their condition, all the youngsters were taken in hand by the health service.

The second transport arrived on December 24. It consisted of a few boxcars out of which stumbled some 400 half-frozen, half-starved Slovakian women, many clutching small children or holding babies. One 9-day-old infant had been born en route. The women had become separated from their men and had hidden out in the woods near Sered until the cold and their children's hunger forced them to give themselves up. The Nazis had shot some on the spot and dispatched the others, many of them seriously ill, to Theresienstadt. The women's first question was, "Are our husbands here?"

There was also a new development concerning deportations from Theresienstadt. On December 8 the SS ordered the Jewish administration to hand over all registers and records regarding these transports. The Russians had already discovered much evidence of the Holocaust in some of the extermination camps in Poland which they now occupied, and the increasingly fearful SS did not want any such evidence in Theresienstadt to fall into their hands as well.

It seemed unlikely, however, that the Soviet troops would get to Theresienstadt anytime soon since the camp did not lie along the line of their advance. However, an official at the Jewish agency in London, S. Adler Rudel, had noticed this and decided to try to do something about it.

Rudel knew that the Russian ambassador to Sweden, Alexandra Kollontai, had a reputation for being sympathetic to Jews. He also knew that she wielded considerable influence in the Soviet government. So he hopped a plane to Stockholm where he asked for and received an audience with her. In the interview, Rudel expressed his fears that the Nazis would exterminate Theresienstadt and with it the remnants of the Jewish intelligentsia in Western Europe. He pleaded for a Soviet effort to take Theresienstadt by surprise before the Nazis could act. Kollontai, obviously moved by his plea, promised she would cable the entire contents of their conversation to Moscow that very day.

Rudel returned to London where a few days later he was called to the Soviet embassy. There an official told him, "The foreign ministry in Moscow has instructed me to inform you that the government has received a report concerning your conversation with Madame Kollontai and that everything will be done to fulfill your request."

As it so happened, the Russians would make no special effort to liberate the camp before the end of the war, and Rudel's fears for its future would prove to be well founded.

38. According to Troller, photos of some of their art work had appeared in the Swiss press and this had triggered the investigation which caught not only the four artists mentioned here but several others as well.

39. Only Haas, his wife and, quite miraculously, Fritta's young son survived the war. The Haas' adopted Tomas when they returned to Czechoslovakia.

40. As to Schliesser, he also knew too much and was not only involved in the food problems but had formed a close relationship with Bartels, the SS economic *Referent* in the camp and a man whom Rahm hated. Rahm had uncovered evidence that the pair were planning to profiteer through some of the camp's production operations. He could not get rid of Bartels, who had close connections with higher-ups, but he could foil his plans by getting rid of Schliesser.

41. An incident depicted by Lederer shows Murmelstein in a slightly softer or more vulnerable light. According to Lederer, Zucker and Schliesser were placed in a separate waiting room at the Schleuse for the first transport. When Prochnik came in and told them they would have a separate carriage on the transport, Zucker refused, insisting they would share the same conditions as the others. Prochnik left. Soon thereafter Murmelstein entered and "with tears streaming down his face" said the Germans insisted. Zucker then agreed.

42. Murmelstein testified later that the discovery of the note was the first time he knew of the transports' destination. Adler calls this "unbelievable," but Mrs. Koralek told me it was true.

43. Suskind, though fully accepted and even revered by the Dutch, was actually half German. He had grown up in Germany where he was a classmate of Ferdinand Aus Der Funten, the Nazi director of jewish affairs in Holland. Aus Der Funten had given him a warm letter of recommendation, but when suskind with letter in hand attempted to approach Rahm on the deportation platform, an overzealous member of the transport commission pushed him back into line. Suskind, his wife, and their young daughter all perished in Auschwitz.

44. In general, however, there appears to have been little homosexuality in Theresienstadt, at least little that was overt. Utitz says he never came across or heard of any instance of it. Lustig says he knew of a few cases, one individual being a Dutch opera tenor. Fredy Hirsch, despite his military manner and athletic ability, was widely thought to be homosexual, but if so, he was apparently quite discreet.

CHAPTER 12
FINAL DANGERS, FINAL DAYS

A new year arrived bringing fresh hopes and fresh challenges. The hopes came from continued Allied advances--the Americans had crushed a last-ditch German counterattack in the soon-to-be-famous Battle of the Bulge--and from continuing indications that the Nazis intended to preserve the ghetto. These same indications, however, also brought the fresh challenges.

Shortly before the year began, the SS decided to refurbish a barracks for their own use. To this end they had ordered the camp's now minimally-manned Technical Department to outfit the building with an elaborate kitchen, an ornate diningroom, a plush lounge, and a cinema. With their regime collapsing, their comrades dying in battle, and their families at home exposed to almost daily air raids, the SS remained committed to its own comfort.

The completion of this construction project brought the challenge of a much greater one. The Jews were ordered to build a special internment complex on the town's embankments. Apparently Theresienstadt was being readied for a substantial influx of new inhabitants.

Whatever differences remained between male and female labor now virtually disappeared as every able and available resident, children included, worked daily from 6:00 A.M. to 9:00 P.M. In the bitter cold they unloaded 4,500 tons of steel from railroad cars, brought it to the embankment, and used it to erect eight separate buildings in the allotted time. The buildings remained empty, however, for although new transports soon began arriving, the existing facilities proved adequate to accommodate those they brought.

The first of these transports arrived on the last day of January, carrying 1,056 Jews from Prague. Over 5,000 others would soon follow. Most were Jews who had hitherto been protected, chiefly by marriage to Aryans, but a few were half-Jews who for some reason or other had lost their protected status. Nearly all were from Prague or from smaller communities in the Reich.

It seems likely that the Nazis intended to bring Jews from the Reich's larger cities as well but the Allied air raids had so destroyed records and disrupted bureaucratic routines in these cities as to make this impossible. The far greater numbers of Jews remaining in these cities would have required the new buildings.

Just why the Nazis were willing at such a late date to tie up trains and manpower to bring Jews to Theresienstadt remains unclear.

Lederer believes that since the new arrivals knew nothing of Theresienstadt's past, and since they were not severely malnourished, they would
make a better impression on the Allies. They might also, of course,
make the disappearance of nearly 88,000 Theresienstadt Jews to the
East somewhat less noticeable. On the other hand, some Nazis may
have been planning or hoping to make these hitherto protected Jews
disappear as well, and were sending them to Theresienstadt as a first
step toward such an end. Events during the following month tend to
substantiate the latter hypothesis.

The new arrivals adjusted to the camp less well than even the Dutch.
To reassure their Aryan spouses and in-laws, as well as to facilitate their
departure generally, the SS had not told them they were going to a
ghetto. Instead they were supposedly going on a "work detail" where
they would enjoy freedom of movement after working hours. They were
also allowed to bring money with them. On arriving at Theresienstadt,
however, they were stripped of their money as well as anything else of
value, first by the Nazis and then by the Jews on the transportation
commission. The latter rationalized their actions by claiming that the
newcomers had been enjoying a privileged existence while they had been
enduring the privations of a concentration camp.

The new residents did receive certain mail privileges and some
portion of their possessions was returned to their Aryan partners. Yet,
says Murmelstein, they showed "little zeal for working, preferring instead
to stand around the streets cursing their fate and the Jewish administration, since they did not dare to curse the SS." Most did not regard
themselves as Jews and many were observant Christians. Some,
especially the half-Jews, even expressed Nazi inclinations and ideas and
would on occasion give the Nazi salute and shout "Heil Hitler."

Despite the problems they presented, they did provide some benefits.
Since most were men, their arrival narrowed the camp's gender gap.
Moreover, many of these men had been working for the Nazi war effort
and hence brought needed manual skills which most of them eventually,
if reluctantly, put to the ghetto's use. Others were accomplished artistes
who injected new vitality into the camp's cultural life. Violinist Paul
Herz, a mixed marriage partner, joined his pianist sister Alisha Herz-
Sommer in a recital of Beethoven's sonatas for piano and violin. Pianist
Hermann Lydendorf became the concertmaster of Peter Deutsch's
orchestra.

The newcomers also gave a great boost to the camp's Christian
community. The Catholics benefitted the most since the newcomers
were more heavily of that persuasion and the Catholic congregation now

moved ahead of the Protestants in numbers. In addition, one new Catholic, a Prague veterinarian named Drucker, gradually took over the congregation's organizational work from the increasingly debilitated Ruschkowitz. With the arrival of the last of these transports, Christians comprised close to one-third of the supposedly all-Jewish ghetto.

January also brought a small, quite unusual, and possibly significant transport from the Reich. It consisted of five former female inmates, two of them teenagers, from the women's concentration camp at Ravensbruck.

The SS put all five in its own jail but treated them well while interrogating them intensely. Guenther and even Eichmann did some of the questioning. The Nazis seemed most intent on finding out how they viewed their own experience at Ravensbruck and how much they knew about the extermination camps. (Ravensbruck itself did not fall into that category.) They were eventually released with warnings to say nothing on such subjects to those they would meet in Theresienstadt. One of the five, Charlotte Freschner Salzberger, later testified that Eichmann told her to keep silent or "you will go up the chimney." His precautions proved unnecessary, however, for although she did talk about the gassings in Poland which she had learned about, no one believed her and some thought she had lost her mind.(45)

The work crew which had been constructing the proposed new Gestapo headquarters in Germany returned to the camp in February. They had built over 100 buildings, some of them designed for Hitler and his staff should the Fuehrer decide to flee Berlin. They and their abilities had been sorely missed.

The most notable event of early February, however, involved not an arrival but a departure. At 4:00 in the afternoon of February 5, some 1,210 well-dressed Theresienstadt Jews boarded a train bound, so they believed or at least hoped, for Switzerland.

A former president of Switzerland, Jean Marie Musy, was chiefly responsible for their departure. Oddly enough, Musy had undertaken such an initiative not because he liked Jews but because he didn't. His hostility to Jews had supplied him with both the motive and the means to now liberate some of them.

As a right-wing politician with pro-Nazi leanings, Musy had over the years developed a cordial relationship with many high-ranking Nazis including Himmler. With German defeat growing increasingly certain, he was now trying to cover up his past by switching sides. One way to do this was to show himself as a friend of their victims. The previous April he had, at the request of an influential Swiss Jewish businessman, secured the release to Switzerland of a Jewish couple being held in a temporary concentration camp in France.

Isaac Sternbruch, the Geneva representative of the Orthodox Rabbinical Association of America, heard of Musy's action and contacted him with the request that he negotiate the release of all Jews in SS custody. Musy, seeing a way that he could emerge from the war as a hero rather than a villain, or at least as a supporter of villains, agreed. In October the 75-year-old Swiss politician and his son Benoit went to Vienna to meet with Himmler.

Himmler proved quite responsive to Musy's request for the SS chief knew that he needed to improve his image far more than did Musy. But Himmler did not want any such leniency to be interpreted as weakness, so in exchange for releasing Jews he asked for trucks and autos which, he said, Germany would use to rebuild after the war. Musy managed to persuade him to accept money instead. The Rabbinical organization had raised the equivalent of 5 million Swiss francs or a little over $1 million, and Sternbruch offered to deposit it in a Swiss bank as a good faith pledge. The head of America's War Refugee Board, an organization Roosevelt had set up in response to persistent pressure from American Jews, also supported Musy's initiative. In January the deal was struck; starting in early February Himmler would release some 1,200 Jews to Switzerland every four days.

Theresienstadt was the natural place to begin such releases since its Jews had endured fewer privations and witnessed fewer atrocities than those of other camps. Thus, on February 3 an announcement was posted throughout the camp inviting the inmates to sign up for a transport to Switzerland.

Initially, most residents reacted with skepticism and scorn. All too many could remember the promises made and assurances given during the fall deportations. (While most still did not realize the real horror that awaited those who had left, they did know that the deportees went to Poland and not the Reich.) The fact that Prominenten, disabled veterans, people with Aryan relatives, and Danes were excluded from this new transport only reinforced their fears. But Rahm went out of his way to promote the transport, giving assurances right and left that it was going to Switzerland and freedom. A more important factor in its favor was that no one was being forced to go. Although every resident was ordered to appear at the processing center at 3:00 A.M. the next morning, each was to be given the right to reject the offer by simply signing a statement of renunciation.

About 2,000 Theresienstadters ended up applying for the trip. The SS excluded all intellectuals, all prominent personalities, and all those whose next of kin had been sent to the East. Such people, so the SS reasoned, were too likely to say too many of the wrong things about the ghetto once they were freed from Nazi custody. The group of 1,200 finally selected were disproportionately elderly, although 48 children were included, and disproportionately Dutch. The latter had signed up in greater numbers than other camp residents for they had had less experience in Nazi double-dealing at Theresienstadt and were also still less well adjusted to camp life.

Those selected were instructed to wear their best clothing and carry "elegant suitcases." A teenager who showed up at the railroad station with shoes tied by ropes received a new pair. All were provided with railroad tickets. Somewhat nervously they boarded the third-class carriages that were waiting for them.

The train had hardly left the station when the Nazis began distributing generous supplies of bread, margarine, sugar, sausage, and dried milk. This was more food than most had received since the start of the war. Even vitamin tablets were given out. These gestures and provisions eased their anxieties, which were further allayed when they saw the train continue through South Germany instead of swerving to the East.

During the trip they were given additional food, including marmalade, jam, and generous doses of Ovaltine. As they neared the Swiss border, the Nazis handed out lipstick and other cosmetics to the women with orders to put them on. On arriving at the border shortly after midnight, a Nazi official announced that in the name of the Fuehrer they were to remove their Jewish stars. Almost immediately the corridors were littered with yellow stars and crowded with people joyously embracing each other.

The train remained at the border for several hours alongside what appeared to be an empty barn. Fear once again began to grip some of the passengers who wondered if the Nazis were planning to take them into the barn and shoot them. But as dawn broke, the train crossed over into the Swiss town of Kreuzlingen. An SS man strode down the corridors declaring, "In the name of Reichsleiter Himmler, you are now free." When the train came to a halt, women from the Swiss Red Cross came aboard distributing apples, chocolate, and cigarettes. When one elderly man said he smoked only cigars, a Swiss Red Cross worker dashed out to the platform to buy one for him. Soon they were allowed to descend from the train. For these 1,210 Theresienstadters, the war had ended.

On the railroad platform they found a group of Swiss journalists eager to question them. The Nazis had told them to say nothing defamatory to the Reich lest they cause unpleasant repercussions to their comrades back in Theresienstadt. All but one obeyed the order. The exception was an elderly woman who was quite deaf and had not heard the order when it was given. She talked freely to the reporters once they learned to shout their questions in her ear.

News accounts were carried not only in the press but also on Swiss radio. As such, the clandestine radio receiver in Theresienstadt picked them up. In this way, and through postcards bearing Swiss postmarks, the ghetto learned that the transport had arrived safely at its announced destination.

Unfortunately, Kaltenbrunner, whom Himmler had kept in the dark about the whole affair, learned of it through the same reports and almost immediately told his fellow Austrian, Hitler. Hitler reacted by reproving Himmler and warning him against any further such moves. The first Theresienstadt transport to Switzerland would also be the last.

It will be recalled that Theresienstadt was designed as a fortress town with its jagged circle of embankments serving as ramparts. These embankments were laced with a network of casements, i.e., within-ground chambers and passageways. These casements were also dotted with holes so that sharpshooters could fire at a besieging enemy.

In early February the SS assigned the Jews two new construction projects. They were to transform a portion of this within-ground network into a place suitable for storing vegetables. They were also to fence off a broad expanse outside one stretch of the embankments for an enlarged poultry farm which would include a large duck pond.

A construction crew of over 80 promptly went to work, but soon questions began to arise as to what the real purpose of these two projects might be. The vegetable storehouse needed a ventilation system, the SS said, but if so, why were the pipes they were to install not designed to lead out to the roof? Also, if ventilation was needed, why was the crew directed to seal up all the sniper holes? And why were airtight doors to be installed that could not be opened from the inside?

The expanded poultry farm with its projected duck pond created still more concern. The Nazis wanted to enclose it not simply with a fence but with a wall 18 feet high covered with broken glass. Was such a barrier necessary to contain ducks and geese, or even to keep out possible poachers? Was it necessary to have only one opening to the enclosed area, and that opening easily blocked off from the outside by the removal of some steps? And was it necessary to have such an expanded area, large enough to hold all the ghetto's inmates? Finally, why were Rahm and Haindl giving these two undertakings so much personal attention and why had high SS officials from Prague and even Berlin come to inspect the work? Could a vegetable storehouse and a duck pond be so important?

The construction crew soon began to suspect that the SS planned to use the "vegetable storehouse" as a gas chamber and the "poultry farm" as a site for mass execution. These suspicions mounted when Rahm stopped the further issuance of Zyclone-B gas used up to now for vermin. He ordered the head of the disinfection station to hand over his keys and then had the gas moved to an embankment chamber near the site of the supposed storehouse. Fears further increased when one of the Jewish engineers helping to create the poultry farm overheard Rahm say to Haindl as they both inspected the site, "From here one can cover the entire area with a single sweep."

By now the entire camp was alarmed. Many thought the SS would take the prisoners from the Little Fortress to the vegetable storehouse for gassing and would march Theresienstadt's inmates to the proposed "poultry farm," possibly on the pretext of a new census, and then machine-gun them down. Baeck told everyone he could to lie down on the ground and refuse to move if ordered to go to the new facilities. He reasoned that the SS simply lacked the manpower to cart off all the Jews to either site. Others started making plans to blow up the new installation and then lead a mass breakout. But meanwhile the camp's engineers decided to call on Murmelstein.

They found him in his office, and Erich Kohn, the head of the technical department, told the Jewish Elder that they would no longer work on the project. If they were going to be killed, he said, they would rather it be done in the camp itself where it could be brought to the world's attention. Murmelstein at first balked at accepting their theory as to the true intent of the two projects, but after a heated discussion which lasted through the night, he agreed to speak to Rahm.

He sought Rahm outside of the customary morning conference and confronted him with what the engineers had said. He also warned the commandant that a mass breakout might well occur and that he, Murmelstein, would be unable to stop it. Rahm exploded in anger and was still furious sometime later when he summoned the engineers to see him. When Kohn refused to retract what he had said regarding the project's real intent and the engineers' intention regarding it, Rahm unholstered his pistol. But then, apparently thinking better about an on-the-spot execution, he used the pistol merely to strike Kohn to the ground. When Kohn still refused to repudiate his statement, Rahm hit him several more times, but then stopped.

Rahm left the next day for Prague, returning two days later. Subsequently, officials from SS headquarters in Berlin inspected the construction site for a second time, this time at night. The project was then discreetly abandoned. Theresienstadt had apparently survived its closest brush yet with total disaster.

While the resistance of the residents almost certainly played a role in the abandonment of the undertaking, other factors may also have helped. Rumors had already begun to circulate in Geneva that the Nazis planned to destroy the camp, and the International Red Cross had instructed its Berlin branch to seek a second visit to Theresienstadt. Also, an SS captain named Dieter Wisliczeny may have played a part. On February 24 Wisliczeny wrote a letter to the Jewish Rescue Committee in Budapest in which he said the following:

I was just in Berlin [when] Prague telephoned Eichmann with the question of what to do with Theresienstadt in case of a Russian thrust. Eichmann explained that of course the Jews must immediately and completely be exterminated.

I told him I was in agreement but wanted to know if he believed that all the traces of such a mass murder could be erased. . . I knew Eichmann well. He was blamed for allowing the gas chambers and crematoria in Majdanek [an extermination camp] to fall undisturbed into the hands of the Russians. Throughout the Allied world there was outrage. Eichmann feared a new scandal. He answered right away, "No, no. I've had enough." He accepted my proposal that in case of a Russian breakthrough, to leave the Jews in their place in Theresienstadt. They would be watched by Czech gendarmes while our men drew back to the mountains.

It was also revealed after the war that the SS had not planned to machine gun the entire ghetto population in the area selected for the poultry farm. They had planned to use flame throwers instead.

The month of March saw further arrivals and departures. The departures consisted of a few small work groups numbering 102 men in all, who left for Bavaria. All eventually returned to Theresienstadt, though the Reich's increasingly confused and crumbling transportation system forced some of them to spend eight days crisscrossing Germany before they reached the camp.

More significant were the arrivals. They included more Jews in mixed marriages, more Slovakian Jews, and the ghetto's first group of Hungarian Jews. The latter, numbering just over 1,000, reached the ghetto on March 11. They had been working on a "Wall" designed to block the Russians from Vienna.

The Hungarians arrived in deplorable condition. Despite the winter cold, many had no shoes and all had gone without food for several days. After some rest, nourishment, and care, most were ready to participate in camp life. Murmelstein proposed giving them a representative on the Council of Elders. The Council agreed but turned down his choice of a Zionist, preferring instead an internationally prominent Hungarian Jew. The Council reasoned that the latter would provide more protection from further Nazi efforts to destroy the camp.

The Slovaks, who also numbered about 1,000, came much later, in early April after the Nazis had closed down their work camp in Sered. They arrived in relatively good shape, bringing with them not just machinery and raw materials from the factories they had been operating for the Nazis, but also considerable quantities of food. The transportation commission quickly robbed them of their food, saying they must have been collaborators in having avoided deportation for so long. However, the Slovakians had avoided deportation only because their leaders had succeeded in bribing their SS overseer, and the latter in turn had convinced Berlin to keep the work camp in operation. The stigma of collaborationism was removed when their leader, a Zionist named J. O. Neumann, provided proof that he had been secretly working with the Slovakian resistance.

The Slovaks asked for representation on the Council of Elders, but Murmelstein remained noncommittal. Undoubtedly he was influenced by Meissner's opposition to any gesture that would seem to sanction the separate nation status of Slovakia. But such representation would probably not have much benefitted the Slovaks in any case, for Murmelstein liked to run a one-man show and had become increasingly used to doing so. This fact was not lost on Neumann, who writes, "At our first meeting, this man, who had taken on all the gestures and speech mannerisms of his Nazi bosses, made a disturbing impression on us. His extremely egoistic way of speaking allowed hardly any of our group to say a word."

The most important arrival occurred on March 5, when Eichmann came to the ghetto. He was, of course, a frequent visitor, but this was his first call since the cancellation of the "vegetable storehouse" and "duck pond" projects. His visit would decide what final steps the SS would now take regarding the ghetto's future. After carefully inspecting the camp, Eichmann expressed satisfaction at what he had seen. Theresienstadt in its present condition, he said, would please anyone. The camp had apparently gained a new lease on life. In fact, it would once again be shown to foreign visitors.

One thing, however, bothered Eichmann: the crematorium along with the funeral urns that had accumulated since the previous November. In those days most religious people, including observant Jews, condemned cremation, and Eichmann told Murmelstein that he had heard of harsh criticisms abroad about this Nazi practice. Eichmann wanted the ghetto to resume the earth burials which it had practiced before the crematorium was built.

Murmelstein, while being careful to say he agreed with Eichmann in principle, pointed out the practical problems this would present, the most serious being the high water level in the burial ground. He also noted that many relatives of the dead would want to take the ashes of their loved ones with them, and that relatives from abroad would also make inquiries. The irony of this exchange was not lost on Murmelstein, who writes, "And so a grotesque situation arose in which a high-placed SS officer, basing himself on Jewish beliefs, defended Jewish burial while a rabbi defended cremation."

Since Eichmann's word was decisive, the ghetto resumed ground interment with the predictable result that the bodies kept rising to the surface. An order to make the graves at least three and a half feet deep failed to arrest or even alleviate the problem. The bodies of the dead continued to bubble up.

During Eichmann's visit Murmelstein came close to losing more than simply his argument over cremation. The rabbi had incurred Guenther's disfavor by disregarding as impractical some of the latter's instructions with respect to the Swiss transport, and also by his perceived closeness to Rahm with whom Guenther was now at odds.

Murmelstein was not fully aware of this, so that when Guenther told him to prepare a thorough account of what had happened in the camp to give to Eichmann, Murmelstein had stayed up most of the night memorizing facts and dates. But the next morning Rahm warned him that a full and factual account would only enrage Eichmann. Instead, he should give Eichmann the same sort of report he would give the anticipated foreign inspection commission, i.e., a falsified one. Murmelstein reasoned that Rahm tipped him off because he saw a link between Edelstein's removal and Seidl's transfer, and feared that Murmelstein's removal would lead to his own loss of position. So Murmelstein prepared and presented the kind of report Eichmann wanted.

Guenther, however, was not yet ready to concede defeat. During their tour of the town, Guenther suddenly sent Murmelstein, who was accompanying Eichmann, ahead so that he could talk to the SS colonel. After 10 minutes, Eichmann called Murmelstein back and asked him if Eppstein's removal had created a negative reaction in the ghetto. When Murmelstein dodged the question, Eichmann mentioned that Eppstein was running another camp and perhaps they should bring him back and send Murmelstein in his place. Rahm and Moehs, however, had joined the group and argued vigorously that replacing the Jewish Elder just before a foreign inspection would create a bad impression. Eichmann then turned to Guenther and said, "So Murmelstein remains here for the time being."

The prospect of a new Red Cross visit produced another beautification effort. Despite Germany's shortage of goods and the trains to carry them, Murmelstein received permission to requisition new materials and promptly did so. The camp's kindergarten had been taken over to lodge recent arrivals, forcing the children to play on the street. Murmelstein now took over another building and made it into what he at least regarded as a model kindergarten. He also renovated an existing youth home and took several other steps to make the ghetto conform more closely to the image the Nazis wanted to present.

Although this second beautification project fell far short of the first in scope or intensity, it did lead to various improvements, including a further invigoration of the camp's cultural life. One of the recent arrivals was Hanus Thein who, in addition to being a prominent Czech singer, was also a former stage director of the Czechoslovakian national theatre. Rahm summoned Thein to his office and bluntly told him, "I need a children's opera." It would be his job to produce one in time for the impending, but as yet unscheduled, foreign visit.

Thein was at first desperate for only the score of *Hansel and Gretel* was at hand and it was too difficult to produce with the time and resources available. But he had heard that Vlasta Schoenova had staged the Czech fairytale *Fireflies* as a dance while she read the text. She at first refused to help revive the production as an opera for she wanted to do nothing that would   aid the Nazi cause. But she eventually yielded to Thein's pleadings and agreed to help.

Rahm also helped by releasing her along with other women artistes from feldspar splitting, abolishing the ban on the use of the Czech language in cultural events, and assigning composer-conductor Robert Brock, another winter arrivee, to compose the music. He gave Brock only three days to do this, but to help him meet such a deadline, he provided him with a private workroom and supplied him with generous quantities of coffee so that he could work through the night.

The new opera premiered on March 20 and scored an immediate success, in part for reasons which the Nazis did not surmise. Brock had smuggled into the score the Czech national anthem, subtly concealed in the contrapuntal middle voices. It took a musical, and Czech, ear to discern it. But this, in addition to the lines, "Spring will soon arrive; May will be here again," brought tears to the eyes of the Czechs who attended the opening. The Nazis, suspecting nothing, rewarded Thein with the most joyfully received gift of his career: a can of liver pate.

The success of *Fireflies* prompted Rahm to summon Thein back to his office. This time the commandant ordered him to stage The Tales of *Hoffmann* y the Jewish composer Offenbach. He then followed up this order by throwing the score of the opera at the astonished Thein's feet. Rahm demanded, however, that he shorten it considerably, a demand which Thein met by eliminating most of the first two acts and incorporating their highlights into the third act.

Other cultural activities also blossomed as the new beautification took hold. A program sheet entitled "Offerings of the Leisure Time Bureau for the Week of March 10" shows one to three concerts every night, most of them recitals by women pianists.

While few plays were now being produced, on March 10 the jurists of the ghetto court unwittingly contributed a comedy of their own. They issued a new, highly detailed criminal code which, among other things, legally and elaborately defined Theresienstadt. With the SS and now, to some extent, Murmelstein making decisions as they saw fit, the court's new code, the product of many hours of examination, discussion, and dispute, would play virtually no part in Theresienstadt life.

The International Red Cross (IRC) was now pressing the Nazis for more access to all of the Reich's remaining concentration camps. On March 12 the organization's president, Carl Burckhardt, met with Kaltenbrunner in Austria and asked him to place all the camps under Red Cross supervision. When Kaltenbrunner refused, Burckhardt sought permission not only to send food but to station representatives at these camps. Kaltenbrunner agreed but with one stipulation: the representatives would not be allowed to leave the camps until the war's end.

The Red Cross subsequently selected a dozen volunteers for this task. A 44-year-old French Swiss named Paul Dunant was assigned to Theresienstadt. On March 23 the SS recanted, telling the IRC that visits to the concentration camps would not be possible for lack of suitable SS monitors. There was one exception, however: Theresienstadt. This "Jewish settlement area" could be inspected in order "to end the propaganda lies of the enemy."

The visit was scheduled for April 6 and in Theresienstadt the pace of beautification now picked up. As was the case with the first foreign visit, walls were whitewashed, flower beds were hastily planted, streets were swept clean and scrubbed. The ghetto bank building was transformed into a headquarters for the Council of Elders and equipped with telephones, furniture, and even Persian carpets. The files of the Jewish administration were combed through and all incriminating papers were burned. Urns containing ashes of the dead were installed in a flower-decorated hall, while in the burial ground outside two monuments were erected and specially treated to look weather-worn. The residents were instructed to give false figures on the death toll and to explain the sparse number of funeral urns by saying that the rest had been taken to the Jewish cemetery in Prague.

The SS conducted a dress rehearsal for the visit, touring the camp and asking the inmates questions in an agreeable, almost affable, manner. When they were answered with mournful complaints and tearful counter-questions concerning the whereabouts of departed loved ones, they decided to take the Red Cross visitors only through unoccupied areas.

Prior to the visit a Red Cross official named A. Schneiper arrived in Theresienstadt bringing four trucks loaded with food from Geneva. He had been instructed to seek the release of further inmates and to find out about the ghetto's need for more food and medicine. Schneiper's small caravan was kept out of the ghetto itself, being allowed only to drive along the perimeter street to SS headquarters. He could speak with Murmelstein only in Rahm's presence and while Murmelstein, who seemed uneasy, signed a paper confirming the shipment's arrival, it was not unloaded in Schneiper's presence. When he asked Rahm about the possible release of residents, Rahm phoned Berlin and then replied,

"No." The next morning Schneiper and his four now empty trucks departed for Geneva.

Four days later the official IRC delegation arrived. It consisted of three Swiss, the IRC's current Berlin representative, O. Lehner, the volunteer representative selected for Theresienstadt, Paul Dunant, and a Swiss diplomat named Buckmuller. Along with them came two officials of the German Foreign Office plus various SS officials including Eichmann and Guenther. Murmelstein greeted them with a carefully prepared address which had gone all the way up to Himmler for approval. (The SS chief had made some corrections before approving it.) They then toured the camp, but the only one of its 17,500 residents they could speak to was Murmelstein.(46)

The delegation inspected several sites, including Murmelstein's own apartment, attended a performance of *Fireflies* as well as a concert, and finally saw the film which Gerron had shot the previous August. It had only recently been put into final form and given the title "The Fuehrer Presents a City to the Jews." They also witnessed the distribution of food sent from Switzerland.

Unlike the previous June, one Theresienstadter managed on this occasion to convey a secret message to a member of the delegation. It was the same nurse from Vienna who had audaciously approached Rahm during a deportation and persuaded him to let her stay. She was on duty when the delegation entered her ward and, when introduced to Dunant, she pressed a piece of paper into his hand. On the paper were the words, *Was Sie sehen hier ist nicht wahr. Bitte helfen Sie uns.* (What you see here is not true. Please help us.)

The Swiss showed considerable interest in deportations from the camp for the arrival of the transport from Theresienstadt in Switzerland the past February had brought news of the massive exodus the previous fall. When they queried Murmelstein about deportations from the ghetto, the rabbi at first hesitated and an SS official stepped in to answer. The latter first put the total deportation figure at 10,000, but under further questioning changed it to refer only to those deported in the fall. He put the total number deported during the camp's entire existence at 18,000, or 70,000 less than the actual figure. When asked why the 10,000 had been sent the previous fall, the Nazis said it was to expand the facilities at Auschwitz. When asked about the present whereabouts of the deportees, the Nazis replied, with a shoulder shrug, that presumably they were now in Russian hands.

The Swiss elicited a promise from the Nazis to deport no further Jews from the town. But as they were preparing to leave, Murmelstein, in thanking them for their visit, expressed some concern over Theresien-stadt's future. His statement could, of course, be interpreted in several different ways.

As with the first such visit the previous June, the visitors were taken to Prague and treated to a lavish dinner. During the evening Eichmann took Dunant into a corner to tell him that the Jews of Theresienstadt were living better than many Germans. Himmler, he said, wanted the Jews "to acquire a sense of racial community through the exercise of almost complete autonomy." Eichmann said he thought Himmler was being too soft-hearted but that he, Eichmann, as a good soldier, was faithfully following his leader's orders.(47)

Lehner sought to have Dunant stay in Theresienstadt as part of the agreement reached earlier with Kaltenbrunner. The Nazis said they would check with Kaltenbrunner on this point. In the meantime, Dunant would have to remain in Prague.

Although Lehner seemed to show more concern for the Jews of Theresienstadt than his predecessor Rossel had manifested during the first Red Cross visit, his report failed to reflect this. In the 4-page document he sent back to Geneva, he said, "The residents of Theresien-stadt have the same [ration] cards as the German civil population. Since they also receive many individual and collective packages, they should generally be better off. . . In fact, the residents of Theresienstadt do not appear undernourished." Pointing out that the group's overall impression of the camp was very favorable, he noted, "We refer to the report of Dr. Rossel and can only add that in the interim nothing has changed."

When it came to the most critical area of concern, deportations, Lehner cited assurances, which he attributed to Murmelstein, that there had been no recent deportations, although 10,000 [not 18,000] had earlier been "transferred" to the East. This, of course, represented a repudiation of Rossel's report that Theresienstadt was an *Endlager* or final destination camp. But the contradiction did not seem to bother Lehner. He described the film they had been shown as having a "lightly propagandistic tone" but did not otherwise comment on it. Once again, a Swiss visit seems to have given the Nazis the result they desired.

Although the inspection had generally gone well for the Nazis, Guenther remained dissatisfied. Rahm had been ill on the day of the visit, so Guenther had joined Murmelstein in leading the visitors through the camp. The joint endeavor seems only to have increased Guenther's antipathy toward the Jewish Elder.

Guenther returned to the camp three days later, and although he had other business to attend to, he used the occasion to accuse Murmelstein of expressing to the Red Cross some doubt about the future of Theresienstadt. He also noted that the rabbi's 9-year-old son Michael had been absent during their visit to his home and wondered if this represented either some sort of protest or if the boy had been smuggled out of the ghetto. He demanded that Murmelstein produce the youngster.

According to Murmelstein's account, his son in fact did not like such encounters and so had purposely stayed away. But now father and son went to SS headquarters where they spent an anxious one and a half hours outside Guenther's office waiting for the latter to appear. Finally, Guenther emerged. After formally interrogating the youngster to make sure he was really Murmelstein's son and that his absence three days earlier was not an act of defiance, he let the matter drop.

The following day, Eichmann paid what would be his last visit to the camp. It was probably just a stopover on his way to Berlin, for he gave no orders and made no changes of any consequence. He did, however, make a statement that would come back to haunt him during his trial in Jerusalem 17 years later. Aware that the end of the Reich might mark his own end as well, he said, "I shall gladly jump into the pit knowing that in the same pit there are five million enemies of the Reich."

Meanwhile, Dunant remained in Prague awaiting Kaltenbrunner's final OK to take up residence in Theresienstadt. On April 12 he heard that the Nazis had destroyed the list of Theresienstadt inmates and fearing that this might be a prelude to destroying the entire camp, he rushed to Berlin. There he was assured that no such plans were in the offing. He then returned to Prague to await the day when he would take up residence in Theresienstadt.

The Swiss were not the only neutrals seeking to demonstrate more interest in concentration camps as the end of Hitler's Reich drew near. The Swedes were also showing more concern for the Nazi regime's victims, and one of their foremost diplomats, Count Bernadotte, though essentially an anti-Semite like Musy, had also, like Musy, begun negotiating with the Nazis in behalf of the Jews. The result of his negotiations came on April 13 when a diplomatic car flying Danish flags drove into Theresienstadt and stopped before the SS headquarters. After a few hours, an announcement was posted: The Danish Jews were going home!

The news thrilled the camp. Though happy for the Danes, whom nearly everyone liked, the residents were also happy for themselves, since the release of the Danes seemed to signal the coming liberation of them all.

Toward midnight two days later a convoy of small buses flying Swedish flags streamed into the camp to take the Danes back. Leavetaking the next day became a joyous event. Although Rahm at first tried to suppress all ceremony, he soon changed his mind. He even lifted the ban on tobacco and ordered the "city band" to play.

As the entire camp assembled under warm and sunny skies to say goodby, Rabbi Friediger hurriedly married off all the eligible Danish men to various Theresienstadt women so that they could be rescued as well. Some of the men had never met their new brides but cheerfully pledged their troth. Comments Emma Fuchs, "Denmark was probably the only country in Europe that got back more Jews than had been deported."

Before the Danes left, some Czechs told them they had spotted large quantities of food in the buses. There was, they said, a chocolate bar and a pack of cigarettes on every seat. As a result, most Danes were easily persuaded to give away their remaining provisions. When they entered the buses and found no chocolate or cigarettes, many were understandably upset at the trick the Czechs had played on them. But some of the younger ones found it amusing and shouted, "The score now stands: Czechs 1, Danes 0." In any event, there was ample food aboard for the trip home.

The Swedish drivers in their white uniforms also added to the uplifting mood. They refused German offers of food and cigarettes and offered cigarettes of their own to the crowd. When Rahm refused to release one Dane who had gone blind in the camp, the Swedes refused to leave until he too was let go. (Rahm probably feared being blamed for the man's blindness.) But the real Swedish contribution to the joyousness of the occasion came when Haindl, the most hated man in the camp, sought to climb aboard a bus to inspect its interior. No sooner was his foot on the running board than a handsome six-foot driver shot out his arm, and barking "Extraterritorial," barred his way. Haindl then slunk off. For those who witnessed it, the incident provided their most exhilarating moment yet in Theresienstadt.

As these April arrivals and departures indicate, Theresienstadt was opening up. The once sealed-off community was almost becoming a visitors' center. Indeed, the day after the Danes departed, two separate non-Nazi visitors called. The first, who arrived in the morning, was Musy's son Benoit. He had heard disturbing rumors regarding the fate of the children and wanted to investigate, presumably with an eye to disproving them. The SS were only too happy to help him, and after he inspected the new kindergarten and received some reassuring if falsified reports, he departed.

The more important and by far more interesting visitor arrived in the afternoon. He was Rudolf Kasztner of the Jewish Rescue Committee in Budapest. Kasztner was the first free Jew ever to call at this or any other Nazi concentration camp or ghetto.

Rahm, Guenther, and other SS officials greeted him politely, without, however, offering to shake hands. They then accompanied Murmelstein as he led his co-religionist on a tour of the town. The group visited various ghetto facilities, including the fire station where Murmelstein staged an impressive drill. (He sounded an alarm and in 45 seconds the company was ready to fight a fire.) Kasztner was also shown the library with its 50,000 books, although Rahm grumbled that the residents actually read little and preferred instead to simply hang around the streets.

A tense moment occurred at the outset of Kasztner's visit when he asked to speak to Eppstein. Told the latter was unavailable, he inquired about some others. When answered with similar responses or with silence, he asked who among those who had signed the letter to him the previous May were still there. Murmelstein mentioned Baeck's name, although Baeck had not been among the signatories. Kasztner then asked to speak to Baeck but was told that would not be possible. (During his tour he did run into Baeck, who was waiting for him on a street corner, and he told the rabbi to reassure the others that the camp would soon be liberated.)

A more fruitful discussion between visitor and hosts centered on what to do with the ghetto since the Nazis were now willing to admit even to a Jew the certainty of their defeat. Kasztner urged them to hand Theresienstadt over to the Red Cross and the SS officials responded favorably, although without committing themselves.

At various moments Kasztner did have a chance to say a few words privately to Murmelstein. One of these moments occurred at the end of his visit. After bidding goodby to the Jewish Elder, he added two words in English which he pronounced with special emphasis: *Captain last*. He then departed.

All these goings and comings as well as continuing reports indicating Germany's impending collapse were having their effect on the camp's spirits. At a communal Passover Seder earlier in the month, at which Murmelstein himself officiated, a group of Slovakian Jews could no longer contain themselves. In a burst of exuberance, they got up in the middle of the ceremony and wildly danced a *hora*. The entire mood of the Seder, recalls Wrencher-Rustow, was one of "unbelievable hysteria."

Seeing the Nazis almost deferentially escorting a free Jew around the camp--several Slovakian as well as Hungarian Jews had recognized Kasztner--further whipped up this feeling of exhilaration. So did the constant sight of Allied war planes flying over Theresienstadt the next day. The population was thus primed for a deception which would lead to a near catastrophic confrontation.

It occurred on the night of April 17, the day following Kasztner's visit. During the evening a one-page mimeographed sheet began circulating through the camp, saying the SS had departed and the Red Cross would take over the camp the following day. The inmates poured out of their billets, cheering, singing, and dancing *horas* on the street.

Awakened by the noise, Murmelstein appeared and with a few others sought to disprove the report and quiet everyone down. Most of the celebrants had returned to their quarters when Murmelstein heard of a further commotion at the barracks of the recently arrived "mixed marriage" men in another section of the town. So he set out with his small band to calm things there as well.

As the group crossed in front of the coffeehouse, they were suddenly blinded by lights flashing in their eyes followed by the sound of Rahm's voice shouting, "Stand where you are or we'll shoot." When they were able to see, they discerned the commandant and about 10 other SS men, all holding submachine guns at the ready. Murmelstein stammered out what he knew about the false report and tried to convince the commandant that he would soon have things under control.

Rahm ordered Murmelstein to walk in front of him, with his hands up, to the site of the new disturbance. On route Murmelstein searched desperately for a way to save the situation and, of course, himself. He recalled how after Kasztner's visit a confused Rahm shook his head, saying, "I just don't understand the world any more." The Jewish Elder now seized on this expression, saying to Rahm as he sought to explain and excuse the unruliness, "They just don't understand the world any more."

When they arrived at the barracks, Rahm ordered the men, who were now inside packing their belongings to go home, out onto the street. There followed a tense moment as Rahm and his SS squad confronted the Jews, most of them still in their underwear. To one side stood

Murmelstein, his hands still raised and his pudgy, terrified face streaming with sweat.

Still clasping his submachine gun, Rahm took a step toward the men, hesitated for a moment, and then said, "*Meine Herren,*" a polite form of address to a male assembly. He then actually asked them to help maintain peace and order. Theresienstadt had weathered yet another brush with disaster.

The SS men with Rahm showed great disappointment at their superior's deference to the Jews, and as they started to leave some began voicing disgruntlement. But Rahm cut them short, saying somewhat defensively, "I know what I'm doing. I have everything under control."

The question now arises as to who printed and began circulating the false report which created the near catastrophe. Although the Jewish administration had a mimeograph machine, very few had access to it and it seems most unlikely that anyone would have used it for this purpose. Even if someone with access to the machine had heard and believed such a rumor, they almost certainly would have checked with Murmelstein before putting out a mimeographed statement. Consequently, the report seems to have been the work of one or more SS men angered and upset over seeing the Reich perish and the Jews survive. One should add at this point that Kasztner's visit had been followed by word from Berlin that Himmler had ordered all camps to be turned over intact to the Allied armies. (Himmler, however, would later change his mind.)

If the mimeographed statement originated from the SS, then Haindl seems the most likely suspect. Known for his extreme viciousness, he had earlier reacted to the cancellation of the "vegetable storehouse" and "duck farm" projects by setting a series of fires, some 12 in all, throughout the ghetto on February 28. He had then sought to restrain the fire department from responding. His public rebuff from the Swedish bus driver two days earlier had undoubtedly only intensified his feelings of frustration and rage. So he may well have put out the report in the hope of getting the Jews to react in a way that would give the SS an excuse to exterminate many of them. If so, he came dangerously close to achieving his goal.

Since his visit on April 6, Dunant had remained in Prague awaiting Kaltenbrunner's permission to move to Theresienstadt. The permission had still not arrived but the Swiss delegate did receive authorization to visit the camp again on April 21. This time he not only inspected the camp but addressed the Council of Elders, assuring them that the camp would eventually be liquidated. When they voiced some alarm at his statement, he quickly assured them that by liquidation he meant liberation. He also told them that the Red Cross had arranged with the Nazis to send inmates from other concentration camps to Theresienstadt and to direct to the camp other Jews passing through or near the Protectorate. Some Allied prisoners of war would also be coming.

The Red Cross representative showed a special concern over deportations from the camp and insisted on knowing if any residents, aside from the Danes, had left Theresienstadt since his previous visit. He had apparently heard rumors, and these rumors were not without foundation, for three days before his arrival the SS suddenly announced a new transport to Switzerland.

The announcement of a second Swiss transport met a mixed reaction. Some, knowing that the first group in February had arrived safely, eagerly signed up. Murmelstein inscribed his wife and son. But others remained suspicious. These suspicions grew when it became apparent that it would include only prominent people. Rahm told Murmelstein to remove his wife and son from the list.

Many of the Prominenten did not want to make the trip. With tears in his eyes, Meissner asked Murmelstein why he should have to return to Prague by way of Zurich. Murmelstein himself was becoming suspicious, and his suspicions as well as those of others increased when Rahm warned the Elders not to say anything to Dunant about the transport during the latter's April 21 visit.

Three days after Dunant's visit, still another transport was announced. This one would consist of construction workers who would travel not to Switzerland but to Bavaria to build barracks. But when Haindl subsequently let slip a remark indicating that the Bavarian-bound barracks builders and the Swiss-bound Prominenten were actually going to the same place, the whole camp became aroused. It seemed apparent that the construction crew was going to build housing for the Prominenten in Germany where the latter would be held for bargaining purposes.

Most inmates, including Murmelstein, were becoming somewhat bolder as the end of their captivity appeared closer. Most now did what they could to block the scheme. Backed by Prochnik, Murmelstein sought to convince Rahm that many of the Prominenten were old and sick and would die before they could be used as exchange hostages. The only result would be an international scandal that would do the Nazis and Rahm himself no good.

Rahm, beset with frequent bouts of illness, began showing less and less enthusiasm for the undertaking. When only a few construction workers showed up for the second transport, he became enraged and struck out at Murmelstein, only to hit an elderly carpenter by mistake. Then, though still furious, he left the scene. Thus, while railroad cars arrived to take both groups, the effort was quietly abandoned. Deportations from Theresienstadt had finally ended.

If the SS had abandoned all further plans for deporting Jews, it nonetheless was showing interest in evacuating one further group of camp residents: themselves. The Nazis had begun slaughtering most of their farm animals and salting the meat for removal. They ordered civilian clothing for themselves from the tailor shop and had the SS insignias on their uniforms replaced with those of the regular army. They also directed the Jews to turn in all their knapsacks. The Jews complied, but removed the cords so that the Nazis could not use them for carrying away their goods.

The SS were also stepping up their efforts to destroy all records, relics, and other things that would shed light on the camp's history. (Fortunately, the chief statistician in the registry office was secretly stashing away duplicate sets of many of the records in the town clock tower.) Then, on April 17, the Gestapo records office which, it will be recalled, had been moved to the camp the previous summer, burned all its files. Since these files covered all of Nazi-controlled Europe, the resulting fire filled the air and littered the streets with charred pieces of paper which the residents were strictly forbidden to touch. Having carried out this final operation, the records office personnel decamped, leaving the ghetto with its regular small SS garrison.

That this garrison with its weaponry could still pose a threat became evident in the confrontation at the Magdeburg barracks that very evening. But this event, in a way, marked the high point of its menace. From then on, its hold on the ghetto steadily weakened, for with their beloved Fuehrer holed up in his bunker as the Russians prepared to besiege Berlin, the SS men had other things on their minds. This did not, however, spell instant relief for the Jews at Theresienstadt, since they now found themselves confronting a new danger. It was posed by their fellow Jews.

A few hours after the Danish convoy had pulled out of the camp on April 15, a handful of Jews arrived from Vienna. It was the last "normal" transport to come to the camp, for even the zealous Eichmann could no longer organize an orderly deportation. In fact, the Russians were already entering Vienna as the transport left and had taken over the city by the time it arrived.

Five days later, the first non-normal transport arrived bringing Jews not from cities and towns within the Reich but from other concentration camps. Dunant had arranged with the Nazis to have Theresienstadt serve as a collection center for Jews from other camps, and from April 20 to May 6 some 15,000 such Jews poured into Theresienstadt, nearly doubling the existing population. Two-thirds of the newcomers arrived in cattle cars but some came on foot.

Nearly all had been half-starved and worn out when they set out for the ghetto. Nearly all were in much worse shape when they arrived. Those who came by train had been shuttled back and forth in the Reich's disintegrating and almost totally disorganized train system and had received little or no food during their journey. One group that came on April 21 from the Flossenburg concentration camp had spent 12 days in open wagons without provisions. Another transport consisting of 2,000 adults and children, had traveled for 30 days. Those who walked to the camp had often experienced the still greater terror of having been shot at by squads of Hitler youth.

Emaciated, half-dazed, and often swarming with lice, the new arrivals staggered into the town. Many collapsed on the street. Others never made it that far, having died en route. Of the 2,000 that arrived by train on May 6, 87 were dead. Given these situations, it was not surprising to learn that acts of cannibalism had occurred. As a survivor of the group that arrived by train from Flossenburg later wrote, "The horrible hunger drove some people to eat the bodies of those who had died . . . I myself saw how they tore away the flesh and consumed it." Some who came on foot had grass sticking out of their pockets, their sole nourishment during the latter stages of their journey.

Many who survived the trip died immediately after they arrived. Some simply collapsed from exhaustion. Others could not digest the bread which sympathetic Theresienstadters gave them. Still others failed to survive the rigors of the delousing process, some 25 dropping dead as soon as the hot water touched their bodies. The stench of putrefaction soon spread over the town as so many corpses piled up that it became impossible to bury or cremate them.

Some of the new arrivals were not newcomers at all but former residents who had previously been deported from Theresienstadt. Two inmates who were carrying one new arrival from a railroad car put him down on the grass for a moment to comfort him. Suddenly, the newcomer said to one of them, "You are Spritzer." The man he addressed looked at him in astonishment and replied, "Yes, but who told you so?"

"Don't you remember me? I am Frank Fein from the bakery."

Horrified, Spritzer and his fellow bearer looked down at the cadaverouslike figure whom they remembered as a young, strong man.

Baeck was told that a typhus patient among the new arrivals wanted to see him. Going immediately to the woman's bedside, he did not recognize her until she addressed him. He then realized it was his grandniece, Dorothea, who had previously been in Theresienstadt with him.

The inmates of Theresienstadt now learned finally and definitively what the Reich's other concentration camps were like. They learned this not just from what they saw but from what they heard. A group of young Greek women being questioned in French screamed when asked about Auschwitz, "FEU, BRULE." Although some Theresienstadters continued to harbor hopes of seeing their deported loved ones after liberation, none could any longer shield themselves from the truth.

Like the Bialystok children, many newcomers regarded the delousing station as a gas chamber and feared to enter it. When taken there, some sank to their knees and begged for mercy. "Let us live," they cried. Even the attempt to group them into marching columns aroused their anxieties. Yet many were too weak to offer any resistance.

The ghetto's inmates initially treated their fellow Jews with kindness and consideration. A Polish Jew who arrived on foot recalls how "the residents surrounded us and silently accompanied us, sharing their beet sugar and roasted potatoes. It was my most joyful moment since the outbreak of war." Another, arriving from Buchenwald, notes how "the Jews spared themselves their short rations to give them to us." A French Jewish woman praises the way the ghetto's nurses took them in hand. All non-essential activities were canceled to accommodate the newcomers. But soon attitudes began to change as it became apparent that these new residents confronted the ghetto not just with problems but perils.

The influx of the refugees coincided with a developing shortage of food supplies. The Nazis were hardly concerned at this time with feeding Jews while growing dislocations in their transportation system were holding up food shipments from Switzerland. As a result, the ghetto had already reduced the rations for its existing residents. Now it had to feed thousands of other Jews as well.

Most of these additional Jews were desperate for food, and some had been reduced to a near-animal state through the deprivations they had already endured. They would grab a sugar cube from the hands of a still weaker person and wolf it down. They would even beat each other for a piece of bread. On reaching Theresienstadt those with any strength left began raiding any place that contained anything they could put into their stomachs. They even broke into the pharmacy and gulped down the medicines, including the contents of two jars of vaseline. Their favorite and most frequent targets were the potato bins, where even rotten potatoes crawling with bugs disappeared down their throats.

The camp was ill-equipped to cope with such a challenge. The Nazis no longer much cared what the inmates did amongst themselves, while the ghetto's own limited number of able-bodied men had all they could do with their own assigned work. Moreover, as we shall soon see, the number of such men was shrinking while the number of new arrivals was growing. Writes one observer, "We sought in vain to erect a chain consisting of young, clean maidens from the Dutch youth corps with their white head towels to hold back this wild horde. But the horde ran around them and even trampled on them. . . They responded to only one thing: food."

Gerty Spies was ordered to guard one potato cellar. Though given an iron pole, she wondered how she, a middle-aged woman, could defend it against these "weakened but ravenous man-beasts." She found she could do so by staring coldly in their eyes while holding the iron bar firmly in front of her. The would-be raiders crouched on the floor before her, but did not attempt to break in.

Their behavior began to affect the attitude of the long-term residents. While some remained sympathetic, others turned hostile. "They are animals in human form. What a scandal for the sensibilities of respectable people," says one. Many blamed their behavior not on their previous suffering but on their ethnic background. "A new species of homo sapiens has appeared in the ghetto, the Polish Jew," writes another.

But if Theresienstadters reacted with disgust and dismay at the actions of the new arrivals, some began to emulate them. With food already scarce and with the new arrivals threatening to consume all that was left, many once orderly residents also began raiding or trying to raid the food supplies. The situation was threatening the ghetto's existence.

But the biggest peril which the newcomers posed came not through malnutrition but through disease. A large number of these refugees were infected with typhus.

Just how many carried the disease remains undeterminable. One figure puts it at approximately 2,500; but since many died before the disease could be diagnosed, the true number was almost certainly much higher. The infected were at first quarantined in a barracks on the fringe of the town. But soon another, more centrally located barracks had to be pressed into service as well. When the second barracks proved insufficient, other housing had to be cleared, forcing many elderly and fragile residents to move. The quarantine itself was only partly successful. Patients kept breaking out, sometimes en masse, and would then form or join raiding parties or simply wander about the streets begging and scavenging food.

Fortunately, the ghetto's medical staff had been partially replenished during the winter with the arrival of the mixed-marriage spouses, many of whom were doctors and some of whom were, or were willing to serve as, nurses. When the influx first began, Murmelstein and Meissner called all the Czech winter arrivees to the courtyard of the Hanover barracks and urged them to do all they could to help the ghetto cope with the crisis. Fortunately, their joint exhortation elicited a generally positive response.

Although the Jewish administration moved forcefully to control the epidemic, it tried to keep the news of its outbreak from the SS, fearing that the latter might use it as an excuse to finally destroy the ghetto. But with the Allied armies drawing ever nearer, the SS had no intentions of doing so. On the contrary, it formally or informally suspended many of its rules. The SS not only lifted the ban on tobacco but on May 1 it actually authorized the distribution of cigarettes. Each adult male was to be given three a day. Non-smokers quickly traded theirs for food, with one cigarette worth two slices of bread.

On April 30 Dunant came once more to the camp. He had apparently heard further rumors resulting from the effort to send the Prominenten to Bavaria, for he showed particular concern over whether there had been any more deportations. Satisfied that none had occurred but still lacking Berlin's authorization to stay in the camp, he returned to Prague.

The day of his visit, however, was also the day of Hitler's suicide. The next day an American plane dropped leaflets on the town saying help was on its way and the following day, May 2, Dunant returned for the third and last time. Though he still lacked formal authorization to take over the camp, he did take up residence and set up an office in the former town hall. The next day he conferred with Murmelstein, Baeck and others on what to do when the camp came into Red Cross hands. Baeck said the Council of Elders should then go out of existence. At the same time, he thanked Murmelstein for his efforts up to now and expressed hopes for his fellow rabbi's further cooperation.

Dunant's assignment also included the Little Fortress where the situation had worsened considerably. Six weeks earlier the guards had casually shot some 30 Jews while they were at work and just the previous day they had executed over 50 young Czechs suspected of having belonged to a communist youth organization. They had then abandoned the prison. Dunant wanted to release most of the healthy prisoners and bring the sick ones to the ghetto. The last group numbered 3,000 in all, two-thirds of whom were infected by typhus. When Baeck assured him that "We can take in 3,000 more," Dunant answered, "Perfect," and ordered the transfer to take place.

The next day 3,000 prisoners, 300 of them Jews, were brought to Theresienstadt. Those not suffering from typhus were lodged in the Sudenten barracks, which had been evacuated ahead of time, while the typhus patients were placed in quarantine. Dunant had also arranged for a Czech Red Cross medical group to come from Prague the same day. Its staff, which included several doctors and 50 nurses, devoted almost all its attention to those from the Little Fortress and showed little concern for the regular residents, especially those who could not speak Czech.

Meanwhile, the ghetto itself was being overwhelmed with its own problems, medical and other. Refugees from other concentration camps were arriving daily, while the camp's work force were showing increasing signs of weariness and restlessness. Murmelstein asked Dunant to put out a bulletin urging everyone to work harder and maintain discipline, but Dunant, probably because he still lacked formal authority and did not want to antagonize the SS, declined to do so. He assured the Council of Elders, however, that food shipments were on their way by truck from Switzerland.

The next day brought the long-awaited phone call from Berlin: Theresienstadt had been officially turned over to the IRC. Dunant was now camp commander. Still, he continued to tread warily. When, after hearing the news, some young Czechs, together with a group of gendarmes, sought to raise a Czech flag over the post office, he ordered them to take it down. The next morning a Red Cross flag flew over the building.

The Czech Jews did proceed to tear down the camp's German signs, replacing them with Czech ones. This did not please all the residents. Tears welled up in the eyes of one young Viennese as she experienced some of the same emotions she had when Hitler took over her country. "Once again," she says, "I felt like an outsider."

Dunant's elevation brought Murmelstein's demission. He resigned saying he was not a deserter but was only trying "to draw the right inferences from the situation." He warned that the situation was deteriorating rapidly. Some 40% of the camp, including a growing number of long-time residents, were now quarantined and the refugees from other concentration camps remained discontented and undisciplined. Another detrimental factor which Murmelstein did not mention was that more and more able-bodied, and hence badly needed Czechs, were leaving. While only five inmates had fled during the month of April, 87 had left during the first four days of May. During the next three days, 547 more would depart. Many Czech spouses and in-laws of mixed-marriage partners were now showing up at the camp to collect their loved ones.

The gendarmes had long ceased to prevent such flights and on May 3 the SS stopped doing so as well for it too was getting ready to leave. The phone call from Berlin saying the camp belonged to the Red Cross prompted Haindl to set his last fire. It was a large, serious one in a barracks on the south side of the town. While the fire department battled its 800th, and last blaze, and while most Theresienstadters not otherwise engaged watched, all but one member of the SS garrison slipped out through the other end of the town.

The one who remained was Rahm who summoned Murmelstein to him for a last conference. The next morning Rahm pedaled on his bicycle through the town, attending to some last minute business. As he made his rounds, thousands of Theresienstadters watched. Though he carried no weapon, and though most of those who observed him hated him, none moved to harm or even yell at him. They simply watched in silence until he too disappeared.

The end of the SS in no way signified the end of the ghetto's problems. As Rahm was leaving, the last trainload of refugees arrived, bringing 87 dead bodies to dispose of and 1,800 half-dead people to care for. Also arriving were some 600 British, Canadian, French, and Belgian prisoners of war.

The Council of Elders issued a bulletin in both German and Czech, the first time both languages had been used in an official announcement. They pointed out that all mail restrictions were now lifted and residents could write to whomever they wished in whatever language they wished. Newspapers, they said, would soon be posted. But the war was still on and it was far safer to stay in Theresienstadt than to travel elsewhere. There was also work to be done in taking care of the martyrs from the Little Fortress and the victims from other concentration camps. Their announcement ended with a plea for all residents to stay where they were, maintain order, and work hard. In this way, they would get home sooner.

The following day, May 7, Dunant appeared on the balcony of the town hall to announce Germany's unconditional surrender. The assembled throng reacted joyfully to the hardly unexpected news. Their jubilation proved a bit premature, however, for the military SS, as well as parts of the regular army, were still not ready to lay down their arms. The German forces were rigorously seeking to suppress an uprising by Czech partisans in Prague to the south, and were also battling Russian tanks coming from the north. Although the war was supposedly over, Theresienstadt now found itself sandwiched between two battle zones.

At 9:00 A.M. the next day shots were heard followed by a burst of gunfire an hour later. German tanks were seen along the perimeter street, first going north and then heading south. At 6:00 P.M. a shell struck a building near the railroad station killing outright a former Czech army colonel and fatally wounding the former Dutch general von Praag. (He would die a few days later.)

Ten minutes later a new burst of gunfire was heard. The residents crouched on the floor, parents holding their young children under them, and nearly all wondering if everything they had endured up to now would be in vain. Heavy German tanks could be heard rumbling along the perimeter street. Then came a period of silence followed by the sound of a single tank coming into town. Peering through the evening darkness, the residents eventually made out its insignia. The tank was Russian. It was 9:00 P.M., but Theresienstadt's long night was over.

---

45. Margaret Wrencher Rustow, who was one of the teenagers--her sister was the other--says the SS guards who brought them from Ravensbruck behaved in a friendly, even flirtatious manner. She recalls being interviewed by Guenther as well as Rahm. The latter showed some solicitude for her welfare, even supplying her with reading matter, although he too cautioned her to keep quiet once she was released. She is not sure why she and her sister were transferred to Theresienstadt but believes it could have been due to the intercession of some influential contacts her family had in South America.

46. Of the 17,500 residents, slightly less than 7,000 were Czechs, 5,500 were Germans, about 1,300 were Austrians, and a similar number were Dutch. Slovaks and Hungarians in near equal numbers made up the remaining 2,100. The Swiss transport in February had disproportionately reduced the ranks of the

Dutch, while the winter transports to Theresienstadt had put the Czechs once again ahead of the Germans.

47. A few days later, Himmler held an unprecedented meeting with a Jew, Norbert Masur of Sweden. With a straight face, he told Masur, "Theresienstadt is not a camp in the ordinary sense of the word but a town inhabited by Jews and governed by them and in which all kinds of work is done. This type of camp was designed by me and my friend Heydrich and so we intended all camps to be."

CHAPTER 13
THE THERESIENSTADT DIASPORA

The Russian tank continued on its way but was followed the next morning by a stream of Soviet tanks and other vehicles passing along the perimeter street. Jubilant Theresienstadters, some waving flags or holding hastily drawn posters, turned out en masse to greet them. The Russians responded by dancing on their tanks and tossing them cigarettes, bread, and other food. Writes one who was there, "No one who has not himself experienced it can understand the joy of that hour of freedom. A [presumably Theresienstadt] band marched through the city; everybody came out and joined the procession. The Internationale was played."

The joyful scene did not transpire without travails. Some inmates had become so intoxicated with elation that they got in the way of the procession and suffered accidents. An elderly man urged them back, saying, "Children, you luckily survived the war. Do you want to lose your life now?" Most heeded his words and no one suffered fatal injuries.

Although most of the Russian troops passed on their way, some remained, camping on the outskirts of town. As in so many locales which the Soviets liberated, instances of robbery and rape, especially the latter, occurred. Starke mentions only one or two isolated incidents, but Fuchs writes, "Our women, skinny and miserable, old and ugly looking . . . became their first spoils of conquest. . . They behaved like wild animals; they knew no restrictions." She points out that no keys existed to the rooms and the women's efforts to barricade the doors with benches were unsuccessful. Still, such episodes were apparently quite limited and quickly ended. On May 10, the day after the Russians arrived, Dunant turned the camp over to a Soviet army major and departed for Switzerland.(48)

The presence of Russian soldiers, English-, French-, and Flemish-speaking prisoners of war, refugees from Eastern Europe, plus the camp's motley assortment of regular residents had virtually transformed Theresienstadt into a Tower of Babel. Yet, according to one who lived through it, "Brotherliness reigned" and "exhilaration prevailed. No more blackouts, evenings the whole town is lit up. . . We sit around laughing, drinking, singing. . . ."

Some even ventured to nearby Leitmeritz. One group of young Viennese who did so decided to enter a cafe. However, they had become so accustomed to Nazi rule that the sight of German-speaking people sitting around not only startled but frightened them. So they remained standing frozen against the wall until a puzzled waitress asked them what they wanted. When one of them muttered "Beer," she replied in a somewhat miffed tone, "So why don't you sit down?" They did so and hesitantly began sampling their first real taste of freedom.

Despite the euphoria of liberation, life was still far from idyllic in Theresienstadt. On May 10, the day after the Russians' arrival, the Jewish-American writer Meyer Levin, now a news correspondent with the U.S. Army, called at the camp. Shortly after arriving, he noticed a wagon coming through a courtyard archway carrying the daily bread ration. "A husky young woman stood in the wagon to carry out the distribution, but she was helpless. The vehicle was instantly mobbed, and from all corners the mob increased; we were caught among the ravenous survivors who, oblivious of the shrieks of women trampled on, or the cries of the camp police for order, unheeding to any appeal or command, raged and tore at each other to reach the wagon." He was told that the soup distribution was better controlled, but with no assurances of further supplies the hungry inhabitants had become frantic with fear. The wild behavior of the refugees was causing more and more of the long-term residents to emulate them lest the former devour everything.

Some of the refugees began plundering other things besides food. This included the sewing machines left behind by the SS and some of the Jewish administration's equipment. A few among the later arrivals went to Leitmeritz to plunder, since many of this city's German inhabitants had fled, leaving behind empty houses and stores, as well as abandoned animals. They looted the buildings and even brought back some horses. The city's mayor came to the camp to protest.

Initially there was little the camp could do to control the situation, for it found itself not only confronting unsettling conditions but also lacking leadership. No one seemed to be really in charge. In addition, more and more of those who had been running the camp were now leaving. By May 10, about 1,000 residents, mostly Czechs, had left; by May 14 another 3,000 had joined them.

The biggest and most threatening problem was the still raging typhus epidemic. It had not only begun infecting the regular residents, especially the doctors, nurses, and employees of the delousing station, but had started to spread to the surrounding towns. It was also exacerbating the tensions between the newer arrivals and the long-term residents. Most of the former had been quarantined and eventually placed behind barbed wire to help keep them from breaking out. Also, they were not receiving adequate care from the overburdened medical staff, some of whom had already left for home. One refugee complained to Levin that their fellow Jews were treating them worse than the Germans had done at Buchenwald. Baeck offered to stay with them to keep them from staging more breakouts. This seemed to mollify them somewhat, for they told him he did not need to sacrifice himself in this way. Yet they remained restless.

The Council of Elders, or all that was left of it, had appointed Jiri Vogel as camp Elder, since Vogel was not only a communist but spoke Russian. But he was more of a technician than an administrator and, in any case, probably no member of the camp community could have brought the situation under control. The camp's Russian commander, Major Kusmin, spoke only Russian and was obviously ill-prepared for his new assignment. Still, on May 13 he addressed the camp's leaders and, with Vogel translating, urged them to stand by their posts. He said all those working in the camp would eventually receive compensation.

Kusmin had earlier sent a plea for help to the local Red Army headquarters, and on the same day he addressed the Elders a Russian medical mission arrived. Its 52 army doctors, some of them Jews, plus 75 nurses and 214 aides and auxiliaries, worked with the Czech medical mission and the ghetto's own medical staff to stamp out the contagion. They deloused between 15,000 to 20,000 residents and gave many of them fresh clothes. (The men received left-behind SS uniforms stripped, of course, of all insignia.) They also set up six additional hospitals in existing barracks and other buildings and placed the entire camp under quarantine.

These measures speedily took effect. In a week's time the number of new typhus cases had dropped from over 100 a day to 50. They had sunk to one or two per day by June 13 when the epidemic was declared ended. Over 3,000 are known to have contracted the disease and of them 500 died. A death rate of less than 25%, especially under ghetto conditions, can be considered another medical triumph for Theresienstadt. It should be pointed out that the death toll included 15 doctors, an equal number of nurses, and 13 employees at the delousing station.

During this time the ghetto benefitted from a new infusion of manpower. One day the startled inhabitants saw a column of young blondish women outfitted in what seemed to be striped pajamas cleaning the streets. The "pajamas" were actually convicts' costumes, for the young women were accused Nazi camp followers or collaborators who had been rounded up by the Russians or by Czech partisans. Men accused of complicity with the Nazi regime were also brought to the camp to work. Although allowed to wear their regular clothes, they had a wide swath shaved through their hair to designate their new status.

Most of these accused collaborators were Germans, either Czech Germans or Germans who had fled from the Reich to avoid the Russian advance. Many had first been locked up in the Little Fortress where the new Czech administration treated them severely, while Soviet soldiers raped the women. At Theresienstadt they received a hostile reception, especially from the newcomers. One Polish Jew called out, "Where are our children? Where are our mothers and fathers?" Another grabbed a stick and began beating a German while screaming, "Gas, Krematorium, Auschwitz." Others, having little or no footwear themselves, began taking their shoes.

The Ghetto Watch intervened and stopped the shoe thefts and any form of physical abuse. The verbal abuse, which had been the most frequent expression of the inhabitants' anger, soon dried up on its own as many began saying, "What good will it do? Our people won't come back."

The Germans were assigned various chores, some of which exposed them to typhus. Wherever they worked, they were under the authority of the camp inmates working with them. Says Spies, "Neither I nor anyone I knew derived any pleasure in giving orders to these people. We dealt with them in the most correct and matter-of-fact manner possible."

By early June Theresienstadt had once again become a functioning community. To be sure, many of those from the other concentration camps were still inadequately clothed and provided for, and so remained prone to breakouts and stealing. But the reestablished Ghetto Watch, aided by some remaining gendarmes, managed to maintain order.

Various relief agencies were now operating in the camp, including the American Joint Distribution Committee, and conditions were improving daily. With the support of a partially revived Youth Welfare office, a Polish Jew set up a home for the refugee children. It supplied the youngsters with wholesome food, clean bed linen, and sympathetic supervision. The children's spirits and health soon improved and they began behaving and sleeping better.

Many other ghetto offices and organizations resumed their activities while the bank, to the delight of its employees, finally acquired a real and useful assignment. The newly formed Czech government had decided to exchange the near-worthless ghetto crowns for Czech crowns and used the facility to carry out the transactions. Thus did the bogus bank end its days as a serviceable institution.

Theresienstadt's last exodus began in early May, continued through the early days of liberation, and even through the two weeks of supposedly strict quarantine when 300 more residents managed to flee. While most of those who left the camp during this month were Czechs, some were not. When Klaus Mann, the son of writer Thomas Mann, came to the camp on May 19 searching for his aunt Mimi, he found she had already left.

The Russians eased the quarantine restrictions on May 28, and the flow accelerated. While most of those leaving were still Czechs, more and more other Jews began going as well. One Berliner pedaled for ten days on a bicycle to fetch his Jewish wife. Another Berliner, a young half-Jew, roared into the camp on a motorcycle, placed his mother securely on the back seat with her arms clasped around him, and then roared off to Berlin.(49)

Most non-Czech Jews left in a more collective and conventional manner. Some of the engineers had built a transmitter which Baeck and others used to broadcast lists of survivors and their home cities, and then to ask these cities to send transportation to bring them home. Soon buses began rolling in from Frankfurt, Dresden, Cologne, and other German cities to retrieve the remnants of their once flourishing Jewish communities. Berlin, heavily devastated and already divided, was the last to respond. Its first bus did not arrive until August 8. Vienna did not respond at all, so Major Kusmin procured a Russian bus for the Viennese. The passengers had to pay for their trip in the new Czech money they had received in exchange for their former ghetto crowns. Some 700 German and Austrian Jews who refused repatriation to their former homeland were taken to a temporary camp in Deggendorf, not far from Munich. When they found themselves once again interned behind barbed wire, they rebelled, forcing the authorities to grant them more freedom.

One former Berlin Jew who could have left early but refused to do so was Leo Baeck. He still had work to do.

A former Chicago newspaperman named Patrick Dolan had been serving as an undercover OSS major in Prague in early May when he received a message to go to Theresienstadt and rescue a Leo Baeck. When he replied, "Who the hell is Leo Baeck?" he was told, "Baeck is the pope of the German Jews." Jewish leaders in England and the U.S., anxious about the elderly rabbi's welfare, had been lobbying for his rescue.

Dolan hurried to Theresienstadt only to have Baeck tell him that he did not want to be rescued, at least not yet. He had pledged to stay in Theresienstadt until the last Jew was saved. So Dolan had to wait until the end of June when, with the epidemic over and with less than 6,000 still remaining in the camp, Baeck let Dolan fly him to England where his daughter and her family awaited him.

Also flying to England were some 1,000 orphan children and adolescents, most from other concentration camps. The Jewish Refugee Committee in London had secured the British government's permission to take them in. They arrived in poor physical condition and were, for the most part, illiterate. But they proved eager to learn, especially English. Their physical condition also rapidly improved. Their first trip to the dentist initially went badly, however, for the youngsters feared the gas which dentists then commonly used as an anesthetic. But after one brave youngster emerged safely from the dentist's chair, the others calmed down.

The Joint Distribution Committee which had helped arrange the trip also arranged travel for those Polish Jews who wanted or at least were willing to return to Poland. It also assisted some 500 others in going to Palestine. Some 428 French Jewish women were taken to Germany in trucks and then flown to France. Those returning to Holland were evacuated by autos but were later transferred to cattle cars in which they had no facilities to relieve themselves. Their return home thus paralleled in some respects their deportation to the camp.

The departures themselves, though generally joyous events, were not without touches of tragedy. Dr. Nellie Stern, a physician who was one of Baeck's nieces, lost her life in a bus accident on leaving the town. A Viennese who boarded a Russian bus in a jubilant mood suddenly grew somber when he recognized the man opposite him. He knew that his fellow passenger, who was observing him with a sad smile, was the sole survivor of a 28-member family.

As the camp's population departed, its various institutions and operations closed down. The Protestant congregation, once again led by its now 72-year-old founder, Artur Goldschmidt, held its last service in June. The Catholic congregation, which had never fully recovered from the previous fall's deportations, had dissolved earlier.

The ghetto library sent its books to Prague. In the process of packing them, Kaethe Starke learned the answer to something that had long puzzled her. A manufacturer among the Danish Jews had come to the library almost daily to spend hours ostensibly reading a set of German books, though he knew almost no German. In working in the section where he customarily sat, she found the set that had so deeply enthralled him. It was a well-illustrated edition of classical pornography which the library staff had not known was on the shelves.

By mid-August only a handful of Jews remained in Theresienstadt and preparations began to receive the town's former inhabitants. By early fall, Czech soldiers were once again stationed in some of its barracks, and by mid-fall the civilian population had started to trickle back. By late fall, Theresienstadt was well on its way to becoming what it had been before the war, and what it is today: a normal Czech town with an army bivouacking center.

As some Berliners were preparing to board a bus for home, they spotted a man sitting on a trunk, his face and most of his body shielded by a newspaper which he had evidently borrowed from the bus driver. A closer look showed the avid newspaper reader to be Benjamin Murmelstein. The Jewish Elder would not, however, be boarding this or any bus. The Czechs had other plans for him.

Before looking at these other plans and what eventually resulted from them, let us first see what happened to Theresienstadt's various non-Jewish, i.e., Nazi administrators.

The fates of Himmler, Kaltenbrunner, and Eichmann, to begin at the top, are well known. The first two committed suicide in Allied custody while the third was picked up by Israeli agents in Argentina in 1960 and brought to Jerusalem, where he was tried and hung. Guenther fled Prague in an automobile on May 5 but had gone only 6 miles when Czech partisans ambushed his car. He was fatally shot while attempting to flee on foot.

We now come to Theresienstadt's three SS commandants, Seidl, Burger, and Rahm.

Seidl was arrested by the Allies in Vienna in July 1945. He insisted that he had only been trying to help the Jews establish a viable community and that when it came to such deeds as the execution of 17 Jews in early 1942, he was simply following orders. He firmly denied knowing anything about the Auschwitz gas chambers. Edelstein, he said, had once asked him about a rumor that a transport from Theresienstadt had been intercepted en route and its passengers gassed. Seidl said he had in turn queried Eichmann, who had firmly repudiated the rumor. Added Seidl, "Since I had the word of a superior officer on the subject, I gave the matter no further thought." Many witnesses testified, however, to his brutality at Theresienstadt as well as at his other assigned posts and the Allies hung him in February 1946.(50)

Burger proved much more elusive. He was not seized until 1947 when Nazi-hunter Simon Wiesenthal stumbled across him while looking for Eichmann in a small Austrian resort town. Wiesenthal had him arrested, but he escaped the following year when he was in Austrian custody. A little over a year later Wiesenthal located him in a Vienna suburb and again had him arrested. This time he was locked up in a prison in Vienna, but in 1951 he escaped once again.

In 1987 Wiesenthal, acting on fresh leads, traced Burger to Munich. There the trail was lost, for the apartment house in which he had lived had been torn down, making it impossible to question his neighbors. By the beginning of the 1990s, his home town had not yet registered him as dead and the possibility existed that he still lived.

Rahm was seized in Austria a year after the war and handed over to the new Czech government which was eager to try him. (Rahm had served the SS for several years in Prague before being assigned to Theresienstadt.) For his trial, which took place in early spring of 1947, the Czechs invited an international group of distinguished observers, one of them from Palestine. They also located 150 potential witnesses. As the son of Czechoslovakia's founder, Thomas Masaryk, put it, "We owe an explanation to this heap of ashes."

The trial took place in Leitmeritz. Standing erect in the witness box but ashen-faced and obviously fearful, Rahm claimed he was only following orders and working for the future of the Third Reich. He constantly tried to save Jews from deportation, he said, by saying they were necessary to keep the camp in operation but he was usually overruled. He was told and believed that they were being sent to central Germany to help in reconstruction and only learned of their fate and that of other deported Jews when he saw an American film on the concentration camps during his imprisonment. (The U.S. Army had put together a documentary on the concentration camps which was shown to Nazi leaders and others. Some were genuinely shocked at what it revealed but it seems unlikely that Rahm was one of them.)

Not only did witness after witness repudiate much of his testimony, but Rahm often seemed to contradict himself. For example, he claimed he harbored no special feelings against Jews but merely regarded them as people of another religion. Yet, at another point, when questioned about a brutal interrogation of a suspected camp smuggler, who in fact had committed suicide by throwing himself out of a window during a respite in the proceedings, Rahm continually referred to the man as "the Jew Pollak" until the exasperated Czech prosecutor told him to identify the man simply by name.

At 2:00 P.M. on April 30 the special court convened for the trial handed down its verdict: Guilty. At 6:00 P.M. Karl Rahm was hanged.

Some months later Haindl was arrested in Salzburg, Austria and brought back to Czechoslovakia for trial. He was hanged in September 1948. Others executed by the Czechs included the commandant and deputy commandant of the Little Fortress and the head of the Czech gendarmes of Theresienstadt, Janetschek. Jaeckl, commandant of the Little Fortress, had earlier testified that Rahm had showed him plans for bringing in 300 SS men to massacre all of Theresienstadt's Jews in the projected "duck pond."

One final note on the prosecution of Nazis involved in Theresienstadt. At the Nuremburg trials the attorney for von Neurath, Hitler's one-time foreign minister who subsequently served as protector of Czechoslovakia before Heydrich's appointment to the post, cited Theresienstadt in his client's defense. The establishment of the camp, he said, showed how his client wanted to help the Jews. His argument apparently failed to impress the judges, who sentenced him, along with most other leading Nazis, to the gallows.

The Czechs' crackdown on Nazis and suspected Nazi collaborators also ensnared Benjamin Murmelstein. When Dunant returned for a final visit to the camp on June 3, Murmelstein asked his assistance in leaving. Dunant offered to evacuate him to Switzerland or to send him to France with a group of French Jews. Murmelstein chose France, hoping to get a job working with the Joint Distribution Committee which had established headquarters in Paris. But the Czechs had other ideas and, by the end of the summer, Murmelstein was behind bars in Leitmeritz undergoing investigation.

In European countries such investigations, especially in important and complex cases, are often quite lengthy. They are presided over by a judge who holds preliminary hearings before deciding to turn over the accused to another judge or panel of judges for a formal trial. The investigation and preliminary hearings in Murmelstein's case lasted well over a year. Then, in December 1946, the prosecutor withdrew his charges, saying, "Murmelstein has been able to disprove all accusations against him."

Although there was no shortage of witnesses against the controversial rabbi, there were also witnesses who spoke on his behalf. Moreover, the judge did not find some of the hostile witnesses convincing. For example, one of them testified that Murmelstein once threatened to throw him out the window. When the judge asked how far the window was from the ground, the witness admitted that the distance was only 3 feet. Another factor favoring Murmelstein's case was his own testimony against Rahm after the former commandant's arrest. As the presiding judge noted, "It must be emphasized that his testimony against Rahm was decisive. Rahm was aware of this and would have spoken out if he knew anything unfavorable about Murmelstein."

Still another factor which undoubtedly aided the accused collaborator was his ability to dispense with an interpreter and defend himself in fluent Czech. His scholarly skills also probably helped him to point out weaknesses in the prosecution's case and to point up strengths in his own. Still another plus on his behalf was the fact that he actually deported few Jews on his own authority for by the time he became Elder, Rahm and Guenther had pretty much taken over the proceedings. The judge concluded, in fact, that he had tried to save Jews.

His clearance of war crimes by the Czech court did not, however, spell the end of his difficulties. After going to Budapest to pick up his wife and son, who had been living there with her family during his incarceration, he journeyed to Rome where he hoped to find a teaching position in a rabbinical seminary. He did not obtain the post, possibly because Baeck may have refused to recommend him.(51)

Murmelstein was offered a congregation in Italy, but it was a small one situated in an outlying area and apparently dominated by a single wealthy congregant. So he decided instead to go into the furniture business. The brilliant scholar-turned-able-administrator proved, however, a poor businessman and his enterprise soon went bankrupt. He then took a position as a traveling salesman for a furniture company and in this capacity traveled throughout Italy and Sardinia while maintaining his home in Rome.

During his time at home he sought to continue his scholarly work, a pursuit which frequently took him to the Vatican library. His presence there gave rise to the rumor that he had converted to Catholicism and become curator of the Vatican's Judaica collection. The rumor is not true.

Following the capture of Eichmann in the early '60s, the Israeli police contacted him as a possible witness. He prepared a detailed statement but was never called to present it either in writing or in person. He therefore, published it as a book in Italian. (See Bibliography.) In 1977 Claude Lanzman interviewed him for several hours for his film *Shoah*. But once again, the opportunity came to naught for Lanzman never used any of the extensive footage he shot.

A few years later Murmelstein suffered a heart attack and his doctor forbade any more interviews regarding World War II. He died in Rome in 1989 at the age of 84.

With the passage of years, hostility toward him, once so pronounced, seems to have diminished. Although nearly everyone who had any contact with him agrees that his deportment was usually deplorable, still most, including Alisah Schiller and Alisa Shek, who today run the Theresienstadt museum and archive at Kibbutz Givat Chaim in Israel, feel that his actual deeds do not differ much from those of other Jewish leaders in similar circumstances. Moreover, his effectiveness as an administrator may have just possibly kept the camp in existence. He was certainly no hero but, within the context of the time, he was perhaps not an infamous villain either.

The Czechs did not arrest Murmelstein's right-hand man, the almost equally disliked Robert Prochnik. After the camp's liberation, Prochnik stayed on for a while compiling an extensive compendium of facts and figures on the camp which he issued under the title, *Jews in Theresienstadt: A Statistical Report*. It covers transports to the camp, deportations from it, figures on illnesses, deaths, and other matters. While his statistics have been emended by others through the years, most of them are substantially correct. He presented his report on July 14; after that, he vanished.

In early fall, Louis Lowy, one of the Theresienstadt Jews who went to Deggendorf and who, because of his knowledge of English, was put in charge of assisting those who wanted to go to America, suddenly received a phone call saying the American Consulate in Munich had opened. The man informing him of this welcome news was none other than Robert Prochnik. Later Lowy and others saw Prochnik in Munich decked out in the uniform of the Joint Distribution Committee. The crude but shrewd Viennese had once again landed on his feet.

When news of his reappearance in Allied uniform reached Vienna, it set off a wave of outrage among the city's Theresienstadt alumni. Some 134 of them signed a petition denouncing the man. Noting that his patron Murmelstein was already under arrest, they asked that Prochnik be incarcerated as well.

In the meantime, the JDC had transferred Prochnik to its Paris headquarters where Lucy Davidowicz remembers him as a heavy-set man with a receding hairline and a bulbous nose who showed a special knack for working with European bureaucracies. When it came to procuring visas, arranging for travel documents, etc., no one could beat him. Nevertheless, when news of the outcry from Vienna reached Paris, the JDC and Prochnik himself found it expedient to separate. He soon landed a position with a business firm in the Alsace, France's border province with Germany, and quickly disappeared from public view.

One Theresienstadt inmate who did not escape the charges and consequences of collaboration was a member of the Zossen work detail named Raffaelsohn. He was denounced by other members of the work group for having actively assisted the sadistic SS man who supervised and grossly abused them. The Czechs arrested Raffaelsohn and, after his trial in which many of his former fellow workers testified, they executed him in 1947.(52)

Though most returning Theresienstadters did not end up in a convict's costume or in an Allied uniform, their homecoming did not lack drama and tension. Karel Klein, the former chief of medical services at Prague's Jewish hospital, left the camp on May 9 with his wife and teenage daughter. Arriving penniless in the city at 10:00 P.M., they found their former apartment still occupied by Nazis. In desperation, they trooped to the home of their former chauffeur and knocked on the door. The chauffeur opened it, welcomed them in, and put them up for the night. The next day they were able to reclaim their apartment, although some of the furniture was missing. Klein later returned to Theresienstadt for a while to help his colleagues stamp out the typhus epidemic.

Clara Eisenkraft got a lift part way to Prague on a Russian armored car and then traveled the rest of the distance on foot. When she reached the city, she stood motionless on a street corner struck by what she saw. "People were walking about casually not realizing what a miracle it was to be able to do that. I sensed that people were looking at me. Suddenly, I felt a parcel in my hand. When I opened it, it was filled with sweets; a kind gesture extended by some kind hand. . . A woman said to me, 'Why such despair? Everything is going to be fine.' A human voice was speaking to me in my awful aloneness. Tears poured down my face."

Gerty Spies, along with other Munich Jews, returned on a special train. As they entered the city, they looked down and saw a group of men working in a railroad shaft. The men looked up and cheerfully waved to them. The returnees could not immediately wave back; they were too startled by the sight of German Gentiles smiling at them.

A delegation of anti-Nazi Germans were on the station platform to greet them with flowers and fruit, along with embraces and welcoming words. Spies then went to a city park, lay down in the grass in the summer sunshine and spread out her arms for joy.

Not all homecomings were so pleasant. Several hundred German Jews who had come to Theresienstadt from Holland wanted to return to their adopted homeland. But on the train back, they confronted the continuing hostility of the Dutch Jews and on arriving in Holland the Dutch military interned them. British authorities secured their release a few weeks later.

Whether in their new or in their old homelands, many were overcome by adjustment problems compounded by what has been called survivors' guilt. Dr. Paul Klaar, a former Viennese police surgeon and decorated World War I veteran, had worked for the Nazis certifying Jews for deportation to Theresienstadt until he was sent there himself. Returning to Vienna, he was made chief police surgeon and given the title of Imperial Councilor as well. But he tried three times to commit suicide before finally succeeding by stepping in front of a trolley.

Still more tragic was the case of Heinz Burger. This young man survived Theresienstadt and then succeeded in getting to America, where he showed great promise as a biochemist. But shortly before obtaining his Ph.D., the 27-year-old scientist committed suicide.

Such suicides were not rare. Three of the seven girls who worked with Netty Vanderpol at the SS farm took their own lives; two of Edith Kramer's four roommates did the same. One man, George Glas, survived not only Theresienstadt but also the Little Fortress, followed by deportation to Auschwitz, only to kill himself after liberation.

Others experienced lesser but still anguishing problems. Ilse Blumenthal-Weiss, a German who immigrated to America, wrote a poem, *Exile*, in 1987 in which she said, "What belongs to me is a non-existent homeland and a language that is not mine." Ernestine Luze, who returned to her native Vienna, wrote, "I soon began to realize that everything had remained exactly the way it had always been. . . While standing on the trolley I eavesdrop on conversations, listening for the word 'Jew.'"

Theresienstadt's 800 surviving children also experienced difficulties in adjusting to normal life. Most of them were Czech and thus returned to Prague. Says Jiri Diament, "Children who were three years in Theresienstadt, beginning as infants, had disturbances in the emotional sphere for a long time: panic, horror of animals [their only contact with them was seeing SS men on horseback], fear that someone would take something from them, such as a toy or food, anxiety when someone left them, and a general distrust of surroundings and people."

Older children, some of whom returned from Auschwitz, displayed somewhat different problems. These included, says Ota Klein, extreme unwillingness to submit to any form of discipline, passivity, lack of initiative and goals in life, difficulty in making decisions, as well as a moral laxness and indifference." Happily, most of these behavioral problems gradually subsided.

Surprisingly, Theresienstadt's children generally showed no great deficiencies in education. The camp's teachers, despite their lack of materials and their inability to function openly, had done their jobs well. The youngsters experienced little trouble in keeping up with their Czech classmates and in some areas even surpassed them. One teenager, Zuzana Ruzickova, became Czechoslovakia's most prominent harpsichordist; another, Kurt Weigel, has become one of Israel's leading orthopedists; still another, Arnost Lustig, has become an internationally recognized writer whose books have earned him laudatory reviews on the coveted front page of *The New York Times Book Review*.

Many adult Theresienstadters also went on to establish successful careers. Once back in Munich, Spies soon found herself a celebrity. Periodicals gladly published her writings and a book of her poems entitled simply *Theresienstadt* became one of the first books of poetry published in postwar Germany. Old and new friends also established contact. Years later she was able to write, "I love the language in which I can write my poems. But most of all it is the wonderful friendships I have made."

Vava Shanova, who dramatized and produced *Fireflies*, went to Israel where, taking the Hebrew name of Nava Shan, she became a leading performer with the Haifa Municipal Theatre. Ze'ev Shek also went to Israel to become one of the bright lights of the new country's diplomatic corps. He died in 1978 while serving as Israel's ambassador to Italy. Shortly before his death he paid a call on his former boss, Benjamin Murmelstein.

Even many of Theresienstadt's elderly survivors went on to lead productive lives. Baeck became president of the World Union for Progressive Judaism. In this capacity he lectured widely and once offered a prayer before the U.S. House of Representative on Lincoln's birthday. Dr. Julius Spanier, who returned to Munich at age 65, was made Director-in-Chief of the city's leading pediatric clinic and was elected president of the Munich medical society. (In this latter capacity he had to inform Nazi and pro-Nazi colleagues that they could no longer practice.) Rabbi Richard Feder, who had lost his wife, his three children, and all of his numerous grandchildren in Theresienstadt--his wife had died in the camp, the others at Auschwitz--returned to Prague to become at 70 years of age the city's chief rabbi. In 1965 he celebrated his 90th birthday, having since his return written seven books on Judaism, four of them for young people. Blind writer Elsa Bernstein (pen name Ernst Rosmer) joined her daughter in Hamburg, resumed her writing and, at the age of 78, learned to type.(53)

Although the final deportations had swept away most of the camp's leading musicians, a few eluded the enforced exodus while a few who didn't managed to survive in Auschwitz. Still others were among the mixed-marriage partners who arrived after the deportations had ended. Most of these survivors went on to establish or resume distinguished careers. Karl Ancerl, the most prominent, conducted the Czech Philharmonic until 1967 when he left to assume a similar position with the Toronto Symphony. Robert Brock became director of Prague's Grand Opera while Karel Froelich became its concertmaster. Peter Deutsch returned to Copenhagen to conduct the country's two major youth orchestras; Leo Pappenheim returned to Holland to lead the Gelder's Orchestra and, as a guest conductor, several German orchestras as well.

Many of those who chose new homelands also fared well. Pianists Alisha Herz-Sommer and Edith Steiner-Kraus became music professors respectively at the Jerusalem and Tel-Aviv Academies of Music. Pavel (Paul) Kling found a position as concertmaster with the Louisville Symphony, and singer David Grunfeld made solo appearances with the Boston and Pittsburgh Symphonies before becoming, under the name of David Garen, a cantor in Huntington, Long Island. Alexander Singer, the Prague tailor whose magnificent voice was discovered and developed in Theresienstadt, did not return to his sewing machine but joined the chorus of the Czech National Opera. He eventually became a cantor in Johannesburg.

Although many Czechs who went abroad changed their names for professional reasons, many of those who returned to Prague and who bore German names changed them to Czech forms. Thus, theatre director Norbert Fried became Norbert Fryd, Otto Abeles became Otto Ambroz, and Rudolf Freudenfeld, who had staged *Brundibar*, became Rudolf Franek.

Much of Theresienstadt's music has also survived and many orchestras have performed it. The first such performance in America occurred in 1971 on a TV program entitled, "There Shall Be Heard Again . . ." *Brundibar*, after several professional presentations in Prague, premiered in Germany during Hamburg's Brotherhood Week in 1967 and in America in 1975 at the Hartford Jewish Community Center. Chiefly responsible for its American premiere was Joza Karas, a Czech-American violinist and music professor at the University of Hartford. (He has also written an invaluable book, *Music in Terezin*.) In 1979 Karas formed a string quartet expressly to play music from the ghetto. The group has performed throughout New England and the mid-Atlantic coast, including one performance at the Smithsonian Institute in Washington.

One notable piece of Theresienstadt music was not discovered until the late 1980s. This was Pavel Haas's *Study for String Orchestra*, which was found in an abandoned suitcase in Prague. It was played in Theresienstadt only once, a month before its composer was sent off to his death.

Mark Ludwig, a violist with the Boston Symphony who had become interested in Theresienstadt music, showed it to Conductor Seiji Ozawa, who decided to perform the piece before he knew the story behind it. The BSO played it at concerts in Boston, New York City, and Los Angeles in early 1991.

Also discovered over the years were many of the camp's paintings and drawings. Some were retrieved from hiding places inside walls or buried in courtyards. In 1950 some 254 aquarells were discovered by accident in a town loft. By the 1980s the Jewish State Museum in Prague had over 2,000 works from various Theresienstadt artists, many done by the multi-talented physician, Karel Fleischmann.(54)

There have been many exhibitions of Theresienstadt artwork in Europe, Israel, and the United States. Three films about the camp have also been made. Two of them, *Transport to Paradise* (1947) and *Night and Fog* (1963), are feature films made in Czechoslovakia; the third, *Terezin Diary*, is a documentary produced by survivor Zuzana Justman and two-time Emmy award winner Dan Weissman. Actor Eli Wallach does the narration. Also, the National Center for Jewish Film at Brandeis University has managed to acquire and put together 23 minutes of Gerron's psuedo-documentary, *The Fuehrer Presents a City to the Jews*.

Although Theresienstadt quickly resumed its role as a normal Czech community after the war, the Czech government did not forget the role it had once played, at least not totally. In 1947 it transformed its crematorium into a monument and some years later erected an obelisk with a text in Czech and Hebrew. Subsequently, the government added some commemorative sculpture including memorial stones.

But the crematorium lies just outside the town and the communist-controlled government did little within the town itself to indicate its wartime function. Hardly any plaques, for example, were put up on buildings to point out the purposes they served during Theresienstadt's days as a concentration camp. Nor was any information center established even during the summer tourist season. The Little Fortress, on the other hand, became a national museum with pamphlets and year-round guides.

The hard-line communist government which took over the country in 1968 showed even less interest in Theresienstadt. Although it kept the Jewish State Museum in Prague operating--the museum was, after all, a major attraction for tourists--it rebuffed efforts in the late 1980s to set up a special Theresienstadt museum in Theresienstadt itself. It claimed it needed the building that had become available for such a purpose for a police museum instead. Just why a national police force based in Prague would need or want a Theresienstadt site for a museum was never made clear.

The fall of the communist regime in 1990 brought an immediate turnabout in government policy. The new Czech government has enthusiastically endorsed efforts to make the Theresienstadt story better known, and in 1991 it transformed the police museum into a Theresienstadt museum.

In the meantime, many Theresienstadt alumni had long been actively trying to make the camp story better known. In the 1960s they set up a small museum and archive known as Beit Terezin at Kibbutz Givat Chaim in Israel. Austrian survivors have put out a *Totenbuch* listing all Austrian Jews who perished after coming to the camp. In Boston, Netty Schwarz Vanderpol and her psychiatrist husband Maurice have set up the Walter Suskind Memorial Fund, one of whose primary purposes has been to promote performances and awareness of Theresienstadt music. Those who survived have not forgotten those who did not.

Finally to be chronicled is the fate of the ghetto crowns. The Czech government ended up with vast quantities of these crowns after allowing survivors to exchange them for Czech crowns following liberation. In 1952 the Czech state bank set aside a portion of these notes for collectors and burned the rest. Many years later an Israeli numismatist summed up the sentiments of many collectors, as well as others, when, in awkward but effective English, he wrote:

It is hoped that numismatists of the future will never have the opportunity to collect notes of their generation with such a background as the Theresienstadt notes; it is humbly hoped that the last notes with such a story and history as those of Theresienstadt have been issued, never to be issued again. This is my hope and it is my optimistic prayer that my hope is heard by all the peoples of the world.

---

48. Years later some controversy arose at an international conference over Dunant's behavior before liberation. Some communist Czech delegates claimed he had been too deferential to the Nazis. Adler vigorously disputes this, stressing the restrictions Dunant was under while the SS was still in the camp. Baeck, one should note, told Dunant before the latter left that "the Council of Elders and , as such, the entire population of Theresienstadt will never forget what you have done for them."

49. This young man is the one who visited the camp more than two years earlier in a bold attempt to see his grandmother. (His mother had not yet been deported to Theresienstadt.) It will be recalled that he had managed to make his way to Seidl's office where the astonished commandant told him to clear out immediately. He succeeded in leaving the camp safely, even though Seidl had refused to give him an exit pass. He would not have been able to see his grandmother in any case, for she had died shortly before his arrival.

50. Raul Hilsberg, who has written what some regard as the nearest thing to a definitive history of the Holocaust, says he was speaking on this subject at a conference in California in the late 1970s when, after the session ended, an attractive woman of about 30 approached him. Her name tag identified her as an English teacher at a Catholic college and gave her name as "Seidl." She asked him about the disposition of Seidl's body and when Hilsberg asked if she was any relation to the man referred to, she did not answer directly but murmured, "We just want to bury him." She then moved off into the crowd.

51. Baker says Baeck refused to recommend a Theresienstadt rabbi for a position because "he has still to prove himself a good man." But Baker does not mention Murmelstein by name, and Baker and Baeck are no longer a live to provide verification. If Baeck did withhold his recommendation, it may well have been on grounds of Murmelstein's personal transgressions, for he is the only rabbi in Theresienstadt known to have engaged in sexual misconduct. As noted in the preceding chapter, Baeck at the time of Murmlestein's resignation officially thanked him for his early efforts at maintaining the camp and expressed hope for his further assistance.

52. The SS officer who oversaw the work group was a 1st Lieutenant named Franz Stuczka. An account by a work group member named W. Goerner offers an example of Stuczka's antics. "on one October Sunday [note: the work detail was supposed to have every other Sunday off] Stuczka staged a special orgy. It had rained heavily the day before, leaving a large puddle in front of the women's barracks.... He ordered his particular "darlings" among the women to sit down in the puddle and use their soup bowls to move the mud to a designated place. The women had to lift their skirts up high so that they were

covered only by their underpants. The men had to take off their shirts [this was, remember, October] and watch them do so. He then made two of the women bathe in the puddle, first lying on their stomachs and then on their backs. As they complied, he stepped on them, first on their stomachs and then on their backs...."

53. Many of Theresienstadt's oldsters lived to advanced ages despite their ordeal. Leon Battel, who was 70 when he arrived in Theresienstadt in 1942, and who lost his wife, brother, sister, and two of his five sons there, observed his 100th birthday in Boston in 1970. He attributed much of his longevity to Baeck, who had urged him to recite some psalms every day to overcome his depression, a practice he had continued to follow ever since. Adolf Schwarz, who also came to Boston to be with his daughter and son-in-law, died at 93.

54. One of the camp's younger artists, Alfred Kantor, had to destroy his artwork before deportation to Auschwitz, but managed to recreate it from memory immediately after liberation. His remarkable paintings, along with a brief account of his stay in Theresienstadt, were published in 1967. (See Bibliography.) He lives today in Yarmouth, Maine.

POSTLUDE
THE LEGACY

Over 154,000 Jews at one time or another inhabited the Theresienstadt ghetto. Of them, about 141,000 arrived in the "normal" transports prior to April 20, 1945. Of these 141,000, less than one-sixth survived. The survival rate of some of the Reich's other concentration camps actually exceeded that of its Privileged Ghetto.

The survivors include the 19,500 regular residents who were in the camp when the Russians came plus the 3,000 to 3,500 who returned from wherever they had ended up after being deported. As a group, the survivors were disproportionately women, younger adults, and Czechs. The non-survivors were disproportionately Germans and Austrians and, on an age basis, the elderly and the young. Of the more than 10,000 children who came to the camp prior to April 20, about 800 were there when the war ended. Less than a hundred others returned from deportation.

In combing through the figures, one can come across all kinds of information. For example, although the elderly fared worst of all, there were nevertheless more than 2,800 residents over 70 years of age in Theresienstadt at the war's end. Of them, 44 were over 85 and four were past 90.

Data such as these, however, tell us little about the true meaning of this oddity of the Holocaust. Another, and far more promising, approach is to determine, if we can, what legacy Theresienstadt's 118,000 dead and 23,000 living have left us.

Thinking in these terms, one tends at first to think of the camp's rather copious output of cultural works, i.e., the poems and prose, drawings and paintings, symphonies and songs. But although much of this effort shows genuine artistic merit--the music is especially noteworthy--the camp's greatest legacy may lie elsewhere, namely, in what it has to teach us. "Theresienstadt," wrote Utitz after the war, "was an experiment, the like of which there never was or never will be." Such an experiment offers lessons to be learned.

The first such lesson may be the amazing ability of cultural activity to survive and even thrive under such seemingly adverse conditions. To this we might add a further lesson, namely, the way such activity can help maintain some semblance of civilization under uncivilized conditions. For while there was a certain amount of coarse and crude behavior among the camp's inmates, certain basic standards and norms were generally observed. The camp's music, drawings, poems, and other outlets for expression almost certainly helped this to happen. Thus,

Theresienstadt seems to support Albert Camus' contention that "Without culture and the relative freedom it implies, even the most perfect society would be a jungle."

Culture was identified earlier as one of Theresienstadt's three areas of significant achievement. As it happens, its two other areas of success, health, and education also have things to teach us.

Its health service found that many, then highly regarded, medicines were unnecessary and that simpler, more natural measures were often more effective. Furthermore, some ailments, such as asthma, certain stomach problems, some forms of diabetes and hypertension, actually improved in Theresienstadt. Moreover, the camp's cancer rate seems to have been unusually low. Many have attributed such encouraging developments to the sharply reduced incidence of smoking and obesity, along with the greatly reduced consumption of fatty and sugared foods. The diminished availability of such drugs as sleeping pills may also have helped.

Unfortunately, these health lessons remained largely unlearned, or at least not acted upon, in the postwar era. So did similar findings from similar places of deprivation. For example, while the simple high roughage diet given prisoners of war and other internees of the axis powers produced nearly everywhere dramatic improvement in those with ulcers, gastroenterologists continued to prescribe "sippy diets" (milk, etc.) for their patients well into the 1980s. Furthermore, while a dramatic fall in cancer rates occurred in many countries where people had to subsist on scanty rations of simple foods, the medical profession showed little interest after the war in utilizing such knowledge, preferring instead to fight cancer with drugs and other "scientific" weapons.

The camp's experience with education also yielded lessons which, at least for a long time, remained unlearned. Although Theresienstadt's teachers demonstrated the value of inspiration, improvisation, and informality in teaching the young, school systems almost everywhere in the postwar years became more formalized and bureaucratized as their administrative and other non-teaching personnel became more numerous and powerful. The teamwork approach adopted by both teachers and students in Theresienstadt has only recently begun to attract interest.(55)

Theresienstadt's three outstanding areas of success offer us collectively still another lesson. Health, education, and culture were the only areas in which women played leadership roles. In health, for example, they not only did most of the nursing but made up about one-fifth of the camp's doctors. It will be recalled that a woman physician headed the camp's medical laboratory, a woman pharmacist headed its pharmacy, and a woman rabbi helped lead its psychological "Assault Squad."

Is it merely a coincidence that Theresienstadt worked best in those areas where women figured most prominently? This hardly seems likely and one wonders what impact a greater presence of women in other sectors of camp life might have had. One cannot help thinking that other camp operations, including the Council of Elders, would have functioned more honestly, more humanely, and, yes, more efficiently had women occupied decision-making positions.(56)

The less successful areas of camp life also provide lessons. To be sure, most of them are of a negative nature but they are no less valuable on that account. One such lesson is the seemingly inherent tendency for institutions, especially governing institutions, to expand and extend their influence. Admittedly, some special factors and forces in Theresien-stadt, such as the desire to provide work for all, encouraged such a trend. But after taking such considerations into account, Adler still views Theresienstadt's experience in self-administration as a warning of the dangers inherent in any creed or approach which tends to foster governmental growth. Unchecked, such tendencies can transform a needed and even essentially well-intentioned administration into a "demonic caricature" that eventually oppresses more than serves those in whose interest it purports to function. While this may be a gross exaggeration when it relates to Theresienstadt, it is worth bearing in mind. As Louis Brandeis observed in a 1929 Supreme Court decision, "I fear the government most when its intentions are beneficent."

Theresienstadt's administrative life also offers at least one other lesson, or rather confirms a lesson already known. This is the seemingly innate inclination of people at work to try to achieve something even when the achievement may not be in their best interest. The first beautification provides perhaps the best example of this. Although the inmates believed that it might bring some benefits, and although they certainly wanted to placate the SS, still many seemed to have developed a genuine zeal for the project's success. In so doing, they may have done more than was necessary or desirable to protect their own interests. Other undertakings, such as the railroad spur or Gerron's film making, show signs of a similar spirit.

A story told about Jews working in a munitions factory at another concentration camp may shed some further light on this problem. These men reportedly worked hard and in reasonably good spirits to help the factory produce goods which, of course, were only enabling the Germans to prolong the war and thus their own captivity. When production temporarily closed down, their Nazi supervisors put them to work carrying buckets of sand from one end of the room to the other, and back again. Forced to carry out such an absurd and meaningless task, which, however, did nothing to help the Nazi war effort, they began developing signs of mental unbalance. Some even committed suicide. As Dostoyevsky once observed, "The surest way to destroy a man is to render his work useless."

Since Theresienstadt was the Nazis' only all-Jewish concentration camp, what if anything can it teach us about Jews? One lesson at least is quite apparent: Jews essentially embody and exhibit the national character of their countries of origin. Generally speaking, the Germans behaved like Germans, the Czechs like Czechs, the Austrians like Austrians, etc. This, as we have seen, led to rivalries and often bitter animosities among these various groups.(57)

Despite their ethnic differences and disparities, do we find any common denominators in the behavior of Theresienstadt Jews which we can distinguish as specifically Jewish? Baeck apparently found at least two. In noting the crowds that jammed his lectures, he wondered whether "there is another people on earth which has such a deep and true connection to the spirit as ours--that although it is facing such humiliation and danger, it asks for the word of the philosopher." Then, the sight of Rahm, unarmed and alone, pedaling his bicycle peacefully through the ghetto streets before leaving, caused Baeck to say to himself, "This can only happen with Jews. Of all these Jewish people here, not one lifted a stone to throw at him. They could have strangled him if they wanted." He attributes this lack of vengeful aggression to the Judaic humanism which Judaism so deeply embraces and enshrines.

Although many will perhaps agree with the rabbi's reflections regarding attendance at his lectures, some might offer caveats regarding his observations on the Rahm incident. The failure of Theresienstadt's Jews to take any action against their hated commandant may have been at least partly due to 2,000 years of Diaspora life. It had taught Jews, once the most rebellious of all peoples under Roman rule, to bow to the uniform. Still, a natural distaste for violence and vengeance may also have figured in their behavior since, with some exceptions, such behavior characterized their subsequent relations with the suspected Nazis brought to the camp after liberation.(58)

Emil Utitz, who as a former philosophy and psychology professor as well as director of the camp library, sometimes shared Baeck's lecture platform, offers two observations of his own on Jewish traits as seen from a Theresienstadt vantage point. He was impressed by the way his co-religionists confronted deprivation and oppression and believes their long years of leading a pariahlike existence in the Diaspora had taught them to cope with such conditions. "The differences became vividly evident to me," he writes, "when right after our liberation some Nazis were handed over to us to help us liquidate the camp in an orderly way. These people were on the whole industrious and willing to work but their spirit was completely broken. This showed itself in their beaten-down demeanor, their carelessness in dress, and in other ways." Their demoralization, he says, did not come from any "crushing feeling of guilt" but simply from their inability to accept their misfortune.

Theresienstadt's Jews, says Utitz, also showed a remarkable ability to learn all kinds of trades. They became good plumbers, carpenters, electricians, etc. But the mastery of one calling seemed to elude them-- that of civil servant (*Beamte*). "One can learn various trades through intensive training," he writes, "but one cannot so easily acquire the character of a proper public functionary." The latter requires one to "treat people not with fawning solicitude as if they were customers, and not with hostility or arbitrariness as if they were pests who are disturbing the orderly routine, but with a calm and composed correctness." He also notes that it was not the camp's professional, i.e., prewar civil servants, but those who had never held public administrative positions before who were chiefly responsible for its overbureaucratization and other administrative failings.(59)

This brings us to a related but much more sensitive issue, corruption in the camp. Was there anything Jewish in the widespread disregard of the public interest in favor of private interests which characterized so much individual behavior? Does it show Jews to be deficient in civic virtue and responsibility?

By no means, for Theresienstadt, like other concentration camps and Nazi-operated ghettos, can in no way be compared to a normal, civil society. As Lawrence Langer has pointed out, moral conduct is a privilege that requires reasonably comfortable living conditions. The moral codes of modern life, he says, were simply inapplicable to concentration camps.

Langer's point seems fully consistent with what other thinkers, as diverse as the 18th century bourgeois Ben Franklin and the 20th century German communist Bertold Brecht, have observed. As Franklin put it, "It is as difficult for a man in want to act honestly as it is for an empty sack to stand up straight." According to Brecht, "*Est kommt das Fressen, dann kommt die Moral.*" (First comes the grub, then comes the morality.)

When we look at the history of other groups functioning under conditions similar to those in Theresienstadt, we find similar behavior. This is seen even in the conduct of groups which have had or should have had more cohesiveness and communal spirit than those of the ethnically diverse privileged ghetto.

In a short story dealing with his experience as a German soldier in a Russian prisoner-of-war camp, Willy Kamp writes, "Envy, greed, worries, and dread accompanied us everywhere--a ghostly choir that by day and more frightfully by night chanted in our ear a constant refrain: just save yourself. (Rette dich selbst.) There is no neighbor; just save yourself. There is no loyalty; just save yourself. There is no God; just save yourself. Just save yourself." Saving oneself over the "bones of another" became the "practice, if secret, religion," writes Kamp.

Kamp in his story shows how a few people yet managed to rise above this level. Theresienstadt's story shows how a great many managed to do so.

Edward Seinfeld notes that while "there were some who behaved badly or even criminally, overall it was a community which organized itself to the extent it was permitted and possible, and considering the diversity of its people, in an extraordinarily positive way." Although a Viennese, he even found the Czech on the transportation commission who handled his arrival to be helpful.

Accounts of other Theresienstadt survivors report example after example of what can only be called exemplary behavior. They speak of women sharing food with others who would never be able to reciprocate, of men undergoing torture while not betraying comrades, of families with children of their own reaching out to care for other children in need. The writers of such accounts, it should be stressed, are almost never describing their own deeds but those of others.

One of these writers is Utitz. While hardly uncritical of the camp and its inmates, he nevertheless reports how "only with the greatest reverence can I, for example, recall the doctors and nurses who under the most difficult conditions performed their demanding and dangerous tasks to the fullest degree. During the last typhus epidemic, brought in by those from other camps, more than 60 of these medical practitioners died.

"I also remember the strange position of toilet warden . Those who held this post were responsible for the cleanliness of the latrines, and among these men were bank directors, lawyers, actors, and others. It was a truly ghastly function but one that was absolutely essential to guard against epidemics. In carrying out their duties, they unselfishly protected the general good. It was also no pleasure," Utitz goes on to say, "for musicians and other performers to enter hospitals and old age homes, there to perform in crowded, unventilated, and stinking rooms where there was always the danger of infection."

In thinking about Theresienstadt in this regard, and in many other respects as well, Camus' novel, *The Plague*, comes to mind. It tells the purely imaginary story of a city, in this case Oran, that is sealed off from the outside world as its inhabitants, somewhat helplessly, confront a strange outburst of bubonic plague. When the plague finally dies out and the quarantine ends, the novel's hero, Dr. Rieux, in recalling the residents' response to their ordeal, concludes that there is more in human beings to admire than abhor. Such a conclusion seems consistent with what we learn of human beings in the very real story of Theresienstadt.

It also seems consistent with the sentiments of one of Theresienstadt's very real heroes, Leo Baeck. As the plane carrying Baeck to England flew over Germany, Captain Dolan, who had become quite fond of the elderly rabbi, pointed down and said reassuringly, "You will never have to see that country again." Baeck, however, turned to him with a smile and replied, "Never have revenge in your heart, Patrick. Only love and justice."

---

55. A survey of corporation presidents in the United States in the late 1980s revealed that they rated MBA graduates of Northwestern University above graduates of other, more prestigious business schools such as harvard and Stanford. The most distinctive aspect of Northwestern's MBA program is its focus on teamwork. In this connection, one might mention a survey of 130 Theresienstadt boys and girls conducted in Prague after the war. Asked whether they had any joyful memories from their experience in the camp, 106 answered affirmatively, nearly all citing the collective life in the children's homes.

56. Those with any doubts on this point may wish to consult the business section of the May 5, 1991 *New York Times*. In two articles on this subject, it points out that women managers have started to lead the way in reducing

hierarchical levels and distinctions, sharing power, and encouraging participation in decision making. As a result, they are getting their employees to work enthusiastically and effectively.

57. To be sure, the inmates might have gotten along better with each other had they been allowed to express their hostility to their real enemies, the Nazis. Of interest on this point is an observation by the black American psychiatrist Alvin Poussaint regarding the early civil demonstrations. He points out that many of these demonstrators were committed to loving their enemies, and as a result they often ended up taking out their hostilities on their comrades instead.

58. An incident involving one of the Jewish women saved by the righteous German industrialist Oskar Schindler in the Sudenten Land may also be of interest. A few days after liberation, she was walking down the street in her wooden clogs when a Czech partisan, in noticing them, ordered a passing German woman to exchange footwear with her. The German woman's shoes fit reasonably well but after the partisan passed, the Jewish woman ran after her and offered to exchange back. The German woman gladly, though not graciously, did so.

59. Some who have visited Israel have come to similar conclusions. Many return greatly impressed with the country's achievements but greatly unimpressed with its bureaucrats, to say nothing of its politicians.

BIBLIOGRAPHY, SOURCES, AND NOTES

BIBLIOGRAPHY

Adelson, Alan, and Robert Lapides. *Lodz Ghetto: Inside a Community Under Siege*. New York: Viking, 1989.

Adler, H. G. "The 'Autonomous' Jewish Administration of Terezin (Theresienstadt)." In *Imposed Jewish Governing Bodies Under Nazi Rule*. New York: YIVO Institute for Jewish Research, 1972.

_____. *Theresienstadt 1941-1945. Das Antlitz einer Zwangagemeinschaft*. 2d ed. Tuebingen: Mohr, 1960.

_____. *Die Verheimlichte Wahrheit: Theresienstaedter Dokumente*. Tuebingen: J. C. B. Mohr, 1958.

Adler-Rudel, S. "Alexandra Kollontai and the Jews of Anderl, Gabriella. "Seigfried Seidl-Anton Burger-Karl Rahm: Die Lagerkommandanten des Juedischen Ghettos Theresienstadt."Unpublished paper, Documentation Center of the Austrian Resistance. Vienna, 1991.

Arad, Yitzhak. *Belzec, Sobibor, Treblinka*. Bloomington and Indianapolis: Indiana University Press, 1987.

Arnold, David. "Quiet Hero of the Holocaust." *The Boston Globe Magazine*, October 21, 1990.

Arsenyevic, Drago. *Otages Volontaires des SS*. Paris: Editions France-Empire, 1974.

Auerbacher, Inge. *I Am a Star*. New York: Simon and Schuster, 1986.

Baeck, Leo. "A People Stands Before Its God." In Eric C. Boehm, *We Survived*. Santa Barbara: Clio Press, 1966.

Baker, Leonard. *Days of Sorrow and Pain: Leo Baeck and the Berlin Jews*. New York: Macmillan, 1978.

Bauer, Yehuda. *American Jewry and the Holocaust: The American Joint Distribution Committee, 1939-1945*. Detroit: Wayne State University Press, 1985.

Beresinen, Yasha L. "Theresienstadt: A Monetary System That Never Was." *The Shekel*, XVI: 2.

Berger, Sam. *Die Unvergesslichen Sechseinhalb Jahre meines Lebens 1939-1945*. Frankfurt: R. G. Fisher, 1985.

Berkley, George E. *Vienna and Its Jews: The Tragedy of Success*. Lanham, MD: Madison, 1988.

Bondy, Ruth. *Elder of the Jews: Jakob Edelstein of Theresienstadt*. New York: Grove, 1989.

Caro, Klara. "Staerker Als das Schwert." Document at the Leo Baeck Institute, 1962. "The Case of Anton Burger." Vienna: Simon Wiesenthal Documentation Center, Bulletin of Information No. 28, Item 15, January 31, 1989.

Davidowicz, Lucy S. *From That Place and Time--A Memoir 1936-1947*. New York: W. W. Norton, 1989.

de Jong, Louis. *The Netherlands and Nazi Germany*. Cambridge: Harvard University Press, 1990.

Edvarson, Cordelia. *Gebrantes Kind sucht das Feuer*. Munich: Hansen, 1986.

Ehrlich, Leonard. *Transkript eines Tonbandes. Interview zwischen Prof. Ehrlich und Ze'ev Shek, aufgenomen in Rom 1977*. Beit Terezin.

Ehrman, Frantisek, et al., eds. *Terezin*. Prague: Council of Jewish Communities in Czech Lands, 1965.

Eichmann, Adolf. For testimony at his trial concerning Theresienstadt, see Transcripts of Sessions 38, 42, and 45. Yad Vashem. Elias, Ruth. *Die Hoffnung erhielt mich am Leben*. Munich: Piper, 1988.

Frankl, Viktor E. "Psychohygiene im Notstand." *Hygiene* (October 1952).

Frankova, Anita. "Deportationen aus dem TheresienstaedterGhetto. Methoden der Abfestigung von Transporten und deren Rueckwirkung auf das Leben der Haeftlinge im Licht eineniger Quellen." *Judaica Bohemiae*, XXIII: 1 (1987).

Fuchs, Emma. *My Kaleidoscope*. Privately printed, 1974. (Available at the Brandeis University Library.)

Goldschmidt, Arthur. *Geschichte der evangelischen Gemeinde Theresienstadt 1942-1945*. Tuebingen: Furche, 1948.

Green, Gerald. *The Artists of Terezin*. New York: Hawthorn, 1969.

Haas, Gerda. *These I Do Remember*. Freeport, ME: The Cumberland Press, 1982.

Haas, Leo. "The Affair of the Painters of Terezin." In *Seeing Through "Paradise": Artists and the Terezin Concentration Camp*. Boston: Massachusetts College of Art, 1991.

Irving, David. *Goering: A Biography*. New York: William Morrow, 1989.

Jacobsohn, Jacob. *Von Berlin Nach Theresienstadt*. Yad Vashem: n.d., 02/373.

Kamp, Willy. "Was Ein Mensch Wert Ist." In *Deutsche Erzaehler der Gegenwart*. Stuttgart: Reclam, 1959.

Kantor, Alfred. *The Book of Alfred Kantor*. New York: Schocken, 1987.

Karas, Joza. *Music in Terezin 1941-1945*. New York: Beaufort, 1985.

Karny, Miroslav. "Das Schicksal der TheresienstaedterOsttransporte im Sommer und Herbst 1942." *Judaica Bohemiae*, XXIV: 2 (1988).

_____. "Ein Auschwitzbericht und das Schicksal des Theresienstaedter Familienlagers." *Judaica Bohemiae*, XXI:1 (1985).

_____. "Das Theresienstaedter Familienlager im Birkenau." *Judaica Bohemiae*, XV:1 (1979).

_____. "Die historische Forschung der Nazistischen 'Loesung der Judenfrage' im sog. Protektorat." *Judaica Bohemiae* XVI, Special Issue.

_____. "Nisko in der Geschichte der 'Endloesung.'" *Judaica Bohemiae*, XXIII:2 (1987).

_____. "Theresienstadt Dokumente. Teil I." *Judaica Bohemiae*, XVII:1 (1981).

_____. "Theresienstadt Dokumente (Teil II)." *Judaica Bohemiae*, XVIII:2 (1982).

Kral, V.A. "Psychiatric Observations under Severe Chronic Stress." *American Journal of Psychiatry* (September 1951).

Kramer, Edith. "Als Aerztin in Theresienstadt." *Tribune*, Heft 92, 1984. Frankfurt.

Kramer, Edith. Untitled, undated typewritten manuscript covering the selection and transport of 1200 Jews from Theresienstadt to Switzerland in February 1945. Vienna: In the files of the Simon Wiesenthal Documentation Center.

Lederer, Zdenek. *Ghetto Theresienstadt*. New York: Fertig, 1983.

Levin, Meyer. *In Search: An Autobiography*. New York: Horizon, 1950.

Lichtenstein, Heiner. *Angepasst und treu ergeben: Das Rote Kreuz im "Dritten Reich"*. Cologne: Bund Verlag, 1988.

Liebrecht, Heinrich. "Therefore Will I Deliver Him." In Eric C. Boehm, *We Survived*. Santa Barbara, CA: Clio Press, 1966.

Lustig, Arnold. *Diamonds in the Night*. London: Hutchinson, 1962.

Lustig, Arnost. *Indecent Dreams*. Evanston, IL: Northwestern University Press, 1988.

_____. *The Unloved*. New York: Arbor House, 1985.

MacDonald, Callum. *The Killing of SS Obergruppenfuehrer Reinhard Heydrich*. New York: The Free Press, 1989.

Marcus, Gerda Brumlik. *Memories of Transport No. AAR 427 Prague-Terezin*. Beit Terezin.

Migdal, Ulrike, Ed. *Und die Musik Spielt Dazu*. Munich: Piper, 1986.

Moser, Jonny. "Theresienstadt, das Altersghetto." In *Totenbuch Theresienstadt*. Vienna: Junius, 1971.

Murmelstein, B. *Terezin: Il Ghetto-Modello Di Eichmann*. Rome: Cappelli, 1965.

Murmelstein, Benjamin. "Das Ende von Theresienstadt: Stellungnahme eines Beteiligten." *Neue Zuercher Zeitung, December 17, 1963. Also in* Die Welt, January 14, 1964.

_____. Untitled, undated manuscript of 65 pages describing his activities in Theresienstadt. Document 064/92, Yad Vashem.

Neufliess, Werner. Document 01/293, Yad Vashem. Penkower, Monty Noam. *The Jews Were Expendable*. Urbana and Chicago: University of Chicago Press, 1983.

Pintus, Liesel. *Die Befreiung 1947*. Typewritten manuscript in Wiener Library, Tel Aviv University.

Presser, Jacob. *The Destruction of the Dutch Jews*. New York: Dutton, 1969.

Richarz, Monika, Ed. *Judisches Leben in Deutschland: Selbtszevonisse zur Socialgeschichte 1918-1945*. Stuttgart: Deutsche Verlags-Anstalt, 1982.

Rothkirchen, Livia. "The Zionist Character of the 'Self Government' of Terezin (Theresienstadt)." Jerusalem: *Yad Vashem*, XI, 1976.

Sadek, Vladimir. "From the Documents Related to the War-Time Central Jewish Museum in Prague." *Judaica Bohemiae*, XVI:1. Special Issue.

Schauer, Peter A. *Filmarbeit in Theresienstadt*. Vienna, 1987. Fifty-page printed manuscript in the files of the Simon Wiesenthal Documentation Center. No publisher or other source given.

Schmiedt, Shlomo. "Hehalutz in Theresienstadt- Its Influence and Educational Activities." In *Yad Vashem Studies on the European Jewish Catastrophe and Resistance*, VII.

Schwertfeger, Ruth. *Women of Theresienstadt: Voices from a Concentration Camp*. Oxford/New York/Hamburg: Berg, 1989.

Seidl, Siegfried. *Testimony Before the Allied Commission in Vienna*. Yad Vashem, Document T/842.

Skochova, J. "Die Jugend in Konzentrationslager Theresienstadt 1941-1945." *Judaica Bohemiae*, XXI:2 (1985).

Skochova, Jarmila. "Literarische Taetigkeit jugendicher Haeftlinge im Konzentrationslager Theresienstadt." *Judaica Bohemiae*, XXIII:1 (1987).

_____. "Theater im Konzentrationslager Theresienstadt." *Judaica Bohemiae*, XIX:2.

Spies, Gerty. *Drei Jahre Theresienstadt*. Munich: Chr. Raiser, 1984.

Squires-Kidron, Pamela. "By the Rivers of Babylon: Music of Theresienstadt." *Israel Scene*, May 1987.

Starke, Kaethe. *Der Fuehrer schenkt den Juden ein Stadt*. Berlin: Haude & Spenersche, 1975.

Troller, Norbert. *Theresienstadt: Hitler's Gift to the Jews*. Chapel Hill: University of North Carolina Press, 1991.

Utitz, Emil. *Psychologie des Lebens im Konzentrationslager Theresienstadt*. Vienna: Continental, 1948.

Vogel, E. "The Strickers at Theresienstadt." In *Robert Stricker*. London, 1950. (Privately printed; no publisher given. Josef Fraenkl is listed as editor.)

York, Dr. Alan. "The Paper Money Used in the Theresienstadt Ghetto: The Inside Story." *The Shekel*, XVI:2 (1963).

In addition to the above-listed books and articles, various newspaper reports have also been helpful. Most helpful of all has been the coverage of Karl Rahm's trial in 1947 by the Czech periodical, *Vestnik Zno*. Ernest Seinfeld has had some of these reports translated into English and kindly sent me a copy.

Regarding other published sources, see the New York *Daily News*, November 7, 1952, for the suicide of Heinz Berger; the *Illustrierte Neue Welt*, February 1987, for a report on Viennese and Berlin productions of Viktor Ullman's opera, "Death Abdicates"; *The New York Times*, January 17, 1990, for a review of Gideon Klein's "Study for String Orchestra"; and *The Boston Sunday Globe*, March 10, 1991, for two review articles on the exhibition of Theresienstadt art. The Jewish Telegraphic Agency carried a report from Geneva on June 23, 1988 on Lichtenstein's strongly critical account of the activities of the International Red Cross in World War II. Finally, *Aufbau*, the excellent newspaper founded by German and Austrian refugees, has published occasional items about Theresienstadt, some of which have been useful.

OTHER SOURCES

Information through interviews and/or correspondence was supplied by the following:

Sam Berger
Yaroslav Drabek
Leonard Ehrlich
Phyllis Ehrlich
Anita Frankova
Lisa Gidron
Gerda Haas
Joza Karas
Sidoni Koralek
Jiri Lauscher
Michela Lauscher
Siegmund Levarie
Ditta Jedlinskly Lowy
Louis Lowy
Arnost Lustig
Karel Margry
Frederick Praeger
E. G. Brockblum
Alisah Schiller
Victor Schroeder
Ernest Seinfeld
Alisa Shek
Netty Schwarz Vanderpol
Kurt Weigel
Ella Weissberger
Margaret Wrencher-Rustow

To be added to the above list are three women survivors who have generously supplied useful information but who have asked not to be identified.

NOTES

Research into Theresienstadt begins of necessity with Adler's *Theresien-stadt, 1941-1945*. This bulky book overflows with facts, figures, and quotations, along with descriptions of events, personalities, moods, and feelings. It is actually longer than its size indicates, for Adler not only uses a system of abbreviations for often-repeated words, but also devotes almost 200 pages of his near 900-page text to notes set in small print, and these notes do not merely annotate his text but provide much additional material. To take just one example, the quotes from refugees of other concentration camps regarding the good treatment they received when they first arrived in Theresienstadt at the end of the war come from these notes.

Adler's book is so massive and seemingly complete that when I first read it, I wondered whether writing a further book on the subject would be worthwhile. But in examining it more closely I saw what others, including most Theresienstadt survivors have seen: Although long in length and copious in detail, *Theresienstadt, 1941-1945* is far from being a definitive work.

There are essentially two reasons why his book fails to meet such a standard. The first is that despite its detail, it lacks much important material. Adler was deported from the camp in the fall 1944 exodus and he shows remarkably little interest in what occurred at Theresien-stadt afterward. Indeed, his account of the camp after his departure is not only skimpy but not always clear. Furthermore, the most recent edition of Adler's book was published in 1960. This was before publication of the books by Ehrman et al., Bondy, Murmelstein, Starke, Haas, Elias, and others, in addition to the numerous research articles in *Judaica Bohemiae*. It was also before the Eichmann trial and its revealing testimony. Consequently, *Theresienstadt, 1941-1945* lacks much important information. It says very little, for example, about the SS, the Czech gendarmes, conditions at the Little Fortress, escapes from the camp, etc. It also treats sparsely the work of the Zionists, for Adler was not a Zionist himself and had little close contact with those who were. So although his book is indispensable, many other sources must be consulted if one wishes to write a reasonably complete account of Theresienstadt.

The second and possibly more important reason for not regarding Adler's account as definitive are his biases. He cared little for most of those in authority in the camp and even calls Edelstein a political opportunist. He also shows little appreciation for the camp's accomplishments. Many survivors such as Alisa Shek, Alisah Schiller, and Ernest Seinfeld believe he was annoyed at not receiving much attention in Theresienstadt and this affected his whole approach. In any case, his many prejudices and generally negative attitude to the camp and most of its leading members greatly limit the value of his work.

Adler's attitude does not appreciably affect his second book, *Die Verheimlichte Wahrheit*, since this work consists primarily of original materials. Among its documents are lengthy excerpts from the reports of Rossel and Lehner, Edelstein's letter to Ullmann, the lengthy memo announcing Edelstein's replacement by Eppstein, excerpts from Gerron's shooting script, etc., etc. The book also contains photographs of Theresienstadt, photocopies of sketches by Theresienstadt artists, and reproductions of numerous administrative documents such as Orders of the Day, memos, invitations, signs, etc.

Adler's last work on Theresienstadt, a talk at a YIVO conference in New York City in 1972, contains little new information. In it, however, he greatly softened and, in fact, virtually retracted most of the harsh things he said about Edelstein in his first book.

Next to Adler's books, *Terezin*, edited by Ehrman et al. and published by the Jewish community of Czechoslovakia, has probably been my greatest source of written material. Most, although not all, of what I have written regarding the Czech gendarmes, the treatment of Jewish prisoners in the Little Fortress, and the two successful escapes from Theresienstadt comes from this work. So do nearly all the excerpts from children's diaries, along with the quotes by Klein, Diament, and Lauscherova, and the reports on how surviving Theresienstadt children fared in Prague after the war. All quotes from Norbert Fryd and Rabbi Feder also come from *Terezin*, as does Rahm's statement to Haindl indicating how easy it would be to slaughter all of Theresienstadt's Jews once they were gathered in the projected "duck pond."

Bondy's well-written, and well-translated, book has been my single best source of material not only on Edelstein and his family but also on the origins of the camp itself. In addition, as citations from the book indicate, it offers some general information about the camp and also about what was happening in the non-Nazi world regarding it. But my best source for such outside activities, including those of Saly Mayer, are Penkower and Bauer, especially the latter. Arsenyevic and Lichtenstein are also helpful on this point, with the latter being much more critical of the International Red Cross. (Lichtenstein, I should add, is not Jewish.)

Murmelstein's writings have frequently been cited and are my chief source for the description of his own activities after the fall 1944 deportations. Although he remains a controversial and far from appealing figure, his written accounts seem generally credible since (1) he never seeks to portray himself as a hero or even as an especially high-minded person, and (2) he usually provides some proof or at least means for external verification for what he says. We should remember that at the time he was writing, in the 1960s or earlier, many survivors who had occupied authoritative positions in the camp were still around to challenge the veracity of any of his factual statements. To my knowledge, no such challenge ever arose.

Goldschmidt's book not only tells the story of the Protestant congregation but gives a good deal of information on the Catholic one as well. However, Liebrecht, who belonged to that congregation, provides still more information, and the quotation comparing the congregants to the early Christians in the catacombs comes from him.

Lustig's books are not only fiction but are not written in a naturalistic style. As far as I can recall, Theresienstadt is not even mentioned by name. Nevertheless, his writings do a wonderful job of conveying some of the atmosphere and mood of the camp as well as that of wartime Prague itself. Lustig's more specific information was obtained through interviews, as noted in the acknowledgments. The poetry and information attributed to Blumenthal-Weiss, Eisenkraft, Trude Groag, and Dormitzer, among others, come from Schwertfeger's book. Professor Schwertfeger has also done an excellent job of translating some of the poetry of the camp's women poets. The deportation of biochemist Eichengruen is mentioned in Richarz's book; the deportation of the poet Pawder is mentioned by Starke.

Turning now to those shorter works whose contributions may not be clear from their titles, Arnold's "Quiet Hero" is Walter Suskind, while Caro's short pamphlet is about life in Theresienstadt as the wife of a German rabbi. Jacobsohn is the observer who noticed on the Berlin train platform the difference between those deportees given an "O" and those assigned a "T". And Karny, in his *Theresienstadt Dokumente*, supplies the quotations from Redlich's diary as well as much other interesting material. The statement of J. H. Fisher, the Israeli numismatist quoted at the end of the last chapter, can be found in Dr. York's article.

Regarding the Eichmann trial, Ansbacher testified in Session 38, Salzberger in Session 42, and Engelstein in Session 45. The latter, an engineer, gave evidence regarding the "duck pond" project.

The quotations from Camus, Franklin, and Brecht in the Postlude are, respectively, from *The Myth of Sisyphus*, *The Autobiography of Benjamin Franklin*, and *The Three-Penny Opera*. Since these works are available in numerous editions, no specific editions have been cited in the bibliography. Lawrence Langer's remarks were made in a talk he gave at the Boston Public Library in the winter of 1992.

Most of those I personally interviewed or corresponded with have already been mentioned in the acknowledgments. I would, however, like to say something here about the contributions of my three anonymous interviewees.

Two of them are sisters from Vienna. One worked as a nurse in Dr. Frankl's clinic and it is she who describes him as "such a good man." She is also the nurse who boldly, and successfully, approached Rahm on the train platform to ask for her release from deportation and who even more boldly passed a note to Dunant warning him that what he was being shown was not true. Her sister is the young woman whom Murmelstein assigned to the Feldspar plant as punishment for "promenading." She is also the Viennese who felt like an outsider at seeing the Czech signs replace German ones and was one of the Viennese who visited the cafe in Leitmeritz shortly after liberation.

The contribution of the third interviewee cannot be indicated without divulging her identity.

ADDENDUM

Shortly after this book went into production, two new publications containing material relevant to its subject came to my attention. One was an article on the Nazis' Theresienstadt film; the other was a book on the activities of the International Red Cross in World War II. (Complete citations of both works will be found at the end of this addendum.)

Since neither publication dramatically added or changed anything in my manuscript, they did not seem to warrant holding up publication of this book to make revisions in its text. But since both did contribute some interesting details and offer one or two minor corrections, they did seem to warrant some mention. Hence this addendum.

The article on the film was sent to me by its author, Professor Karel Margry of the University of Utrecht. As noted in the Acknowledgments to this book, Professor Margry had previously given me some valuable assistance with my own account of this Theresienstadt event. His article makes a further contribution.

According to Professor Margry, the real title of the Nazi film was *Theresienstadt: Ein Dokumentar aus dem Juedischen Siedlungsgebiet* (Theresienstadt: A documentary film of the Jewish Settlement area). The title usually ascribed to it, *Der Fuehrer schenkt den Jueden eine Stadt* (The Fuehrer presents a city to the Jews), was apparently, says Margry, "coined--with a clear sense of irony--by the Jewish inmates themselves during the time that the film was made." It is, he says, "another example of the same black humor with which the prisoners treated many other aspects of ghetto life."

The decision to shoot the film was made in December 1943, before Kurt Gerron arrived at the camp, and although Gerron became its principal creator, many others were also involved. The background music, for example, was selected by the Danish conductor Peter Deutsch, who also conducted the orchestra for the sound recordings. All the music was written by Jewish composers.

Margry attributes the idea of making the film to Hans Guenther, the head of the Prague Gestapo, and he says Guenther embarked on the project without consulting Eichmann. Himmler also seems to have had little direct involvement in the project.

Margry's findings mean that the film was not originally conceived to aid Eichmann's negotiations with

Saly Meyer, since these talks did not begin until April 1944. Nevertheless, while Eichmann appears to have been initially annoyed at
Guenther's rather bold initiative, his subsequent need during the
negotiations to show that the Nazis did have living Jews to exchange for
trucks may have caused him to change his attitude. Serious work on the
film did not get underway until the trucks-for-Jews proposal was actually
made in August.

According to Margry, historians have generally overestimated the
staged character of the film. The film's *visual* authenticity, he says, is
much greater than most people think. "In the final analysis," he
concludes, "the film's blatant dishonesty turns on what it did not show:
the hunger, the misery, the overcrowding, the slave work for the
German war economy, the high death rate and, most of all, transports
leaving for the East."

The book on the International Red Cross (IRC) was written by
Professor Jean-Claude Favez, a highly respected historian at the
University of Geneva. It is an admirable work of scholarship--so, for
the matter, is Margry's article--but it suffers a bit from the fact that
most of the major participants were no longer alive to fill in the gaps in
the written records and provide additional background.

According to Favez, some Red Cross officials wanted to visit
Theresienstadt as early as the autumn of 1942 to make sure that mail
packages plus other supplies were actually being distributed. The
Vatican also expressed an interest in having its papal nuncio in Berlin
visit the camp as well. When the opportunity for such a visit arose in
1944, however, they were less interested, for they suspected that in
making such a visit they might only play into the Nazis' hands. Roland
Marti, who was Rossel's superior in Berlin, had shown quite a bit of
sympathy for the Jews and had maintained good contacts with Riegner
of the World Jewish Congress. But he allowed his subordinate, Rossel,
to go instead.

Rossel had to promise the SS in advance that he would not *publicly*
divulge what he saw in Theresienstadt. In any case, what he did write
in his official and supposedly confidential report was, as we have seen,
fully in line with what the Nazis wanted him to say to his superiors.
Jean-Etienne Schwarzenberg, who headed the Red Cross Division of
Special Assistance, doubted certain aspects of Rossel's report but did
show it, apparently without comment, to representatives of various
Jewish organizations in Geneva.

Favez's book indicates that as early as the fall of 1942 the International Red Cross had some awareness of Hitler's intention not just to deport but to destroy the Jews. But its information was fragmentary and most of its officials may not have correctly assessed the real scope and intensity of the Fuehrer's plans. According to what Favez has told me, it was only in the spring of 1944 that the Red Cross launched a serious and sizeable effort to aid the Jews, and even then its leaders were motivated in part by fears of what the world might say about them after the now seemingly inevitable Allied victory. They were also being pressured, Favez added, by the War Refugee Board which Roosevelt had recently set up. (The Red Cross felt, with some justification, that Roosevelt had only established the Board for political reasons, i.e., to aid his re-election in the fall.)

I interviewed Favez in Geneva where I had come across his book. His statement about the IRC's somewhat less than ardent efforts to aid the Jews prompted me to ask him about possible IRC anti-Semitism. He replied that in combing through the records he did find a slight strain of what might be called a genteel anti-Semitism. (*Une note d'anti-Semitism de bon ton* was the way he put it.) It apparently took the form not so much of a pronounced dislike of the Jews but of simply a feeling that they were a distinctly different people.

To be sure, the International Red Cross, as Favez's book brings out, was established essentially by well-meaning members of Geneva's Protestant aristocracy. No Jews and hardly any Catholics had ever sat on its governing committee.

One should also keep in mind that the IRC was not set up to deal with such situations as genocide. Rather, it was designed to protect and assist such groups as prisoners of war and interned civilian aliens. Furthermore, the Nazis had made it clear that they would tolerate no outside involvement, and only the most limited inspection, into their methods for solving their "Jewish problem." When the IRC delegate in Salonika began showing concern and making inquiries about the fate of that city's large Jewish population, he was sent packing back to Geneva.

As a result of all these factors, most Red Cross officials felt justified in focusing their efforts in those areas where they might be useful, such as helping certain groups of non-Jewish internees. Although some officials did make an extra effort to help the Jews, if only to pass on information to the Geneva representatives of Jewish organizations, most did not.

This indifference is seen all too vividly in Rossel's report on his 1944 visit to Theresienstadt. Although Rossel, as Favez's book brings out, may not have believed all that he saw in the camp, and may have written his report knowing that the Nazis would soon get a copy of it, it nevertheless shows a callous attitude toward the Theresienstadt Jews and a most superficial appraisal of their situation. To a somewhat lesser degree, so does the report by Lehner, who visited the camp in April 1945.

Such attitudes and appraisals seem to be generally reflective of the organization itself. For although the International Red Cross was certainly not hostile to the Jews, it allowed certain opportunities to help them slip by. One of the more conspicuous of such missed opportunities was its failure to show any interest in inspecting the Theresienstadt "family camp" at Auschwitz following Rossel's visit to Theresienstadt itself in June 1944. Had the organization shown such an interest, many more of the family camp's inmates might have survived the war.

BIBLIOGRAPHY

Margry, Karel. "Theresienstadt (1944-1945): The Nazi Propaganda Film Depicting the Concentration Camp as Paradise." *Historical Journal of Film, Radio and Television*, Vol. 12, No. 2, 1992.

Favez, Jean-Claude. *Une Mission Impossible? Le CICR, les déportations et les camps de concentration Nazis*. Lausanne: Editions Payot, 1988.

1. Jacob Edelstein (courtesy of YIVO Institute for Jewish Research, New York.

2. Otto Zucker (courtesy of Beit Terezin, Kibbutz Givat Chaim, Israel).

3. Paul Eppstein (courtesy of Beit Terezin, Kibbutz Givat Chaim, Israel).

4. Karl Schliesser (far right--the other two men are not identified) (courtesy of Beit Terezin, Kibbutz Givat Chaim, Israel).

5. Egon (Gonda) Redlich (courtesy of Beit Terezin Kibbutz Givat Chaim, Israel).

6. Fredy Hirsch (courtesy of Beit Terezin, Kibbutz Givat Chaim, Israel).

7. Aron Menczer holding a birthday cake given him in Vienna prior to his deportation to Theresienstadt (courtesy of Professor Yacov Metzer, Hebrew University, Jerusalem).

8. Courtyard in Theresienstadt. Drawing by Nobert Troller (courtesy of Leo Baeck Institute, New York City).

9. Courtyard in Theresienstad, artist unknown (courtesy of Leo Baeck Institute, New York City).

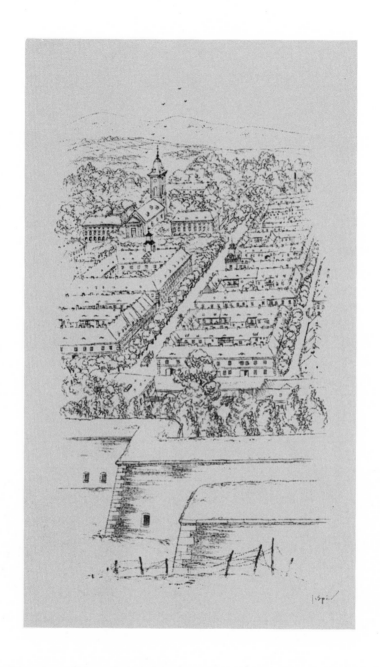

10. Drawing of Theresienstadt by the Dutch artist Jo Spier (courtesy of Leo Baeck Institute, New York City).

11. Still photo from the Nazi propaganda film on Theresienstadt. Note shrubbery and bushes put up especially for the film (courtesy of National Center for Jewish Film, Brandeis Univesity).

12. Sign pointing to the library. Still photo from the Nazi propaganda film (courtesy of the National Center for Jewish Film, Brandeis University).

13. Still photo from Nazi propaganda film (courtesy of National Center for Jewish Film, Brandeis University).

14. Meeting of the Council of Elders. Stading, left to right, Zucker, Eppstein, Murmelstein. Note: this photo may have been especially staged for Nazi propaganda purposes (courtesy of Leo Baeck Institute, New York City).

15. Karl Rahm, who lost considerable weight during his incarceration, testifies at his trial in Leitmeritz (courtesy of Beit Terezin, Kibbutz Givat Chaim, Israel).

16. Photo of Theresienstadt taken after the war (courtesy of the Leo
Baeck Institute, New York City).

Index

HITLER'S GIFT:
The Story of Theresienstadt

As the shadow of Nazism spread over Europe, a small town in Czechoslovakia suddenly became the continent's outstanding outpost of learning and culture. Here, inside an area nine blocks long and five wide, one could enjoy the finest, and free-est, music, hear the best lectures and receive some of the best medical care in Hitler's Europe. For here, living virtually side by side, were many of Europe's more distinguished composers and conductors, statesmen and soldiers and scientists and scholars, along with numerous celebrities from stage, screen, concert hall and other walks of life.

These prominent personages shared one common characteristic: all were Jews who had failed to flee the Nazi menace in time.

Because of their stature and connections--both within their own countries, and often internationally as well--these Jews were not earmarked for execution, at least not right away. Their total disappearance might occasion disturbing inquiries abroad as well as within the Reich itself. Instead, they, along with certain other groups of Jews, would supposedly be given an "entire city" in which to establish the first all-Jewish community of modern times. The "city" was Theresienstadt (Terezin in Czech), and the Nazis described it as the Fuehrer's "gift" to the Jews.

In this way, Theresienstadt became a Nazi show place, a unique concentration camp designed to cover up the Jewish extermination program. Its inmates were not only allowed to receive packages from Aryan friends and relatives, but also from Jewish relief agencies operating in neutral countries. On two occasions, Swiss Red Cross representatives "inspected" the camp and went away impressed with what they saw.

But Theresienstadt, as Professor Berkley vividly shows, was essentially a Potemkin village, a fabricated community behind whose flimsy façade destitution and death ran rampant. Most Jews deported to Theresienstadt were not distinguished and most of them either died there or were sent on to the gas chambers of Auschwitz. Even many of the camp's prominent Jews eventually perished. In the words of one of the camp's few survivors, Theresienstadt was a theatre of the absurd.

The gripping story of this *theatre of the absurd* is being told objectively and completely for the first time. In researching his book, the author reviewed records, memoirs and testimony, interviewed survivors and traveled to Israel, Vienna, Prague and Theresienstadt. The result is an often dismaying but never disheartening chronicle of contradiction and conflict, villainy and virtue, defeat and success. Ultimately, it is a story of human decency managing, under inhuman conditions, to survive and, finally, to triumph.

About the author:

Political scientist George E. Berkley received his master's degree from Harvard University and his PhD from Tufts. A Professor Emeritus from the University of Massachusetts at Boston, he is the author of several books, the most recent of which is *Vienna and Its Jews: The Tragedy of Success*. A member of B'nai B'rith and the Workman's Circle, he lives in Brookline, Massachusetts.